FAMILY VIOLENCE

DATE DUE

NOV 17 97	APR 8 2003		
SEP 2 4 98	MAR		
APR 12 99	JUL 14 2003		
NOV 3 00			
APR 18 00	OCT 3 0		
APR 25 00	NOV 1		
APR 17 01			
9 01			
OCT 6 01			
APR 26 2002			
AUG 2 200			
FEB 2 4 2003			

Other Books in the Current Controversies Series:

FAMILY VIOLENCE

David L. Bender, *Publisher*
Bruno Leone, *Executive Editor*

Scott Barbour, *Managing Editor*
Brenda Stalcup, *Senior Editor*

A.E. Sadler, *Book Editor*

Cover Photo: © Edward Lettau/FPG
© Arthur Tilley/FPG

Library of Congress Cataloging-in-Publication Data

Family violence / A. E. Sadler, book editor.
       p. cm. — (Current controversies)
     Includes bibliographical references (p.   ) and index.
     ISBN 1-56510-371-8 (lib. bdg. : alk. paper).—ISBN 1-56510-370-X
(pbk. : alk. paper)
     1. Family violence—United States. I. Sadler, A. E. II. Series.
HQ809.3.U5F335   1996
362.82'92'0973—dc20
                                                                    95-35485
                                                                    CIP

© 1996 by Greenhaven Press, Inc., PO Box 289009, San Diego, CA 92198-9009
Printed in the U.S.A.

Every effort has been made to trace the owners of copyrighted material.

Contents

Chapter 3: Who Are the Victims of Family Violence?

substantially higher than men, radical feminists distort the statistics in an effort to create a sexist judicial system that penalizes men while allowing women perpetrators to go free.

Chapter 4: How Can Family Violence Be Reduced?

Increasing Specific Efforts Can Reduce Family Violence

Increasing Certain Efforts Will Exacerbate Family Violence

Foreword

By definition, controversies are "discussions of questions in which opposing opinions clash" (Webster's Twentieth Century Dictionary Unabridged). Few would deny that controversies are a pervasive part of the human condition and exist on virtually every level of human enterprise. Controversies transpire between individuals and among groups, within nations and between nations. Controversies supply the grist necessary for progress by providing challenges and challengers to the status quo. They also create atmospheres where strife and warfare can flourish. A world without controversies would be a peaceful world; but it also would be, by and large, static and prosaic.

The Series' Purpose

The purpose of the Current Controversies series is to explore many of the social, political, and economic controversies dominating the national and international scenes today. Titles selected for inclusion in the series are highly focused and specific. For example, from the larger category of criminal justice, Current Controversies deals with specific topics such as police brutality, gun control, white collar crime, and others. The debates in Current Controversies also are presented in a useful, timeless fashion. Articles and book excerpts included in each title are selected if they contribute valuable, long-range ideas to the overall debate. And wherever possible, current information is enhanced with historical documents and other relevant materials. Thus, while individual titles are current in focus, every effort is made to ensure that they will not become quickly outdated. Books in the Current Controversies series will remain important resources for librarians, teachers, and students for many years.

In addition to keeping the titles focused and specific, great care is taken in the editorial format of each book in the series. Book introductions and chapter prefaces are offered to provide background material for readers. Chapters are organized around several key questions that are answered with diverse opinions representing all points on the political spectrum. Materials in each chapter include opinions in which authors clearly disagree as well as alternative opinions in which authors may agree on a broader issue but disagree on the possible solutions. In this way, the content of each volume in Current Controversies mirrors the mosaic of opinions encountered in society. Readers will quickly realize that there are many viable answers to these complex issues. By questioning each author's conclusions, students and casual readers can begin to develop the critical thinking skills so important to evaluating opinionated material.

Current Controversies is also ideal for controlled research. Each anthology in the series is composed of primary sources taken from a wide gamut of informational categories including periodicals, newspapers, books, United States and foreign government documents, and the publications of private and public organizations. Readers will find factual support for reports, debates, and research papers covering all areas of important issues. In addition, an annotated table of contents, an index, a book and periodical bibliography, and a list of organizations to contact are included in each book to expedite further research.

Perhaps more than ever before in history, people are confronted with diverse and contradictory information. During the Persian Gulf War, for example, the public was not only treated to minute-to-minute coverage of the war, it was also inundated with critiques of the coverage and countless analyses of the factors motivating U.S. involvement. Being able to sort through the plethora of opinions accompanying today's major issues, and to draw one's own conclusions, can be a complicated and frustrating struggle. It is the editors' hope that Current Controversies will help readers with this struggle.

"Many families could use a lot more outside interference."

Barbara Ehrenreich

"The issue is not just about 'saving children'; it is about family preservation."

Karen Radko

Introduction

"Family violence" broadly refers to physical and/or sexual violence between people who are intimately associated. Spousal abuse, elder abuse, and child abuse are the types of violence most frequently falling under this label. However, the category is often expanded to include violence between gay men, lesbians, and unmarried heterosexual partners, as well as siblings. Family violence, then, is a general designation encompassing various forms of violence occurring within numerous types of relationships. It is most difficult to detect, however, when children are its victims, according to emergency room physician Patricia Salber, because "often the victims cannot speak for themselves."

Americans' traditional love of privacy, in the minds of some mental health professionals, worsens this situation by contributing to the perception that any involvement or inquiry by nonfamily members is intrusive. Thus people are hesitant to voice concern when they see a child with suspicious-looking bruises or other indicators of abuse. According to educators Sally A. Lloyd and Beth C. Emery, "The physical abuse of children is indirectly supported by the cultural norm of family privacy." And because the American home is beyond the reach of most mechanisms for social control, they contend, it is where those vulnerable to abuse experience the most danger.

Efforts to combat the obstacle presented by family privacy emerged during the 1960s in the form of mandated reporting laws, adopted by both federal and state governments. Restricted to instances involving child abuse, these measures require that people who work in child-related fields, such as education and health care, report all suspected cases to local government authorities. Many health and child welfare professionals, however, still worry that situations of family violence persist unacknowledged, and therefore unabated. "We know only about reported cases," writes Harris Meyer in *American Medical News*, adding that it is likely that many incidents go unrecorded.

Some inside the federal government argue that a national surveillance system is needed to collect adequate data on the problem, the same systematic approach used by the scientific community in times past to fight diseases such as smallpox and polio. "Surveillance may answer questions such as whether potential victims can be identified before violence occurs and how severe the long-term consequences of abuse really are," writes Rebecca Voelker. "This information can lead to the next step in the public health approach against violence—intervention."

Intervention involves social workers directly contacting those families in which abuse is suspected. Such contact can range from brief, irregular home visits to the actual removal of children from their parents. In some instances, parental rights may be terminated and the child placed for permanent adoption with another family. These actions follow the traditional philosophy of child protection services, which discourages leaving a child in a home with an abuser on the grounds that this simply involves too much risk. According to Michael Petit, deputy director of the Child Welfare League of America, "When a child is being abused by an adult, two options are open: to remove the child or to remove the adult." Such intervention has its supporters. Among these is *Time* magazine essayist Barbara Ehrenreich, who argues that "many families could use a lot more outside interference in the form of counseling and policing, and some are so dangerously dysfunctional that they ought to be encouraged to disband right away."

Opponents claim intervention—especially the removal of children from their parents—violates parents' constitutional rights and actually harms, rather than benefits, the child. They criticize these policies as blatantly antifamily and argue that the government is overreacting to the possibility of child maltreatment, citing the large number of reported cases of abuse that prove unsubstantiated. "Why are there so many state investigations and so few confirmed reports of abuse?" demands Karen Radko, a board member of a local Florida chapter of VOCAL, Victims of Child Abuse Laws. "Why must so many families defend their innocence against false allegations of abuse or neglect?" Yet people are hesitant to argue for reducing intervention, she points out, because they fear being labeled proponents of child abuse. "The result," she concludes, "is unnecessary state intervention into private family matters and grief to innocent parents and their children." She sees a need to recognize parents, not government agencies, as the "experts" in knowing what is best for their children: "This issue is not just about 'saving children'; it is about family preservation."

Many child protection agencies are responding to parental rights activists like Radko and have begun to embrace "family preservation" programs in which the family undergoes therapy and intensive home visitations from social workers while the child remains in the home. "We all have to change," says Anne Cohn Donnelly of the National Committee for the Prevention of Child Abuse, advocating that social workers employ alternatives other than removal of the child. She endorses home visitation, a component of the family preservation strategy, as such an alternative. "No [other] program holds such promise," she maintains. Charles Wilson, director of Child Welfare Services in Nashville, Tennessee, argues that being removed from the family can cause more trauma for a child than remaining in an abusive home. "You are removing them from their dog, from their school, from their back yard," he states. Wilson cautions, however, that the family preservation approach is not a "one-size-fits-all" panacea, contrary to what some of its supporters seem to purport. In his opinion, foster care remains "the only answer sometimes for very dangerous situations."

The most effective response to child abuse is just one of the issues addressed in *Family Violence: Current Controversies*. This anthology follows the ongoing debates among social scientists and others who seek to map the territory of abuse in American families—its nature, its scope, and its potential solutions.

Chapter 1

Is Family Violence Defined Too Broadly?

CURRENT CONTROVERSIES

Chapter Preface

The term "family violence" often seems to function as social science's kitchen sink—everything and anything deemed "violent" and involving familial relationships gets tossed in. Such generic labeling makes for problematic discussion, let alone definition.

One problem in defining exactly what family violence is, in language that is understood and accepted universally, stems from the difficulty in distinguishing precisely where normal or healthy behaviors cross over into abuse. In discussions of such topics as corporal punishment, for example, participants are split into intensely polarized factions.

Many people have long considered spanking unruly or disobedient children as American as apple pie. Eighty-three percent of readers who responded to a 1993 survey by *U.S. Catholic* magazine, for example, had been spanked as children. And while approximately 80 percent of respondents agreed that spanking children is potentially harmful and that there are equally effective alternatives, 55 percent had themselves used spanking as a form of discipline.

"Saying adults should never hit kids is about as dumb as saying that adults should always hit kids," wrote one respondent. "Spanking . . . can reinforce a rule or modify a behavioral problem, sometimes better than any other way." Another reader wrote in to say that he had been spanked and that rather than resenting his parents for this action, he commended them for it. He relates the details of the happy and stable life he has gone on to achieve as a confident, well-adjusted adult.

Other people believe corporal punishment is intolerable. "Hitting and spanking only teach children to use force to settle disputes," Alice McCarthy advises parents in her "All in the Family" newspaper column. Jordan Riak of the organization Parents and Teachers Against Violence in Education (PTAVE) describes being spanked as a "degrading, humiliating experience." He quotes anthropologist Ashley Montagu, to whom "any form of corporal punishment or 'spanking' is a violent attack upon another human being's integrity."

Debate over whether or not corporal punishment is abusive represents only one aspect of the argument over how family violence should be defined. The following chapter explores the issues and questions arising from various attempts at definition.

"Domestic Violence" Is Not Clearly Defined

by Ann Jones

About the author: *Ann Jones is a journalist, activist, and the author of* Women Who Kill *and* Next Time She'll Be Dead, *from which this viewpoint is excerpted.*

"Domestic violence" is one of those gray phrases, beloved of bureaucracy, designed to give people a way of talking about a topic without seeing what's really going on. Like "repatriation" or "ethnic cleansing," it's a euphemistic abstraction that keeps us at a dispassionate distance, far removed from the repugnant spectacle of human beings in pain. We used to speak of "wife beating"—words that brought to mind a picture of terrifying action, a big, heavy-handed man with a malicious eye, and a slight woman, dazed and bent, raising her arms against the blows, and crying out, "No!" Or we called it "wife torture," the words of Frances Power Cobbe [Irish reformer and feminist of the late 1800s] that conjure the scenes *between* beatings: the sullen husband, withdrawn and sulking, or angry and intimidating, dumping dinner on the floor, throwing the cat against the wall, screaming, twisting a child's arm, needling, nagging, manipulating, criticizing the bitch, the slut, the cunt who never does anything right, who's ugly and stupid, who should keep her mouth shut, who should spread her legs now, who should be dead, who will be if she's not careful. Charles Dickens drew such scenes, and Thomas Hardy and D. H. Lawrence, Fyodor Dostoevsky and Émile Zola, Doris Lessing, Toni Morrison, Margaret Atwood, Alice Munro, Alice Walker, Joyce Carol Oates. But we prefer to speak of "domestic violence."

A Veil of Words

I suspect that some academic researcher coined the term, dismayed by the fact that all those beaten wives are *women*, and reaching for some pretentious and gender-neutral "objective" term. During the Carter administration, when women's issues enjoyed a heady moment of legitimacy in the nation's capital, professionals in mental health and justice, equipped with professional vocabularies, took up the problems of "spouse abuse," "conjugal violence," and "marital aggression"—and a great renaming took place, a renaming that veiled once again the sexism a grass-roots women's movement had worked to uncover. Even feminist advocates for women, who called their cause "the battered women's movement," eventually succumbed; they adopted "domestic violence" in their fund raising proposals, so as not to offend men controlling the purse strings by suggesting that men were in any way to blame for this "social problem." So well does the phrase "domestic violence" obscure the real events behind it that when a Domestic Violence Act (to provide money for battered women's services) was first proposed to Congress in 1978, many thought it was a bill to combat political terrorism within the United States.

Obscuring Violence

It's difficult to face up to the sexism behind the "social problem," for the public mind, like the individual, is apt to minimize, deny, repress, and forget the bad news. Women in particular may have trouble facing the facts of sexist violence against women. Psychiatry professor Judith Lewis Herman observes: "Most women do not in fact recognize the degree of male hostility toward them, preferring to view the relations of the sexes as more benign than they are in fact. Similarly, women like to believe that they have greater freedom and higher status than they do in reality." Nevertheless, it's absolutely necessary to keep that sexism in sight if we hope to make sense of battery, for the immensity and viciousness of male violence aimed specifically at women are otherwise incomprehensible.

Any battered woman, who has surely been called a lot of bad names, can tell you that words have the power of blows; but the words we commonly use to discuss battering aren't up to the task. Male violence disappears in euphemism. The old term "wife beating" named only one piece of male violence and only one relationship—marriage—between assailant and victim; and it focused attention on the victim, not the perpetrator. But at least it suggested what goes on. Current terms like "domestic violence" and its academic progeny "partner abuse," "familial dysfunction," and "spousal dissonance" obscure its nature altogether.

> " 'Domestic violence' is . . . a euphemistic abstraction that keeps us at a dispassionate distance, far removed from the repugnant spectacle of human beings in pain."

On the other hand, the term "battered woman"—adopted by the battered women's movement from nineteenth century feminist campaigns against "wife beating"—suggests a graphic picture, but one that may also mislead: the picture of a woman more or less constantly subjected to serious physical assault, a helpless victim. It alludes to only one form of male violence against women in the home, and it seemingly excludes so many others that most "battered women," sizing up their own circumstances, don't see themselves as "battered." Again, in emphasizing physical damage, the term "battered" masks the real nature and purpose of the "batterer's" behavior.

The terms "battered woman," "domestic violence victim," and "abused woman," which emphasize a woman's situation as the victimized object of another's actions, also obscure her subjectivity and actions. They suggest that "battered" woman is *all* she is, that "victim" is her identity. Yet women who have lived through such violence, who know the immense daily expenditure of strength and attention and self-discipline it takes to survive, rarely identify themselves as "victims." They think of themselves as strong women who can somehow "cope." Many who escape speak of themselves as "formerly battered women" or "survivors" or "veterans" of violence, but these terms suggest a status achieved after the fact; they do not describe the active woman in the day by day process of coping with, combating, and escaping her "partner's" violence.

> *"In emphasizing physical damage, the term 'battered' masks the real nature and purpose of the 'batterer's' behavior."*

Deceptive Terms

The term "partner," by the way, is a politically correct addition to the academic lexicon, neutral not only in terms of gender but also sexual preference. It subsumes battering in lesbian and gay relationships under the discussion of heterosexual violence as if it were the same thing, when in fact the cultural context in which the violence occurs raises very different problems for victims in straight and gay "partnerships." On one hand, history and culture clearly support old-fashioned wife-beating, giving it a legitimacy that sets it apart from "partner abuse" within the marginalized homosexual community. On the other hand, the cultural repression of homosexuals trivializes violence within the homosexual community and writes off its victims, presenting immensely complicated problems to those who need help and must seek it from public authorities. In short, the word "partner" gives a nod to homosexuals while ignoring their real concerns. The usefulness of the term lies in its gender neutrality, for it conveniently hides one undeniable fact: that despite the real problem of violence committed by women against women, the assailant in almost all heterosexual *and* homosexual violence is a man.

The label "battered woman" is dangerously deceptive in other ways as well. The word "battered" names what someone else *did to her*, but since the battering agent is omitted from the phrase, the word "battered" somehow attaches to the woman as if it were an attribute, or part of her own nature—as in *deceitful* woman or *ambitious* woman. The implication built in to the form of the phrase is that *battered* is what she somehow chose to be. Somewhere in the back of our minds, just behind that American folk hero the "self-made man" lurks his dutiful counterpart, the seemingly "self-battered" woman.

The term "battered woman," which puts the focus on her, also encourages us to overlook her children; but there can be no doubt that male violence inflicts terrible damage upon them. Uncounted millions of children live in households dominated by violent men. Millions of children see and hear their mothers beaten repeatedly, a traumatic experience that many experts regard as in itself a form of child abuse. Some studies suggest that children who witness battering may suffer long-term consequences; both as children and as adults they may be particularly anxious, depressed, or aggressive. And one major review of psychological studies of batterers found only one point of common history: many batterers witnessed the battery of their mothers when they were boys. Millions of children become targets of violence as well, for the man who batters a woman is likely to abuse the kids, too. Two studies found that between 53 and 70 percent of men who battered a wife or girlfriend also abused a child; and in households with four or more children, 92 percent of the batterers abused the children. Two other studies of children who received hospital treatment for abuse found that between 45 and 59 percent of their mothers were battered women. Such children, too, are likely to become depressed, anxious, or aggressive; and the physical and emotional damage that will freight their adult lives is beyond calculation and repair.

Minimizing Male Violence

The term "battered woman" also sets apart women who are victims of one form of male violence, as though there is something peculiar about *them*, and obscures the universal pattern of male dominance. (This is another reason why battered women themselves resist the label.) Labeling separate categories of male violence—battering, rape, incest, pimping, murder, and so on—makes each "problem" seem smaller than it is, a local condition, or a personal one.

In fact, the categories of male violence interpenetrate and merge. What the batterer does inside the family, the rapist and pimp and murderer do outside the family. What the incestuous father does inside the family, the child molester does outside the family. The batterer subjects his wife or girlfriend to a process of seduction and coercion (known as "romance"), while the pimp uses an *identical* process of recruitment and indoctrination (known in the trade as "seasoning") to "turn out" a prostitute. In fact, the batterer often is a pimp, forcing his wife to have sex with other men or with animals. The batterer often is the molester of his own child or stepchild, or of his girlfriend's child. Batterers rape and rapists batter. Many women suffer male violence sequentially at the hands of various men: the girl beaten or sexually abused by her father, stepfather, or older

> *"The word 'partner'... conveniently hides one undeniable fact: ... the assailant in almost all heterosexual and homosexual violence is a man."*

brother runs away only to be picked up by a pimp, raped and battered, and turned into prostitution from which she may try to escape by marrying a batterer if she is not first murdered on the job. In California in 1981 Victor Burnham was convicted of marital rape after not one but three of his wives testified to rape, battery, torture, and captivity (which the prosecutor likened to the experience of prisoners of war) dating back to 1964. He is different in degree but not in kind from the dozens of serial sexual killers who roam the United States slaughtering one woman (or child) after another. Indeed dominance and violence have become so inextricably bound up with male sexuality that some observers see the serial sexual killer as merely the logical extension of what it means these days to be a man. Thus, even to speak of male violence as a "problem" is euphemistic, suggesting that what women and children experience as a fundamental, universal condition of life is discrete and readily overcome or solved, and that it is a malaise rather than an accumulation of undeterred criminal acts.

A Vocabulary of Damaging Inadequacy

In short, when it comes to a discussion of "family violence," we are stuck with a vocabulary too flimsy for the subject, a vocabulary powerful only in this one respect: its insidious subversion of our understanding. I use *battering*, *battery*, and *assault* to name acts of physical violence, although the profound psychological damage men do to women in addition to, or in lieu of, physical violence—the damage implicit in Cobbe's "*torture*"—leaks out around the hard edges of those legalistic words. And when I quote a court decision, a newspaper article, an academic study, a legislative proposal, or a sermon, we are set adrift again on the warm and featureless seas of *domestic violence*.

We are likely to be betrayed by syntax as well, ambushed all at once by the passive voice, just as women *are beaten*, wives *are abused*, children *are abandoned*. By whom? In the scholarship of sociology and psychology, and even in the columns of the local papers, women are less likely to be assaulted by men than by a deadly mob of abstract nouns. Women are victimized by *abuse*, they are threatened by *aggressive behavior*, they are battered by *the relationship*, they are done in by the *cycle of violence*, they are mutilated by *spousal hostility* and murdered by *domestic incidents*. Women are victimized by amorphous verbs, too. Women experience battering. They *suffer* abuse. They *undergo* assault. Rarely in the authoritative literature does a man hit a woman: in the gut, for instance, or the face, with his fist, hard—hard enough to split her lip, loosen her teeth, break her nose, lace her eyeball with a red web of ruptured veins—hard enough to make the blood run down the page. In real life it happens all the time.

Domestic violence, *battering*, *wife beating*, *woman abuse*—call it what you will—is something greater than and different from what the terminology and the standard syntax suggest. We must look at the thing itself—at what is really going on.

Child Abuse Is Defined Too Broadly

by David Rieff

About the author: *David Rieff is a regular contributor to* Harper's Magazine *and the author of* Los Angeles: Capital of the Third World.

Imagine a country in which millions of apparently successful people nonetheless have come to believe fervently that they are really lost souls—a country where countless adults allude matter-of-factly to their "inner children," who, they say, lie wounded and in desperate need of relief within the wreckage of their grown-up selves. Imagine the celebrities and opinion-makers among these people talking nightly on TV and weekly in the magazines not about their triumphs but about their victimization, not about their power and fame but about their addictions and childhood persecutions.

A New National Narrative

Imagine that this belief in abused "inner children" dragging down grown-up men and women has become so widespread as to exert considerable influence over the policies of such supposedly practical bodies as corporations, public hospitals, and boards of education—which, in turn, have taken to acting as if the greatest threat facing their various constituencies is a nexus of addictions and other self-destructive "behaviors," ranging from alcoholism and drug addiction to the more nebulous, if satisfyingly all-encompassing, category of "co-dependency," a term meaning, in essence, any reliance for one's sense of self on the opinion of someone else, someone more often than not plagued by his or her own addiction. One would be imagining a place, then, where nearly *everyone* is identified—is identifying himself or herself—as some sort of psychological cripple.

In this country, it is taken for granted that no blame for these addictions or dependencies can be assigned to those who exhibit them. Terms such as "character," "weakness," and "individual responsibility" are no longer deemed appropriate. Those who drink too much, take drugs, or destroy themselves (and their co-dependents) in other ways suffer either from a disease (like alcoholism) or

Excerpted from "Victims All?" by David Rieff, *Harper's Magazine*, October 1991. Reprinted by permission of Wylie, Aitken & Stone, as agents for the author.

from difficulties that are the direct, ineluctable result of the faulty upbringing to which they had been subjected as children.

A desperate creed, and yet this country is not—as, upon hearing it, an outsider might have had reason to suppose—on anything approaching its last legs. It has neither been bombed by fighter aircraft so technologically advanced as to be undetectable to its air defenses nor has its morale been unhinged by the rigors of prolonged triple-digit inflation, an austerity program imposed by the World Bank, the emigration of its skilled professionals, or inter-communal savagery. To the contrary, here is a country that, although scarcely without its difficulties, remains one of the richest countries on earth, indeed one of the richest places the world has ever known. . . .

> *"Terms such as 'character,' 'weakness,' and 'individual responsibility' are no longer deemed appropriate."*

Those drawn to the idea of their wounded "inner child" are doing pretty well. Many have life stories that hew to what has long been the country's favorite narrative about itself: rags to riches. But now there has developed a new narrative: from addiction, through discovery of the "inner child," to recovery. In this country, this is the story men and women are increasingly telling themselves and one another. The country is the United States of America. . . .

Everyone Is a Victim

Proponents of recovery do not think in group terms. They claim that virtually everyone in the country is, in some essential sense, a victim—a victim, mostly, of abusive parents. Moreover, the recovery advocates say they have the statistics to back up this sweeping assertion. "What we're hearing from experts," John Bradshaw, one of the recovery movement's leading figures, confidently told an interviewer not long ago, "is that approximately 96 percent of the families in this country are dysfunctional to one degree or another.". . .

It will be obvious that Bradshaw is not a man to shrink from extremes. For him, not only are the personal and the political one and the same but so are the historical and the psychological. Borrowing liberally from the work of the Swiss child psychoanalyst Alice Miller, he argues that Nazism was the direct result of Hitler's having been abused as a child. Hitler, too, it would seem, was a victim. "Hitler," Bradshaw writes, "was re-enacting his own childhood, using millions of innocent Jews as his scapegoats." Small wonder, then, that Bradshaw and those who accept his arguments believe that recovery work is far more important than any more conventional social activism. As Bradshaw puts it, "Hitler and black [sic] Nazism are a cruel caricature of what can happen in modern Western society if we do not stop promoting and proliferating family rules that kill the souls of human beings."

More than anything else, it is this bleak, totalizing view of the world that distinguishes the message of most recovery books from that contained in the other self-help volumes with which they share space on bookstore shelves and best-seller lists. The message is not Coué's "every day, in every way, I'm getting better and better," or Norman Vincent Peale's "power of positive thinking," or even Eric Berne's rather more tentative "I'm okay, you're okay." These authors offered little direct criticism of society in those books. Contrast their messages with John Bradshaw's unyielding assertion that "our family life is killing the souls of human beings" and his recommendation that since "most families are dysfunctional because our rules for normalcy are dysfunctional. . . . The important issue is to find out what species of flawed relating your family specialized in. Once you know what happened to you, you can do something about it."

And the one thing that all the recovery writers insist upon is that, whether an individual remembers it or not, *something did happen.* According to Dr. Charles Whitfield, one of the most successful recovery writers, only between 5 and 20 percent of Americans grew up "with a healthy amount and quality of love, guidance and other nurturing. . . ." The rest—and, unsurprisingly, most recovery writers favor Dr. Whitfield's lower figure for those raised in healthy homes—did not receive anywhere near enough of the aforementioned psychic nutrients to successfully "form consistently healthy relationships, and to feel good about themselves and what they do." If the result is not a substance addiction like drink or drugs it is likely to be a "process" addiction taking the form of either too much interest in some activity or too much reliance on some other person or thing for an individual's sense of identity—the dreaded co-dependency.

A Proliferation of Labels

In their book *Adult Children: The Secrets of Dysfunctional Families*, John and Linda Friel provide a list of recovery groups—an incomplete list, they advise—that maps (or begins to) the contours of contemporary American addiction and victimhood. Beginning with AA [Alcoholics Anonymous], the Friels go on to note Al-Anon (the organization founded as a sort of ladies' auxiliary to AA, in the period when it was all male, to help the wives—later, more ecumenically, any loved one—of alcoholics), Alateen, Al-Atot, Narcotics Anonymous, Cocaine Anonymous, Overeaters Anonymous, Bulimics/Anorexics Anonymous, Sexaholics Anonymous, Sex Addicts Anonymous (the recovery movement is full of mysteriously fine distinctions), Adult Children Anonymous, Adult Children of Alcoholics, Gamblers Anonymous, Spenders Anonymous, Smokers Anonymous, Debtors Anonymous, Fundamentalists Anonymous, Parents Anonymous, Child Abusers Anonymous, Workaholics Anonymous, Shoplifters Anonymous, Pills Anonymous, and Emotions Anonymous.

> *"Proponents of recovery . . . claim that virtually everyone in the country is . . . a victim—a victim, mostly, of abusive parents."*

Whew! And, of course, such a list is infinitely expandable. For if there is really not all that much difference between working too hard and abusing your children (and the Friels' decision to place them side by side suggests that, in the recovery context, there really isn't), then any conduct that can be engaged in enthusiastically, never mind compulsively—from stamp collecting to the missionary position—would be one around which a recovery group could presumably be organized.

> *"It is clear that the next decade will give rise to any number of new subsets of the victimized, the impaired, and the addicted."*

And new categories are, indeed, cropping up all the time. . . . The list goes on and on, and it is clear that the next decade will give rise to any number of new subsets of the victimized, the impaired, and the addicted. . . .

"Victimhood" Is Expanding into Meaninglessness

For people like Whitfield and the other recovery writers to insist that we are all victims is pretty much the same thing as asserting that no one is a victim. Either way, the civic voice is muffled, if not blotted out; it is up to you or to me, but not we. Of course, such an outbreak of self-pity among the affluent classes as recovery has spawned all but ensures that the real victims in American society—those who will never be affluent enough or have enough free time to work it out with their "inner children"—will not get the attention that is the necessary first step to any improvement in *their* lives. . . .

The recovery writers insist that nearly everyone in the United States has been the victim of some instance of child abuse. One would think that if a term like "child abuse" is to have any real meaning, it must be limited to some variant of sexual violation or battery. The recovery movement would have it otherwise. They talk of mental abuse, of parents' abusing their children by "invalidating their experiences," even of abusers who thwart "the child's spirituality," to quote Charles Whitfield. So much for life in its full, honest imperfection.

In recovery workshops, as well as at home in the living room, recovery workbooks opened, people are encouraged to try to get in touch with that "inner child" and discern, through a dialogue with it, whether he or she was abused: "Memory work," it is called. One might reasonably ask if someone moved to do such memory work were not, in some way, predisposed to uncover evidence of abuse—some explanation of their addiction or emotional unhappiness. But this is not a question to be entertained. Steven Farmer writes in his book *Adult Children of Abusive Parents*, "No matter how abuse is defined or what other people think, you are the ultimate judge: If you think you were abused, you were. If you're not sure, you probably were."

What matters is the story that you arrive at. Thus, to imagine is to make it so, or, as the title of an anthology of postwar American women writers would have it,

"We are the stories we tell." Bradshaw's story is, as he says in *Homecoming*, that we are "divine infants in exile," a nation of E.T.'s desperate to come home. And it seems that increasing numbers of Americans are beginning to agree with him.

But *are* we the stories we tell? During the period that I was reading little but recovery books, I kept remembering an encounter I had seen once on television between reporters and the grieving father of one of the passengers killed when Sikh terrorists blew up an Air India flight over the Irish Sea in 1985. The weeping father had been shown coming out of the makeshift morgue that the Irish police had set up in a small coastal village, and no sooner had he done so than he was surrounded by the hacks who bombarded him with questions. "What are you going to do?" one called out. To which, with astonishing dignity, the man replied simply, "Do? What do you expect me to do in this dirty world?"

The point that he was trying to make through his sobs was precisely the one that the recovery movement is most anxious to deny. Life may be whatever story you invent in a Bradshaw seminar, but only very affluent, very cut-off people could persuade themselves, at least once they have "returned home," that this is really the way things are. A quick way of seeing just how specific the recovery idea is to prosperous Americans in the late twentieth century is to think how preposterous it would seem not only to a man whose daughter had just been killed by a terrorist bomb, or someone who was hungry, but to someone, anyone, in Croatia, the former Soviet Union, or South Africa. It is a safe bet that they are more worried about what will befall their real children than what has befallen their inner children. It is a measure of the continued economic success of the United States that so many of its citizens could be so buffered from the real harshness of the world that they can spend their time anatomizing the state of their own feelings and speculating, often deep into middle age, about whether or not their parents always behaved as well as they should have.

> *"If a term like 'child abuse' is to have any real meaning, it must be limited."*

In most of the world, though, people's thoughts are elsewhere. Beyond our innocent shores, it is understood that the past is not always knowable and never recuperable, that there is sometimes nothing to be done, and that reality conforms neither to our desires nor to our schemes, psychic or material. There is chance, and fate, and tragedy.

Abusive Parenting Is Defined Too Broadly

by Dana Mack

About the author: *Dana Mack writes regularly for* Commentary, *a conservative monthly magazine, and is an affiliate scholar at the Institute for American Values, a research organization focusing on issues affecting the American family.*

Not so long ago, parents were generally looked upon as repositories of wisdom and rectitude, and they were the unchallenged custodians of their children's welfare. But today parents are relentlessly assailed as abusive, and unworthy of their authority over children.

Just take television, where during the 1993 season alone, Americans have seen and heard countless tales of parental cruelty and lasciviousness—child beatings, sexual molestations, and even murder. From the testimonials of the Oprah Winfrey show, to the movie *Child of Rage*, to the *Prime Time* segment devoted to "Satanic Child Abuse," TV has spread the disconcerting impression that everywhere sick and/or evil parents are brutalizing the young lives so carelessly entrusted to their care. . . .

The Scapegoating of Parents

Then, too, there is an exploding "self-help" literary genre which specializes in parent-bashing. Perhaps the best-known example is Susan Forward's *Toxic Parents* (1989). Forward, one of the first psychotherapists to charge that there is widespread child abuse going on in America, has made a veritable science of ferreting out ways in which parents can oppress children. The behavior she assails in her book as "abusive" ranges all the way from incest to occasional moralizing, from life-threatening beatings to the demand that children show up for Christmas dinner. Whether horrific or harmless, every parental demand is treated by Forward as a display of power hunger. Subtle psychological pressures, in her view, can be just as destructive as brutal beatings. "Many civic authorities," she warns, "have come to recognize the need for new procedures to deal with . . . physical and sexual abuse. But even the most concerned authorities can do nothing for the verbally-abused child. He is all alone.". . .

When one stops to consider that the parents now derogated as so abusive are for the most part those who raised the baby-boom generation, one's head can begin to spin. For the baby boomers grew up in a charmed era for children—an era in which a truly gentle child-rearing ethos began to permeate society at all levels.

A Shift Towards Greater Permissiveness

At the source was Sigmund Freud, whose discoveries had given rise to the idea that, as early as infancy, parental mistakes could wreak lifelong damage upon a child. Then came Dr. Benjamin Spock, the pediatrician whose book *Baby and Child Care* (first published in 1945), exerted a greater influence over the parents of the first postwar decades in America than any other. The key to raising happy children, said Spock, was to relinquish the "biblical" model of parenthood and relieve children of those pressures of parental power and authority which supposedly created dependent and inhibited adults. Traditional discipline—with its harsh sting of anger and reprobation—was Spock's great bugaboo. In *Baby and Child Care*, for example, he suggested that parents might respond to school-age stealing by "thinking over" whether their child might "need more . . . approval at home," and even a raise in allowance!

It is important to recognize the extent to which Spock and his disciples stood the ideal of good parenthood on its head. For them, "good" parents were not those who got their children to behave, but those who understood why their children might *not* behave. Good parents did not depend upon wielding power in rearing their children. They did not demand; they did not rage; they were careful not to react to provocation with anger. Rather, they empathized with the arduous process of psychic development, and coped with—rather than fought— the passing stages.

Much of the popular child-rearing advice that followed Spock's amounted to an elaboration of this essentially psychoanalytic model of parenthood. The most famous child-rearing authors of the late 60's and early 70's, Haim Ginott and Thomas Gordon, wrote their books at a time when the baby boomers had grown into rebellious teenagers, and were testing parental tempers to the limit. Ginott and Gordon advised that parents try to bridge the generation gap with therapeutic and counseling techniques—that they turn themselves, in effect, into therapists.

> *"'Abusive' ranges . . . from incest to occasional moralizing, from life-threatening beatings to the demand that children show up for Christmas dinner."*

Thus, the traditional arsenals of parental authority—shouting, chiding, slapping, and threatening—were no longer regarded by "enlightened" thought as immutable prerogatives for making kids behave. In fact, this new attitude had long since spread into education, social work, and even the mass media. Parents who continued to rely on physical punishment or verbal rebuke as means of child management learned from such TV shows as *Father Knows Best* and *Leave It to Beaver* that a powerful cultural elite considered them backward.

Not surprisingly, this permissive school was due to come in for some criticism. The late 60's and early 70's were, after all, a period when a fair number of people who had granted their children "voting rights" and power to negotiate all the household rules found themselves forced to rescue these same children from the dreadful embarrassments of drug busts, religious cults, and arrests for political subversion. Indeed, by the 80's, faced with statistical evidence of ever-rising substance abuse, violence, delinquency, and teen pregnancy, a new school of child-rearing experts was calling for a return to more authority and discipline in child-rearing.

> *"Parents who continued to rely on physical punishment or verbal rebuke . . . learned . . . that a powerful cultural elite considered them backward."*

Not that the theorists of the so-called "assertive-discipline" school relinquished the therapeutic notion that children who misbehaved were unhappy rather than naughty. Nor were they prepared to give up on the idea of parenthood by social contract rather than by natural authority. Demanding obedience, displaying anger, spanking, reproving, or moralizing, the new theorists continued to make clear, were ignoble ways of managing children.

What then should parents do? They should "withhold friendliness" or "remove special privileges" when their children acted up, and they should "encourage good behavior with rewards . . . and with promises of more rewards." So advised a slew of new books on the subject of "assertive discipline." Their model was the personnel-management techniques of the workplace.

The Unconscious Urge to Abuse

The "assertive-discipline" school of child-rearing still boasts a number of adherents today, especially among teachers and behavioral psychologists. But it, along with the Spock-Ginott line, has been eclipsed by the work of a Swiss psychoanalyst, Alice Miller. Two of Miller's books, *For Your Own Good: Hidden Cruelty in Child-Rearing and the Roots of Violence* and *Thou Shalt Not Be Aware: Society's Betrayal of the Child* (the first published here in translation in 1983, and the second in 1984), dealt shattering blows to the optimistic notion that parents, with a few tips, could be taught to raise their children without doing them permanent harm.

Miller presented the analytic community with a devastating critique of modern advice for parents. Parenthood, Miller insisted, was not a rational, conscious process dictated by a set of beliefs about how children should be raised. It was an un-

29

conscious power struggle between adults and their children, and one which invariably ended with the former emerging victorious and the latter crushed.

The roots of all hatred, violence, and criminality, Miller argued, were to be traced to one source and one source alone: the pathological acts of sadism perpetrated every day, and in every home, by parents on their children—regardless of their child-rearing philosophy. Parents could not *choose* to be good or bad. For they were unwitting slaves to the dark secrets of their own childhoods.

"The individual psychological stages in the lives of most people," Miller wrote, "are . . . to be hurt as a small child, . . . to fail to react to the resulting suffering with anger, to show gratitude for what are supposed to be good intentions, . . . [and] to discharge the stored-up anger onto others [namely, one's own defenseless children] in adulthood. . . ."

According to Miller, even parents who never uttered a harsh word, much less raised a hand to their children, visited upon them unbearable psychological pain and cruelty. By the mere exercise of their instincts, parents promulgated a process of submission to authority and self-denial that amounted to "soul murder." Thus was a legacy of abuse haplessly transmitted from generation to generation, with neither parents nor children aware of its cruelty. Religion, education, even psychoanalysis, she charged, encouraged children to idealize parents for mistreating them, and the child-rearing conventions of Western culture congratulated parents for abusing their offspring in the names of discipline and civilization. . . .

An enthusiastic reception of Miller's ideas in the American academic community had long been prepared. Her depiction of bourgeois family life as an authoritarian political model was already quite familiar to social thinkers here from the writings of the neo-Marxist scholars of the Frankfurt School. But what was to guarantee the success of Miller's ideas among the broader public was not their affinity to an academic school of thought, or the sponsorship of several stars of the therapeutic world—among them the renegade Freudian, Jeffrey Masson. It was their ready *solution* to the putative evils of family life.

> *"Eighty percent of substantiated cases of child maltreatment pose no serious physical danger."*

While theorists of the family who came before Miller seemed unable to offer any remedy for its shortcomings except social revolution, Miller promised more immediate help through the "inner revolution" undertaken on the psychoanalytic couch. Psychoanalysis, she proposed, must concentrate on helping patients release their pent-up "narcissistic rage" against the parents who had mistreated them. Patients who by means of psychoanalytic catharsis reexperienced the sources and intensity of their childhood angers and resentments could then disengage themselves from the impulse to victimize their own children as they themselves had been victimized. . . .

30

America's Preoccupation with the Dysfunctional Family

In the late eighties, the entire complex of Miller's ideas was adopted with alacrity in the therapeutic profession and among self-help gurus. From Ellen Bass and Laura Davis's book, *Courage to Heal* to John Bradshaw's *On Family*, the nuclear family was pronounced "dysfunctional," "shaming" and "abusive." The result has been a rash of accusations of physical and sexual abuse against parents by grown children—accusations which (as is more and more coming to be recognized) are at least as likely to be the result of therapeutic suggestion as of actual abuse. . . . The consequence has been embittered and broken family ties, with no one knows how many innocent aging parents now denounced for crimes they never committed.

Another consequence of the new ideas has been an explosion of communal activism and publicity intent on convincing parents of the present generation of their need for therapeutic help. In my own community—a small town in Fairfield County, Connecticut—invitations to join parent "support groups," to attend lectures on parental "styles" and "stresses," to take advantage of the services of school psychologists and social workers, and particularly to avail oneself of information on "codependency" and "abuse," flood mailboxes and constitute a good portion of the literature sent home with children from the public schools.

Even parents' magazines propound the by-now popular view that conscientious mothers and fathers will seek help from psychotherapeutic resources as a preventive measure in child-rearing. Recently, a publication specializing in advertisements for birthday-party entertainment and nanny-referral services goaded parents to consider the benefits of family and twelve-step therapy, whether there were problems at home or not. Pointing to the ever-increasing suicide rate among teen-agers, the article blamed parents who had not submitted themselves to the psychotherapeutic experience. . . .

> *"Parental foibles which used to be the object of good-natured jibes—chastising . . . demanding too much . . . —are now widely depicted as abusive."*

Children, too, are being targeted. My community newspaper recently printed a front-page article advertising the hotline services of a nearby Kids-in-Crisis center. The center expects children to call not only in cases where they are physically maltreated or demoralized by family conflict, but also when they might simply be "afraid to go home because of a problem at school"—that is, when they are looking for someone to defuse the force of parental discipline. Teachers also now commonly set aside daily or weekly time for the purpose of unveiling the specters hanging over each child—from the high tragedy of parental desertion to the low comedy of resented bedtimes.

Most of the time, such exercises in the confessional mode are performed within the context of "comprehensive-health" or "life-skills" curricula mandated by state governments. These programs instruct children in the delicate subjects of pedophilia, alcoholism, drug addiction, and other dangerous negative propensities of adults—and this introduction to the big, bad world of grown-ups begins in kindergarten.

For example, the *Here's Looking at You, 2000* comprehensive-health curriculum, now used in thousands of school districts throughout the nation, features a cuddly parrot puppet by the name of Miranda who instructs children in almost all the ins and outs of family pathology. In the opening lesson for second grade, Miranda implies that when adults scream at children, it usually means they have had one too many bottles of beer. Through songs, stories, films, and "role-playing," she encourages kids to check the family cupboards for alcohol, nicotine, and

> *"The underlying impetus of the movement to 'liberate' children from parental control and impositions has little to do with concern for the welfare of children."*

other "poisons," share their "feelings" about the "war" that is their "home life," and confess "problems at home" by "writing secret messages" to the teacher.

My own eight-year-old worries now that her parents drink wine with dinner, that our marital spats will lead to divorce, and that we lack the wherewithal to handle an emergency properly. For that eventuality, she has memorized a host of 1-800 numbers given to her by her teacher.

The Numbers Do Not Add Up

There is no evidence that child abuse has reached epidemic proportions in America. Owing to massive public awareness campaigns on the issue of child abuse, reports of child maltreatment skyrocketed between 1976 and 1993 from 669,000 to nearly 3 million. In the same period, however, the percentage of such reports which could be substantiated upon investigation by child welfre authorities drastically declined. According to Douglas J. Besharov, founding director of the National Center on Child Abuse and Neglect, each year well less than 40 percent of child maltreatment reports are substantiated, and around 80 percent of these substantiated reports turn out to pose no serious danger—either physical or psychological—to the children involved. In fact, on average today, only 3 percent of substantiated reports involve an injury requiring medical attention.

Indeed "substantiated" child-abuse cases cannot be taken at face value, since they have in recent years run the gamut of what most of us would consider pretty innocuous practices. Parents have actually been convicted of such "crimes" as restricting television viewing, or taking a child out of school for a few days for reasons unacceptable to school authorities. Even those parental foibles which used to be the object of good-natured jibes—chastising too much, demanding too much, worrying too much—are now widely depicted as abusive.

Is, then, the veritable hysteria over child abuse perhaps a symptom of increased sensitivity to the welfare of our children? Not according to Richard Elkind, who argues in his interesting book, *The Hurried Child* (1988), that the underlying impetus of the movement to "liberate" children from parental control and impositions has little to do with concern for the welfare of children. On the contrary, he writes, "Our new family styles (divorce, single parenting, two-parent working families, and blended families) make it next to impossible for the majority of parents to provide the kind of child-rearing that goes along with the image of children as in need of parental nurture."

Here we may have the key to the puzzling obsession with child abuse: by imagining that even their own highly permissive parents were authoritarians who abused them; by buying into the theory that parenthood is inherently pathological; and by assuming the competency of schools and communal institutions to raise children or, worse, of children to raise themselves—the notoriously self-regarding baby-boom generation, now become parents themselves, can also imagine that they are doing the right thing in failing or refusing to accept full responsibility for the physical care and the moral education of their own children.

None of this is to deny that far too many children in contemporary America suffer—as children everywhere have, from time immemorial—the whims of ill-willed, immoral, vindictive, and even vicious parents; nor is it to deny that many small cups are filled to the brim with bitter oppression. But the truth is that many more children among us suffer from the opposite offense. For if there is a widespread criminal disposition to be feared in the current generation of parents, it is not their tendency to exceed the proper limits of their authority; it is their readiness to abdicate the parental role. And indeed, according to the National Center on Child Abuse and Neglect, parents today are far more likely to neglect their children than to abuse them. Which, no doubt, explains why there has been so much talk about abuse and so little about neglect.

Properly Executed Spanking Is Not a Form of Violence

by John K. Rosemond

About the author: *John K. Rosemond is a family psychologist and author of several books, including* Parent Power! *and* John Rosemond's Six-Point Plan for Raising Happy, Healthy Children. *He serves as director of the Center for Affirmative Parenting, an educational and research resource for families and mental health professionals.*

Discussion (hah!) of this volatile topic generally begins with someone asking, Do you *believe* in spanking children? Strange—as if spanking is some sort of religious principle or experience. There are some, in fact, who would have parents believe that by spanking children on a regular basis, they are pleasing God and doing His (this is definitely a guy-God) will, but I am not one of those.

Speaking for myself, spanking has never been a religious experience. I do not believe that one spoils the child by sparing the rod, or switch, or belt, or hand. But, true confession time, I have, on occasion, spanked my children. When they were much younger, that is (they're both adults). And, in retrospect, given the same situations and outrageous behaviors, I would probably do so again. I have no regrets. But I don't *believe* in spanking.

Spanking Is Not Abusive

I am not of an extremist persuasion on this issue. I issue that disclaimer realizing that by admitting I've taken an occasional hand (and only a hand, I assure you) to my children, I join, in the minds of some, the ranks of the vile. Nonetheless, I do not believe that spankings are necessary to the proper rearing of children. Nor do I believe that spankings are, in and of themselves, abusive.

So, what *do* I believe? I believe that spankings are a lousy form of discipline. In fact, I believe they do not warrant being classed as discipline at all. At best, a spanking is nothing more, nothing less, than a dramatic form of nonverbal communication. It is a means of getting the attention of a child who needs to give that attention quickly; of terminating a behavior that is rapidly escalating out of control; of putting an exclamation point in front of a message the child needs to hear.

The spontaneously delivered (as in without warning) spank to the child's rear end says, "Stop!" and "Now hear this!" Having terminated the behavior in question (a tantrum, for example), having secured the child's attention, it is necessary that the parent follow through with a consequence of one sort or another. The spank is merely the prelude to the consequence. In the final analysis, the spank is, therefore, inconsequential. The follow-through is what's important. Without proper follow-through a spanking is, at the very least, stupid.

> "*A spanking is nothing more, nothing less, than a dramatic form of nonverbal communication.*"

The parent might send the child to his or her room for a time, or take away a privilege for the remainder of the day, or simply give the child a stern reprimand. For the most part, and for the purposes of our discussion, the form the consequence takes is fairly arbitrary. All-important is that the spanking not be the consequence, the end in itself. When spankings are treated as an end in and of themselves, parents misuse, overuse, and edge ever closer to abuse. No doubt about it, spankings can be administered abusively.

But, then, banishing a child to his or her room can be done abusively. It would be abusive, for instance, to lock the child's door and keep the child in confinement for days. And one can reprimand a child about his or her misbehavior abusively. It would, for example, be abusive to refer to the child as a "little shit." But sending children to their rooms and reprimanding them are not, in and of themselves, abusive. Nor are spankings. But, in the wrong hands, they can be.

At this point, the naysayer is probably inclined to say, Given that there's no way of knowing in advance who will spank abusively and who will not, let's just bypass the risk by making spanking illegal. The same argument can be made for sending children to their rooms and talking to them, thus it is absurd, rhetorical (as all the naysayer's arguments will prove to be).

Spanking as a First Resort

The term *corporal punishment* is problematic to this, uh, discussion because a properly administered spanking is not, strictly speaking, a punishment. Nor, for that matter, is a wrongly administered spanking. According to the scientific definition, a punishment is a consequence that renders the behavior that preceded it less likely to reoccur. But people who believe they can spank certain behaviors out of existence are going to discover otherwise. Their frustration is likely to drive them to spank more often and harder. Almost inevitably, these folks wind up spanking abusively. But it is important to understand that these are not necessarily abusive people. Often, perhaps more often than not, these are people who want to do right by their children. The proper intervention here is education, not legislation.

When I am asked, by the courts or social services, to counsel parents who have spanked a child or children abusively, I rarely waste time attempting to persuade these folks to stop spanking. Instead of trying to paddle back up the stream of their upbringing, I advise them on how to spank *strategically*, as in occasionally, at carefully selected times, and only to secure the child's attention. This has not won me friends at social services (where one can generally find one of the largest concentration of emotionally charged zealots in the free world), but has definitely reduced recidivism among these clients.

It is appropriate, at this point, to define what, in my estimation, constitutes an appropriate manner of applying a spank to a child's rear end. I believe (that word again) in spanking as a first resort; in spanking in anger; in spanking only with one's hand; in spanking only the child's rear end; in administering only one, certainly no more than two, spanks at a time. I also believe that the more often one spanks, the less effective the spankings will be at terminating undesirable behaviors and securing the child's attention. In order to retain a spank's effectiveness, parents must spank only once in the proverbial blue moon.

Spank as a first resort? That's right. Spontaneously. As soon as you see that the child is losing control or as soon as the child commits whatever completely outrageous act (e.g., spitting on an adult). Whack! "Now hear this!" Send the child to his room.

> *"Sending children to their rooms and reprimanding them are not, in and of themselves, abusive. Nor are spankings."*

Done. As one builds up to a spanking with warning and threat, one builds frustration. When, under those "last resort" circumstances, the spanking finally comes, it is likely to consist of a whack, whack, whack, whack, whack, whack, whack, whack, whack. That's when spankings become abuse.

Spank in anger? That's right. If you're going to spank a child's rear end, it is rightful to make perfectly clear you disapprove of the child's behavior. You are displeased, as in angry. Not in a rage, however. You are not in a rage because you've spanked as a first resort. You are just angry, and you are able to communicate that emotion clearly.

Add the hand only, not belts, switches, spoons, or whatever. Add to the child's rear end only, not thighs, face, arms, or whatever. Add once, maybe twice. Add the message and the consequence, the follow-through, and you've got a properly administered spanking. But I don't *believe* in spanking. You can do without them, if you choose.

The Harmfulness of Spanking Is Unproven

"So, then, let's do without them!" No, I said *you* can do without them. You choose for you. I'll choose for me. You accept responsibility for your behavior, but do me the favor of not trying to accept responsibility for mine, okay? I'll handle that myself, thank you.

You see, what really, truly bothers me about the naysayers is they think they know what's best for everyone. Beneath the veneer of social concern, they're pseudointellectual, politically correct megalomaniacs. If you don't agree with them, they want to pass laws that make you agree, or at least conform to their ideas of what constitutes appropriate behavior. They believe they are ordained, by virtue of moral superiority, to create a perfect world, and have a right to impose that vision on us all, by whatever means necessary.

> *"I believe . . . in spanking as a first resort; in spanking in anger; in spanking only with one's hand; in spanking only the child's rear end."*

They say spankings are abusive. Why? Because they are acts of violence. I say not necessarily. Spankings can be violent. On the other hand, spankings can simply be dramatic. But the naysayers' swollen egos prevent acceptance of any other point of view. There is but one proper point of view. Theirs.

They say that spankings teach children that violence is an acceptable means of responding to interpersonal conflict. This, they assert, is "proven" by the "fact" that violent and/or abusive adults, almost to the person, were abused as children. Accepting the truth in the latter, it nonetheless proves nothing about spanking. By assuming, a priori, that spankings are abusive, the argument violates one of the precepts of rational inquiry. Furthermore, the argument fails to consider the many, many, many people who were spanked as children (some, like myself, fairly often) who are not, as adults, violent or abusive. (I realize, however, that by admitting I was spanked as a child and that I spanked my children, I've "proven" their argument.)

They wave research that "clearly proves" that spanking destroys self-esteem, promotes violent behavior, and so on. The research stinks. All of it. There is not one study into the effects of spanking on children that's worth the paper it's written on. Every single one of them (I've reviewed them all, I think) is rife with design problems. This so-called research would be ridiculed in a sophomore course in experimental psychology.

In the first place, there is no research that tracks children who were spanked properly as opposed to improperly. To my knowledge, that distinction has never been made by any researcher. That reveals something important about many, if not most, of these so-called researchers. They're not doing research at all. They're trying to promote their own personal agendas. And they cloak this promotion, this shameless propaganda effort, in the guise of "science."

But as long as we're talking lousy research, I'll bring out some of my own. We'll compare lousy research with lousy research. That way, we'll stand on equal ground. My lousy research involves me and my two children. As I said, I spanked them. They're fine, thank you. They're achievement oriented, but not compulsively so. They're responsible, but do not take life seriously. They're gregarious, but not self-centered. They've never given one indication of an inclination toward violence. They're not perfect. They have their share of problems, as do we all, but not big ones. Just typical ones, the ones that come with lack of experience and maturity. Therefore, the research—my research—disproves all the other research. My research "clearly proves" there is a proper way of spanking children that is not abusive, that does not result in damage to a child's self-esteem or significant emotional damage of any other description.

Politics—Not Spanking—Is the Real Issue

When all is said and done, this argument isn't about spanking, or corporal punishment. It's about people. It's about people who want to create a perfect world. It's about politics and political correctness. It's about people who want to impose their ideology on everyone, by hook or crook. And the more frustrated they become, the more outrageous they become, the more dangerous they become. That's the problem with moral superiority, in any form. Frustrated, it inclines toward totalitarianism.

The problem with spanking is not spanking, it's people. It's a people problem that will not be solved through legislation. It will, in fact, never be completely solved, only mitigated. It can be mitigated through education. So, let's begin the education, keeping in mind that the best, most effective educators, the ones who cause people to truly want to listen, inquire, and learn, don't promote extremist points of view.

Some Cultural Traditions Are Incorrectly Identified as Child Abuse

by Leslie Berger

About the author: *Leslie Berger is a staff writer for the* Los Angeles Times *newspaper.*

Her first thought when police arrived was that her two youngest children were in trouble. Then the recent immigrant from Ho Chi Minh City realized that *she* was the reason for the visit, prompted by concern over the angry-looking red streaks on her 6-year-old son's neck and temples.

Luckily, it didn't take long for authorities to confirm that the marks were from coining, a common Vietnamese practice of massaging away fevers and aches with a heated coin or piece of metal that draws blood to the surface of the skin.

"Everybody has it done. You feel good after," the Northridge, California, woman explained recently.

Instead of being prosecuted on abuse charges or having her son placed in foster care, the middle-aged mother of nine received three visits from a Vietnamese social worker from the Los Angeles County Department of Children's Services. They chatted in their native tongue and he explained some American dos and don'ts on parenting. Meanwhile, following routine procedure, he discreetly made sure the child was safe.

Case closed.

Custom vs. Abuse

As Southern California's immigrant population and cultural diversity continue to swell, authorities are getting better at differentiating misunderstood customs from potential abuse, and at working with parents who have yet to learn that some child-raising practices in their homelands are not socially acceptable here.

As a result of culture clashes and a 24% increase in calls to the Department of Children's Services hot line in recent years, the agency now emphasizes bilingual skills when recruiting workers and requires training in cultural sensitivity. (Department Director Peter Digre estimates that his staff encounters up to 16 languages regularly, although English and Spanish predominate.)

When trouble arises, the department's 18 general family preservation programs allow children to remain at home while pairing families with caseworkers who know their language and culture.

Some local experts attribute the increased calls to an overall rise in family strains caused by a bad economy and to heightened public awareness, but also to the racism and ignorance simmering within the county's cultural potpourri.

"The suspicion of people who are different sets up a predisposition to see parental neglect where it would not be seen if the people were like yourself," said Rino Patti, dean of USC's School of Social Work.

The Department of Children's Services, which does not keep statistics on all ethnic groups represented among its clients, says immigrants are only a fraction of the families it monitors.

But sorting out misperceptions makes the role of culture "extremely important and challenging and complex and . . . one of the big priorities we struggle with every day," Digre said.

Perplexing Practices

The innocent but sometimes baffling practices confronting police, social workers and judges can range from coining to arranged teen-age marriages to swatting unruly children with sticks, as common in some cultures as was spanking with belts in Depression-era America.

For example, one case of alleged sexual abuse involved a rare custom practiced by a San Gabriel Valley man originally from an island off Taiwan. In "the kissing of the flower," the father held up his 6-year-old daughter before relatives and briefly kissed her vagina to mark the passage from infancy to childhood.

Years later, the father, whom police describe as a professional, was arrested and his then-preteen daughter was briefly placed in foster care after she described the experience at school to horrified friends and teachers.

"Authorities are getting better at differentiating misunderstood customs from potential abuse."

Los Angeles County sheriff's Sgt. Tom Sirkel, who investigated the case, said he was perplexed at first. But after a few interviews and a little research, he concluded that there was nothing secretive or sexual about the gesture, which is openly performed with boys as well. The charges were dropped.

"We have had some dilemmas," said Sirkel, who is assigned to the child abuse detail. "Does the cultural behavior constitute a crime when done in the state of California? It may be parentally inappropriate in our eyes, but does it violate the law? Even if it violates the law, is prosecution the best answer?"

Some advocates for unassimilated parents say that despite the county's best efforts, some of their clients remain victims of Western, middle-class bias.

"There's dozens of cases in which the system, which is a white, Anglo-Saxon, Protestant-oriented system, has made bad calls," said attorney Pete R. Navarro, whose private practice includes defending immigrant parents in the county's Juvenile Dependency Court—where families monitored by the Department of Children's Services are divided and reunited daily in one gut-wrenching hearing after another.

> *"The innocent but sometimes baffling practices . . . can range from . . . arranged teen-age marriages to swatting unruly children with sticks."*

Navarro cited a Latina preschooler who was placed in foster care for two weeks after a day-care worker assumed that the birthmarks on her back were bruises and, adhering to the state's mandatory reporting of suspected child abuse, notified the department.

"The child had what we call . . . 'la Mancha Mogolica,'" Navarro said, a Mongolian spot—a large, purplish birthmark usually seen among Asians, Native Americans or Latinos with Native American ancestry. He said the badly traumatized girl was returned to her parents after he initiated a court-ordered exam at Childrens Hospital in Los Angeles.

"The kid was released to her parents and DCS *still* wanted to intervene because of the emotional reaction she had to being separated . . . to give counseling," Navarro said.

Difference Draws Suspicion

One Pacoima-based therapist recalled a large family from rural Mexico that became a Department of Children's Services case after a school nurse found lice on one daughter—considered to be a warning sign of neglect. The children were allowed to remain at home, family counselor Alicia Trelles said. The mother and father—mortified at having their personal hygiene and housekeeping under official scrutiny—were referred to parent education classes and to Trelles, who works with El Nido, a nonprofit group that is part of the department's family preservation network.

"That father's role in the family and his power was completely reduced to nothing," Trelles said. "He felt so embarrassed that he didn't know how to do things in the city, in this country."

Had lice been found on a white, middle-class child, the nurse probably would have sent home a note explaining how to kill the common pest and that would have been that, said attorney Jo Kaplan, whose nonprofit, county-funded firm handles dependency cases for indigent clients.

For "people with language barriers, who are frightened and not used to dealing with people in authority, those cases are treated differently and the worst is presumed," Kaplan said. . . .

Sometimes, it is difficult for department workers to separate the effects of poverty and culture. For example, do parents sleep with their children because they can't afford more space or because in some countries a shared family bed is the norm? Either way, Kaplan and Navarro said, it can be held against them and children are often kept in foster homes until their parents get them their own beds.

(A department official said sleeping arrangements alone "would never be an obstacle for a child returning home." The issue should only arise in cases involving alleged sexual abuse, said department Police Director Renee Powers.)

"Does the cultural behavior constitute a crime . . . ? It may be parentally inappropriate in our eyes, but does it violate the law?"

Institutional bias against poor Latino and Asian parents recalls the experience of Southern and Eastern European immigrants at the turn of the century, USC's Patti said. Back then, he noted, scores of children were taken from their parents in Boston and New York and sent to work on Midwestern farms by Protestant charities who were aghast at the way immigrants' children were raised.

"A great deal has been written about the use of 'child protection' as a way of expressing in not-so-disguised fashion the racism or repugnance of the dominant white society for the habits of particularly southern, Catholic Europeans," Patti said.

He also sees a parallel in that era's anti-Catholic movement with today's backlash against illegal immigrants and concern "that they're taking jobs that should properly go to Americans."

"In those days, people feared Italians were taking jobs the good, sturdy white Americans should have had," Patti said. "So the whole sense of these people was a sense of them threatening the American way of life, of diluting the values that good white Protestant Americans had created."

Today, ironically, it is immigrant parents who are often appalled by American values and this country's relatively lax standards of discipline.

Disciplinary Matters

Other factors can complicate matters. Under California's broadly worded child protection laws, only simple spanking is generally considered appropriate; the use of a belt or a slap to the face, under certain circumstances, can be grounds for court intervention. Thus, corporal punishment generates many of the child abuse reports against unsuspecting immigrants who, like some Americans, may hit disrespectful children with sticks, shoes and fists—the way their parents punished them in their own countries.

The pressures of assimilation often aggravate friction between children and parents, authorities say. "A lot of over-disciplining is due to the frustrations of what the Western world is doing to these kids," said Los Angeles Police Detective

Mike Houchen, who oversees child abuse investigations in West Los Angeles and the San Fernando Valley. Many cases he sees involve Middle Eastern families.

"It's very difficult to deal with parents and tone them down and say, 'Hey, when in Rome . . . ,'" Houchen said. "All of a sudden, the police are involved in what has been a private domain for eons, especially in the East, where family matters are handled by family."

In screening the 90 to 150 reports his office receives each month, Houchen looks at three main issues: whether marks were left on the child, the intent of the parent, and a history of complaints. It is common for him to leave matters with underlying cultural issues, especially first-time offenses, to the Department of Children's Services rather than opening criminal investigations.

The county's child welfare bureaucracy is also less inclined to separate families in which there is no clear-cut risk of physical or sexual abuse. Parents reported for hygiene, folk remedies, even corporal punishment are prime candidates for the family preservation programs, which emphasize education over separation. Joined with networks of community groups, the projects also help families gain housing, clothing and other essentials to help keep them together.

So far, the 18 such projects involve about 3,000 children of all backgrounds in a third of the county, in areas that generate the most foster care candidates.

Working Against Ignorance

Fieldworkers also receive what the department calls "ethnographic training," or instruction in the cultural nuances that can lead to tragic misunderstandings.

Among some cultures, for example, direct eye contact is considered rude and well-mannered people avert their eyes during conversation. But to an uninitiated American investigating possible abuse, that type of behavior could be misinterpreted as a sign of guilt or evasiveness, said Cecilia Reza, who heads the department's American Indian Family Preservation Program.

That is the kind of miscommunication that the department is hoping to avoid. In the case of the Northridge mother who had coined her son, there was little room for misunderstanding, for instance, because her caseworker and his supervisor were Vietnamese. During the last of the social workers' visits, the woman's home, with its dimly lit shrine, simmering broth and crowing pet rooster, evoked the scents and sounds of their homeland, and everyone seemed relaxed.

> *"A great deal has been written about the use of 'child protection' as a way of expressing . . . the racism or repugnance of the dominant white society."*

The men smiled knowingly as the woman demonstrated coining. First, she dabbed a strong-smelling oil onto an adult son's back, then she briskly rubbed his skin with a piece of metal until a pattern of red streaks emerged. He said it did not hurt.

"When you catch the bad wind, you have to get the wind out," the woman explained through workers Bao Truong and Phuoc (Frank) Nguyen, who heads the Asian/Pacific Island preservation project. What she meant, they said, was that the massage draws out the illness.

The woman added that although she still planned to coin her husband and grown children, she would no longer practice the home remedy on her school-age sons, as Truong and Nguyen had advised her. They smiled, satisfied that their mission was accomplished.

"We try to bridge the gap," Nguyen said. "We don't try to accuse."

Verbal Battering Is a Form of Abuse

by Jean Guarino

About the author: *Jean Guarino has been a freelance journalist for over 20 years and is a frequent contributor to* U.S. Catholic *magazine, the* Chicago Parent *magazine, and several other religious, parent, and family-oriented publications.*

When children are young, parents protect their physical health by teaching them to stop and think before they cross a busy street or do anything that might cause bodily harm. Yet in moments of stress, how often do parents fail to stop and think to themselves before saying hurtful things to their children—things that can have a devastating impact on their emotional health?

Words Can Harm

According to Stephanie Ferrara, a Chicago psychotherapist specializing in family therapy,

> Many parents put their mouths on automatic and just say the first thing that pops into their heads without thinking of the terrible effect their words have on their children. Adults who are more resilient and can shrug off the put-downs of their bosses and co-workers think their young children should be able to do the same. They don't realize that, as parents, they are larger than life figures to their children, who accept as fact everything their parents tell them. If their parents say they are dumb, no good, and a failure, then it must be true.

How often do parents make these or similar comments to their children: You're more trouble than you're worth! You're pathetic! You can't do anything right! Get out of here! I'm sick of looking at your face! I wish you were never born! You disgust me! Just shut up! You're a failure just like your father!

And although most parents regret these remarks later when they've had a chance to cool down, by then the damage has been done. Like a virulent weed growing in a beautiful garden, this verbal abuse can only be uprooted by the determined effort of the person responsible for planting it.

Excerpted from "'Don't Call Me Stupid': How to Avoid Hurting Your Kids with Words" by Jean Guarino, *U.S. Catholic*, September 1992. Reprinted with permission of Claretian Publications, 205 W. Monroe St., Chicago, IL 60606.

For instance, Jennifer is a pretty 12-year-old who cheats, lies, steals, and avoids schoolwork. She doesn't believe she can do the work, so she copies the work of others. She gives money or things she has stolen to other kids hoping it will make them like her. This is due to the fact that Jennifer doesn't believe she is worth anything to anyone. Since she was a little girl, her parents have told her: "You can't do anything right. You're stupid. I'll do it myself; you'll ruin it." Her brothers and sisters also pick on her the same way.

Jennifer is a victim of emotional child abuse. Her bruises, invisible to her teachers and other authorities, will remain undetected and untreated. Yet eventually these unseen wounds will leave scars far more damaging than the welts and cuts on a child who has been physically abused.

Judy Keith-Oaks, director of the Center for Personal Recovery in Jonesboro, Tennessee, asserts, "While emotional abuse cannot directly kill, its effects are insidious. Instead of murdering the child, the result is a destruction of the spirit, a loss of the sense of self, a reflection on the ability to succeed, and a barrier to healthy interaction with people."

Self-Worth Requires Praise

This sense of self, or lack thereof, reveals itself in the story of John. John's dad has very clear ideas about how to run things in his house—John, 7, should be kept on his toes. His dad joshes John a lot in front of family and friends; and to keep John jumping, he plays games with him. If John wins a game, his dad makes fun of him for being an egghead; if he loses, he makes fun of him for being a dummy. Unfortunately it's the same with affection. John's dad will call him over for a hug; and when John responds, his dad pushes him away telling him he's getting to be a sissy. John literally cannot win.

Everyone yearns to be loved, accepted, and heard. And people desire worth, esteem, and praise. Everyone wishes to be a somebody. The roots of a person's "somebodiness" lie in his or her childhood. Parents, siblings, grandparents, aunts and uncles, teachers, coaches, friends, and neighbors all feed into people's beliefs about their basic sense of worth. . . .

"Many parents . . . say the first thing that pops into their heads without thinking of the terrible effect their words have on their children."

Nathaniel Branden, author of *How to Raise Your Self-Esteem*, says that a healthy self-esteem—the value we place on the self—leads to a childhood and adulthood of happiness, success, wise decisions, good friendships, confidence, hope, outreach to others, and a close relationship with God. Lack of self-esteem, on the other hand, brings irresponsibility, internal conflicts, rocky relationships, poor choices, confusion, loneliness, spiritual bankruptcy, and a tendency to perpetuate a pattern of emotional abuse on one's own children—which is the most damaging effect.

"What I remember most about my childhood is my father calling me stupid," says Janice, 24. "He'd ask me to read for him; and if I stumbled or missed a word, he'd say, 'You're so damn stupid!' I remember crying about that. His words hurt a lot." But in high school Janice learned that her father was illiterate. Therefore, when he called her stupid, he was project-

> *"The roots of a person's 'somebodiness' lie in his or her childhood."*

ing his negative feelings about himself onto her. When parents label their children fat, lazy, dumb, or ugly, they may need to come to grips with their own lack of self-esteem.

The Trap of Verbal Abuse

Janice admits that she picked up her father's hurtful habits and began verbally abusing her own son. "I started calling my son stupid, bad, and lazy when he was around 3 years old. Finally when he was 5, he said to me, 'Don't call me stupid. I don't like it.' When he said that, I flashed back to my own childhood and started crying. I resolved to change the way I was dealing with my son."

How do parents prevent the words that hurt? How do they stop the patterns of behavior that lead to emotional maltreatment?

Bob Noone, director of Family Services in Wilmette, Illinois, says,

> The first step a parent must take to begin to heal the damage that has been done to the child is to assume some responsibility for the conflict.
>
> Next they have to resolve to change whatever it is in their lives that is poisoning their relationship with their son or daughter. Whatever the stresses are that cause them to lash out at the child must be changed. It isn't easy, and it requires a high level of determination. But nothing will change unless the parent consciously wants it to change.

. . . But even when parents love their children and want to do well by them, families can become caught in a vicious cycle of harsh words that poison a family's time together. It's frightening for both parents and children to think that they are locked into a system of anger and fear that seems to have a life of its own and is out of control.

Stopping the Abuse

Help is only as far as the phone for parents under pressure who have slipped over the edge and chronically vent their anger on those around them least able to defend themselves—their children. They can call other parents who have learned to control their own abusive behavior. . . .

However, in many cases, it is not necessary to use the services of either a hotline or professional counselor. There are many common-sense things people can do to help defuse the tensions in their homes without seeking outside help.

The first and most obvious step is for people to re-evaluate their priorities. Stress is necessary to keep people energized and motivated. But if they find themselves subject to massive amounts of stress and feel burned-out, it's time to eliminate some of the pressures that cause them to blow a fuse.

What situations cause people the most stress? Can they free themselves from some situations that are not really important to them?

"I never learned to say 'no'," says a harried mother who works full-time, serves on the school board, is a den mother, and then committed herself to directing the parish variety show. "The pressure made me a crazy woman," she admits. "I was yelling at the kids every time they opened their mouths. Finally my husband just said, 'Enough!'

"I'm honoring my commitment to direct the show," she says, "but that will be over in another month. But I resigned from the school board, which was very time-consuming. Now I enjoy being a den mother, and I can finally talk to my kids without snapping their heads off."

Parents must learn to listen to their children. And they must give their children positive attention. If all they've done in the past is react to negative behavior, they should try complimenting their children when they do something well. Parents should tell their children they are smart, pretty, handsome, clever, resourceful, fun, a good sport, and kind.

> *"Families can become caught in a vicious cycle of harsh words that poison a family's time together."*

"When my son was little, I never told him I loved him or that he was smart," says Janice. "I do it now, and he responds to me better. He gets higher grades and is more cooperative."

When things happen that can set off an explosion, parents need to take time out. They shouldn't let the explosion happen. Parents must wait. And then wait some more. When people hold their tongues until the heat of the moment has passed, it's a lot easier to respond with love and guidance rather than with anger and harsh words.

And parents need to be people that their children know they can count on. This doesn't mean that they never get angry. But it does mean that a child needs to know that his or her parents love him or her even when one or both of those parents are angry. Parents need to be flexible and willing to stop and peek in on their child's world. The child will feel more valuable because of it. . . .

Guarding One's Words

There are some words that people should never say to each other in a family. Words such as stupid, dummy, idiot, worthless, freak, dope, and jerk have no place in the interactions of parents and their children.

As parents, people should avoid absolute statements, such as "You never . . ." or "You always . . .". They should have a sense of good manners with their families. However, this doesn't mean that parents must avoid all conflict or can't set limits.

Signs of unconditional approval by a parent should be evident to a child. Unconditional love doesn't mean parents always approve of a child's behavior, but it does mean they care no matter what. One way of showing acceptance is through undivided attention in such a way that the child feels truly loved.

> *"Words such as stupid, dummy, idiot, worthless, freak, dope, and jerk have no place in the interactions of parents and their children."*

One mother of four says, "Every month we give each of our boys a chance to do something alone with us. It's his special time when he knows he can spout off about things he might not want to talk about in front of his brothers, and he knows we'll listen."

These special times don't have to be elaborate or expensive. They can involve such simple activities as riding bikes, stopping for a snack, seeing a movie, going to a ball game, or working on a scout project. The important thing is that children feel cherished during their special times.

Admitting Mistakes

And parents need to let their children hear them acknowledge their own mistakes. They need to risk being humble. Parents should dare to say "I'm sorry" to their children when appropriate. Apologizing reveals that the truth is larger than their egos and feelings are more important than their pride.

Children need to witness their parents confronting their shortcomings and strengths. It's all right for parents to lose their cool and yell at their kids with little provocation. But the important thing is to apologize once they've calmed down. If parents do, they will have taught their children an important lesson. . . .

The potential for the most destructive action is present in each of us. . . .

We can escape the temptation to abuse simply by walking into another room or getting a baby-sitter and going out. Escape can come through parenting classes, activities with friends, conversations on a hotline with other parents, or professional counseling.

But most of all, escape will come through prayer and an absolute faith that God has not abandoned us.

Emotional Battering Is a Form of Abuse

by Marti Tamm Loring

About the author: *Marti Tamm Loring directs the Center for Mental Health and Human Development in Atlanta, Georgia, teaches at Georgia State University, and is the author of* Emotional Abuse, *from which this viewpoint is excerpted.*

Vulnerability to emotional abuse generally has its origins in childhood experiences. Babies and children who experience consistent empathy, understanding, and validation from a nurturing figure develop a sense of security and a comfortable pattern of attachment. The safe haven provided by certainty that the nurturer will be there in a kindly and warm manner most of the time endows the child with feelings of trust and hope for the future. When the nurturer mirrors back positively the child's responses to her environment, the seeds of her sense of self are planted and nourished. She feels unique and confident, excited about her own abilities and skills. Attachment to the nurturing parent provides a secure base from which to venture forth and explore the world.

Securely attached children hold onto nurturers tightly and are, in turn, consistently embraced with firmness and warmth. Even when the nurturer is occasionally unavailable or sad, the certainty of physical and emotional reunification (consistently established over time) remains, and no harm is done. The child is not panicked or traumatized by such infrequent physical and/or emotional absences. Generally this ebb and flow of secure attachment is carried over into adult relationships. Partners who establish the trust and certainty of being there for each other during difficult times fulfill their individual needs as well.

Insecurity Begins in Childhood

Infants and children who lack this secure and empathic foundation may become, in the words of J. Bowlby, "anxiously attached." This pattern is sometimes established when illness or depression limits a parent's physical or emotional accessibility to the child, or divorce or separation consumes a parent's emotional resources for a long period. Similarly, the prolonged hospitalization or death of one parent often disrupts the development of normal attachment; the child may grow up emotionally abandoned. In childhood and in later life, this sense of abandonment can result in . . . desperate clinging. . . .

Bowlby's studies of children physically or emotionally separated from their parents for considerable periods of time reveal this pattern of "anxious attachment" and strong clinging behavior under the following conditions:

- When one or both parents either consistently fail to respond to or actively reject the child's efforts to elicit parental care
- During discontinuities of parenting occurring more or less frequently (for example, periods of hospitalization or divorce in which the nurturing figure is emotionally and/or physically absent)
- When a parent persistently threatens to withdraw his or her love as a means of discipline
- When one parent threatens to abandon the family, either to punish the child or to coerce the adult partner
- When one parent threatens to desert or kill the other parent or to commit suicide
- When guilt is induced by telling the child that his or her behavior will cause a parent's illness or death

Fantasies of Intimacy

Bowlby found that a child blamed for a parent's depression will blame herself and become prey to anxiety and fears of abandonment. She will cling all the more desperately to the parent or, in his or her absence, to reassuring fantasies of closeness. If an emotionally distant parent persists in pushing the child away and punishing her, a vicious circle is likely to ensue: the child reaches out for affection and validation again and again, and the nurturer pushes her away in each instance. Each time the cycle is repeated, the child feels more anxious and clings more desperately.

Joanie is a five-year-old whose mother, Susan, experienced sexual abuse as a child. Susan still suffers periodic bouts of depression. During what the family calls "one of her spells," she shuts herself in her room and cries until her husband returns from work. Meanwhile, Joanie's eleven-year-old brother fixes his sister's lunch and takes care of her. When her mother emerges, Joannie rushes to her and hangs on her skirts, sometimes jerking on them to gain attention. The attention, when it

> *"A child blamed for a parent's depression will blame herself and become prey to anxiety and fears of abandonment."*

comes, is harsh: Susan screams at the child, "Leave me alone!" But Joanie clings all the more tightly. She also bids for her mother's attention by trying to engage her in conversation, demanding to be fed frequently, and complaining of frequent stomachaches and headaches.

For children like Joanie, repeated experiences of emotional abandonment induce deep yearnings and unfulfilled hopes for more consistent closeness. The child develops ambivalent emotions: a desperate hope for intimacy, and a despairing suspicion that she will never attain it. Moreover, she has experienced a repetitive cycle of reaching out and being rejected that can set the pattern of her adult life.

The emotionally abused child—and, later, the same child as an emotionally abused adult—treasures the precious nuggets of warmth and understanding she receives from the abuser. They are her lifeline and the basis of her sense of worth. She holds tenaciously to these occasional moments of empathic connection. When they are withdrawn, she mourns their loss and tries desperately to regain them. Recapturing them and transforming them into a more consistent, empathic, and lasting connection becomes her major quest in life. . . .

> *"The [emotionally abandoned] child develops . . . a desperate hope for intimacy, and a despairing suspicion that she will never attain it."*

Thus the emotionally abused adult is caught in a dilemma. By choosing for her life partner a person as incapable of consistent empathic bonding as her parent, she is attempting to reconstruct a lost childhood. Although victims often report tantalizing moments in which the abuser seems to connect with genuine empathy and encouragement, such moments do not last. The longed-for bond with a consistently warm and responsive partner is simply not available in an emotionally abusive relationship. Yet the quest goes on. As one victim explains, it is "a struggle to collect crumbs of warmth and not let them get away."

Most couples, of course, experience periods of conflict and times when one partner's preoccupations separate him or her from the other. The harsh, unrelenting assaults and withdrawal in an emotionally abusive relationship are very different. They often have a scriptlike pattern. . . .

Using withdrawal as a mechanism of control is emotional abandonment. The victim feels betrayed and isolated by the unilateral disconnection. As her need for connection grows, her attempts to engage the partner increase in frequency and intensity, and she clings harder. Although her efforts fail, the trauma of pain and terror leave the victim with no choice but to continue trying. Jean Baker Miller argues that

> the most terrifying and destructive feeling that a person can experience is isolation. . . . It is feeling locked out of the possibility of human connection. This feeling of desperate loneliness is usually accompanied by the feeling that you, yourself, are the reason for the exclusion. . . . And you feel helpless, powerless, unable to act to change the situation. People will do almost anything to escape this combination of condemned isolation and powerlessness.

The attachment is so essential to her that the victim may obey the abuser's orders to commit illegal acts; to disobey him is to risk abandonment or emotional assault. Threats of abandonment create fear, uncertainty, and confusion for a victim whose sense of self is destroyed and who cannot therefore think through a problem effectively, nor comfort herself in moments of sadness. In this type of emotional abuse the victim's judgment is confused, and the abuser uses coercion to control her feelings of safety and well-being. . . .

There are several reasons why . . . the typical victim does not view leaving an emotionally abusive relationship as an option. Usually she is unaware that what is occurring is emotional abuse. Even if she complains about her partner's verbal attacks, she usually lacks a full understanding of their impact on her. Furthermore, her complaints are often weakened by the abuser's denial and projection of blame. Desperate and despairing, she is likely to blame herself for the conflicts in the relationship.

> *"Many victims of emotional abuse have never experienced a . . . consistently warm relationship and so cannot see any alternative."*

Furthermore, the pervasive erosion of the self wrought by the abuse has left her unable to break out of the relationship. Her self-esteem is so diminished that the abuse is an echo of her own self-criticisms. Thoughts of severing her already diminished self from what she perceives as its only anchor are likely to precipitate panic attacks. Moreover, many victims of emotional abuse have never experienced a kinder and more consistently warm relationship and so cannot see any alternative to the present situation.

With help, victims of emotional abuse can begin to recognize the violence of the "terrible kind of attachment" that permeates their lives. They can learn that the abusive mechanisms diminishing their sense of self are not the necessary cost of a human connection. They can begin to envision new and different ways of bonding. As their quest for warmth and validation in one-sided attachments becomes a search for a mutually empathic connection—a place where she will be appreciated and allowed to flourish—the victim can move toward becoming a survivor.

Exposure to Domestic Violence Harms Children

by Betsy McAlister Groves, Barry Zuckerman, Steven Marans, and Donald J. Cohen

About the authors: *Betsy McAlister Groves is an assistant clinical professor of pediatrics and director of the Witness to Violence program at Boston University School of Medicine and Boston City Hospital. Barry Zuckerman is a professor and chairman of the Department of Pediatrics at Boston University School of Medicine/Boston City Hospital. Steven Marans coordinates the Child Development–Community Policing Program in New Haven, Connecticut, and serves as the Harris Assistant Professor of Child Psychoanalysis at Yale University's Child Study Center. Donald J. Cohen teaches child psychiatry, pediatrics, and psychology at the Yale University School of Medicine and is director of the university's Child Study Center.*

The crisis of violence in the United States has expanded to include more than the traditional emphasis on the victim and perpetrator. We would like to bring attention to a previously underrecognized group of victims in this public health epidemic: the children who witness the violence. These usually silent, indirect victims show no physical sign of harm and are commonly overlooked. . . .

At least 3.3 million children are at risk for witnessing parental abuse each year. This is probably a conservative estimate because of underreporting of domestic abuse. These children witness the range of abusive behavior, from hitting, punching, or slapping, to fatal assaults with guns or knives.

While a good deal of attention has been focused on children and adolescents who are direct victims of violence, less attention has been paid to children who witness violence. What is the impact on these children? How does exposure to violence affect their development, their view of the world, and their future relationships?

Witnessing Violence Victimizes Children

In a 1992 book, James Garbarino and colleagues make comparisons between the children they have studied in Chicago and children of war in Mozambique, the West Bank, and Cambodia. Exposure to violence adversely affects children's development in many areas, including their ability to function in school, emotional stability, and orientation toward the future. These effects may be long lasting. The severity of a child's reactions to trauma is related to the proximity to the violent event, the victim's relationship with the child, and the presence of a parent or caretaker to mediate the intensity of the event. Children who have been exposed to violence may also display symptoms associated with posttraumatic stress disorder, such as diminished ability to concentrate in school, persistent sleep disturbances, flashbacks, disordered attachment behaviors with significant caretakers, sudden startling and hypervigilance, and a nihilistic, fatalistic orientation to the future, which leads to increased risk-taking behaviors.

> *"Children who witness domestic violence may be particularly vulnerable to emotional and developmental problems."*

Most studies on the effects of traumatic exposure to violence on children have focused on elementary-school-aged children and adolescents. Preliminary evidence, however, suggests that preschoolers may be especially vulnerable to the effects of traumatic exposure to violence. . . .

The World Is a Dangerous Place

During the early years, children turn to their parents as the most immediate source of stability, control, and protection. When these same adults are the wounded victims, out-of-control combatants, or emotionally distraught casualties of violence, the world of the young child is no longer safe or stable. The calm, reassuring voice of the parent has little currency or is absent when parents themselves are frightened and insecure. Young children who have witnessed violence bear the additional burden of being least able to communicate their fears and reactions in words. Perhaps because of an inability to understand the language of young children, adults may have a tendency to deny the serious impact that witnessing violence will have on development, assuming—or wishing—that young children will not understand and will forget what they have seen.

Children who witness domestic violence may be particularly vulnerable to emotional and developmental problems. Studies have not yet been conducted to compare the range, type, and severity of problems between children who witness violence in the home with those who witness it outside the home. However, based on our clinical experience, it appears that witnessing violence between parents in the home results in more severe consequences. Data are available showing that children who witness violence in the home identify along gender lines with their parents' relationship. Boys become more abusive as adults; girls become victims. Children of both sexes may come to see violence as an appropriate means of resolving conflict and as an integral part of a close relationship.

The drawings and play of young children who are exposed to violence reveal that this exposure has a deep effect on how children perceive their world. Children fear their own destruction and vulnerability. One little boy who witnessed the death of his mother draws pictures of boys with gaping mouths, screaming silently. The boys in the picture are unable to communicate their terror. . . . Children also tell us about their fear of repeat trauma. A child builds jails to house the killers of his mother. However, the jail walls crumble. He builds them up, only to have them fall again and again. This child does not feel safe. Finally, these children express anger at the failure of adults to protect them. Some of the anger is irrational, rooted in a child's need to believe that parents and adults are invincible. Unfortunately, they discover at a young age that adults cannot protect them from the terror of violence. . . .

Parents' fear about . . . safety . . . communicates powerful messages that the world is an essentially hostile and unpredictable place. While parents are often creative and heroic in their attempts to mediate this dangerous world for their children, the restrictions and the fear that inspires them may exact considerable costs to the child's development.

Society Must Help

We believe the crisis of children's exposure to violence makes demands of us in our practices, both at the individual patient level and at the advocacy/social-policy level. First, children of all ages must have an opportunity to talk about the violence in their lives. Physicians should inquire about violent events in their patients' lives during routine history taking. . . . To verbalize a terrifying or overwhelming experience can be therapeutic. For example, a 10-year-old girl awakened one night to see someone attempting to crawl into her bedroom

> *"These children . . . discover at a young age that adults cannot protect them from the terror of violence."*

through the window. She presented at a pediatric visit with a number of posttraumatic stress symptoms, including sleeplessness, inability to concentrate in school, and increased dependence on her mother. The physician facilitated her detailed recollection of the event, her reactions to it, and how she thought she might cope with worries in the future. The girl and her mother reported a decrease in symptoms after the visit. The physician's intervention may have offered the first chance for the girl to review the events and for the parents to fully understand the significance of the trauma from the child's perspective. . . .

Second, there is a need for specialized mental health services and for psychotherapists who are trained to treat children who experience trauma and/or symptoms of posttraumatic stress disorder. . . . Children who are exposed to violence are often kept in an anxious state by the burden of seeing parents who are themselves overwhelmed by violent events. Attending to the parents' needs and providing specific information and support to respond more appropriately to their child is an equally important focus of intervention in treating young patients. For example, a 4-year-old who witnessed the murder of his mother would frequently fall to the floor, lie motionless, and stare upward with a fixed gaze, to reenact his mother's murder. His caretakers were horrified and forbade him to play in this manner. However, once they understood that this reenactment was a necessary part of the boy's attempts to manage the trauma, the caretakers changed their response to the child, saying to him that he must be thinking about his mother. . . .

Finally, there is a need for intervention that goes far beyond the clinical setting and involves society's responsibility to insure that children grow up in a safe environment. The quantity and quality of violence that we live with is a national disgrace. Our inability to secure tougher gun-control laws is but one example of this country's failure to come to terms with the violence that surrounds us all. We need

> *"There is a need for intervention . . . to insure that children grow up in a safe environment."*

to consider carefully what it means to be raising a generation of young children who must, out of necessity, become numb to the violence around them. Children who think that their lives are so vulnerable and tenuous may fail to take care of themselves. They may seek relief from the intolerable feelings of fear and anxiety through alcohol and other drug abuse; and/or they may become the perpetrators of violence. Children who witness violence must be added to the clinical and policy discussions regarding the consequences of violence. They are victims and need treatment.

All Spanking Is a Form of Violence

by Murray A. Straus

About the author: *Murray A. Straus is a professor of sociology and codirector of the Family Research Laboratory at the University of New Hampshire.*

The laws of every state of the United States permit parents to hit children for purposes of correction or control. Eighty-four percent of a national sample of Americans agreed with the statement that "It is sometimes necessary to give a child a good hard spanking." Study after study shows that almost 100 percent of parents of toddlers use spanking and other kinds of "corporal punishment." There are many reasons for the strong support of spanking, but most of them are myths. . . .

Myth 1: Spanking Works Better

There has been a huge amount of research on the effectiveness of corporal punishment of animals, but remarkably little on the effectiveness of spanking children. That may be because almost everyone assumes that spanking is effective and therefore they don't feel a need to study it. In fact, what little research there is on children agrees with the research on animals in finding that spanking is *not* more effective than other modes of correcting misbehavior, and there are some studies that show it is less effective.

Ellen Cohn and I studied 270 students at two New England colleges. We asked them to tell us about the year they experienced the most corporal punishment. Their average age that year was eight, and they recalled having been hit an average of six times that year. Next we asked them about the percent of the time that the corporal punishment was effective. It averaged just over half of the time (53 percent), which also means that corporal punishment was not effective almost half the time it was used.

Dan E. Day and Mark W. Roberts did an experiment on three-year-old children given "time out." Half of the mothers were assigned to use spanking as the mode

Excerpted from *Ten Myths About Spanking Children* by Murray A. Straus, a 1992 study from the Family Research Laboratory, University of New Hampshire, Durham, NH. Reprinted with permission.

of correction if the child did not comply with "time out" and left the time out place (sitting in a corner). The other half put the child who did not comply behind a low plywood barrier and physically enforced the child staying there. Keeping the child in the barrier area was just as effective as the spanking in correcting the misbehavior that led to the "time out." A longitudinal study by Robert E. Larzelere also found that a combination of *non*corporal punishment and reasoning was as effective as corporal punishment and reasoning in correcting disobedience.

Jill Crozier and Roger C. Katz, Gerald R. Patterson, and Carolyn Webster Stratton et al. all studied children with serious conduct problems. Part of the treatment used in all three experiments was to get parents

> *"Spanking is **not** more effective than other modes of correcting misbehavior."*

to stop spanking. In all three, the behavior of the children improved after spanking ended. Of course, many other things were part of the intervention in addition to avoiding spanking. But, parents who on their own accord do not spank also do lots of other things. It is these "other things," such as setting clear standards for what is expected, providing lots of love and affection, explaining things to the child, and recognizing and rewarding good behavior, that account for why children of parents who do not spank tend to be easy to manage and well behaved. What about parents who do these things and also spank? Those children also tend to be well behaved, but it is illogical to attribute that to the spanking since the same or better results are achieved without the spanking. . . .

Parents who favor spanking can turn this around and ask "If spanking doesn't work any better, isn't that the same as saying that it works just as well? So what is wrong with a quick slap on the wrist or bottom?" There are at least three things that are wrong:

- Spanking becomes less and less effective over time, and eventually becomes physically impossible.
- For some children, the lessons learned through spanking include the idea that they only need to be good if Mommy or Daddy is watching or will know about it.
- There are a number of very harmful side effects—for example, a higher probability that the child will grow up to be depressed or violent. Parents can't perceive these side effects because they only show up in the long run.

Myth 2: Spanking Is Needed as a Last Resort

Even parents and social scientists who are opposed to spanking tend to think that it may be needed when all else fails. There is no scientific evidence supporting this belief. It is a myth that grows out of our cultural and psychological commitment to corporal punishment. . . .

Take the example of a child running out into the street. Almost everyone thinks that spanking is appropriate because of the extreme danger. Although spanking in that situation may help parents to relieve their own tensions and anxiety, it is not necessary or appropriate for teaching the child. It is not necessary because spanking does not work better than other methods, and it is not appropriate because of the harmful side effects of spanking. The only physical force needed is to grab the child and get him/her out of danger, and, while hugging the child, explain the danger.

Ironically, if spanking is to be done at all, the "last resort" may be the worst time. The problem is that parents are usually very angry by that time and act impulsively. Because of the high level [of] anger, if the child rebels and calls the parent a name or kicks the parent, the episode can escalate into physical abuse. Indeed, most episodes of physical abuse started as physical punishment and got out of hand. . . . Most instances of spanking do not escalate into abuse. Still, the danger is there.

The second problem with spanking as a last resort is that, in addition to teaching that hitting is the way to correct wrongs, doing so impulsively teaches another wrong lesson—namely that being extremely angry and "beyond yourself" justifies hitting.

Myth 3: Spanking Is Harmless

When someone says, "I was spanked and I'm OK," they are arguing that spanking is not harmful. This is contrary to almost all the available research. One reason the harmful effects are ignored is because most of the harmful effects do not become visible right away, often not for years. Even more important is the fact that only a relatively small percentage of spanked children experience obviously harmful effects. . . .

> *"What is wrong with a quick slap on the wrist or bottom? . . . [A] higher probability that the child will grow up to be depressed or violent."*

Another argument in defense of spanking is that it is not harmful if the parents are loving and explain why they are spanking. The research does show that the harmful effects of spanking are reduced if it occurs in a context of a loving family in which parents explain their actions. However, although the harmful effects are reduced, a study by Larzelere and my own research show that they are not eliminated. . . .

Even in a loving context, and perhaps even more in such a context, spanking teaches that hitting others is morally correct. Of course, it is only correct if the other person is doing something seriously wrong and won't stop. The irony of this can be seen by examining the circumstances under which a child hits another child. It is very rare for a child to simply walk up to another child and hit him or her. Rather, children hit other children when the other child is doing something that they think is seriously wrong—such as "squirting water on me" and refusing to stop, or "taking my doll" and not giving it back. So it is no wonder that hitting a child for misbehavior increases the probability the child will hit siblings and other children. They are faithfully following the rules learned from the example of their parents' behavior. My 1991 study shows that when the child grows up, spanked children tend to spank their own children, which is hardly surprising. What may be surprising is . . . that they also have a higher rate of hitting their spouse. However, it should not be surprising because spouses may also "misbehave" and "not listen to reason." Other findings from the same study show that the more a child is spanked, the greater the probability that he or she will assault someone outside their family. . . .

> *"Most episodes of physical abuse started as physical punishment and got out of hand."*

Corporal punishment makes it more difficult for parents to influence a child later on, especially in adolescence. This is partly because in adolescence children become too big to control by physical force, but also because each use of spanking chips away at the bond between parent and child, and children are more likely to do what the parents want if there is a strong bond of affection with the parents.

Ellen Cohn and I asked the 270 students mentioned earlier to tell us about their reactions to "the first time you can remember being hit by one of your parents" and the most recent instance. We used a check list of 33 items, one of which was "hated him or her." That item was checked by 42 percent for the first instance of corporal punishment they could remember and by the same percentage for the most recent incident. The large percentage who hated their parents for hitting them is important because it is evidence that use of corporal punishment does chip away at the bond between child and parent.

Contrary to the "spoiled child" myth, children of non-spanking parents tend to control their behavior on the basis of what is right and wrong rather than to avoid being hit. This means that if parents avoid spanking, they are likely to have children who are easier to manage and better behaved. That is ironic because almost everyone thinks that the opposite is the case.

Research on the women and men in the National Family Violence Surveys I conducted in 1992 finds that the more corporal punishment experienced, the greater the probability of being depressed and the greater the probability of having thought about committing suicide during the 12 months preceding the interview. Another analysis found that the more corporal punishment experienced, the greater the alienation, and, holding constant social class of origin, the *lower* the occupational and economic achievement. I interpret the lowered occupational and economic achievement as one of the consequences of the higher rate of depression and alienation associated with corporal punishment.

Myth 4: One or Two Times Will Not Cause Any Damage

The evidence does indeed indicate that the greatest risk of harmful effects occurs when spanking is very frequent. However, that does not necessarily mean that just once or twice is harmless. Unfortunately, the hypothesis that even once or twice increases the probability of psychological damage is not addressed by most of the available research. This is because the studies seem to be based on this myth. They group children into "low" and "high" frequency of having been hit, thus preventing the "once or twice is harmless" myth from being tested scientifically because the "low" group may include parents who spank as often as once a month. The few studies that did classify children according to the number of times they experienced corporal punishment . . . show that even one or two instances are associated with a higher number of depressive symptoms later in life, although only slightly more. . . .

Myth 5: Parents Cannot Stop Without Training

Although everyone can use additional skills in child management, there is absolutely no evidence showing that it takes some extraordinary training to be able to stop spanking. The most basic step in eliminating corporal punishment is for professionals concerned with children, such as psychologists and pediatricians, to make a simple and unambiguous statement that hitting a child is wrong and that a child should never be hit. That is, just as we tell children to never hit another child, parents need to be told to never hit their own child— *never*, ever, under any circumstances.

Almost without exception that idea has been rejected. Parent educators and social scientists I have talked to argue that it would turn off parents and it could be harmful because parents don't know what else to do. They say that parents need to learn alternative modes of discipline before we can withdraw use of spanking. That may be true for some incompetent parents. . . . However, . . . most parents *already* use a wide range of non-spanking methods, such as explaining, reasoning, and rewarding. The problem is that they also spank. Given the fact that parents already know and use many methods of teaching and controlling, the solution is amazingly simple. In most cases, parents can do just what they were doing to correct the misbehavior, but leave out the spanking! . . .

> *"Spanking chips away at the bond between parent and child."*

Myth 6: If You Do Not Spank, Your Children Will Be Spoiled or Run Wild

It is true that some non-spanked children turn out to be problems, but when this happens it is not because the parent didn't spank. It is because some parents think that the alternative to spanking is to ignore a child's misbehavior, or to replace spanking with verbal attacks such as, "Only a dummy like you can't learn to keep your toys where I won't trip over them." The real alternative is to take firm action to correct the misbehavior, but not by spanking. Just firmly condemning what the child has done and explaining why it is wrong is usually enough.

Suppose the child hits another child. Parents need to express outrage at this or the child may think it is acceptable behavior. The expression of outrage and a clear statement about never hitting another person will do the trick in most cases. That does not mean one such admonition will do the trick, any more than a single spanking will do the trick. It takes most children a while to learn such things, whatever the methods the parents use.

The importance of how parents go about teaching children is clear from the classic study of American parenting, *Patterns of Child Rearing* by Robert R. Sears, Eleanor C. Maccoby, and Harry Levin. This study found two behaviors that are linked to a high level of aggression by the child: Permissiveness of the child's aggression, i.e., ignoring it when the child hits another child, and use of spanking to

> *"Parents need to be told to never hit their own child—never, ever, under any circumstances."*

correct misbehavior. The most aggressive children are those . . . of parents who permitted aggression by the child and who also spanked. The least aggressive children are . . . [those] whose parents clearly condemned acts of aggression, *and*, by not spanking, acted in a way that exemplified the principle that hitting is wrong.

There are other reasons why, on the average, the children of parents who do not spank are better behaved than children of parents who spank. Non-spanking parents tend to:

- Pay more attention to their children's behavior, both good and bad, than do parents who spank. Consequently they are more likely to reward good behavior and less likely to ignore misbehavior.
- Do more explaining and reasoning. This teaches the child how to use these essential tools to monitor their own behavior, whereas children who are spanked get less training in thinking things through.
- Treat the child in ways that tend to bond the child to them and avoid acts that weaken the bond, including

  More rewarding of good behavior

  Greater warmth and affection

  Less verbal assaults on the child (see Myth 9)

  By not spanking, they avoid anger and resentment over spanking.

When there is a strong bond, children identify with the parent and want to avoid doing things the parents say are wrong. This amounts to the child developing a conscience and letting that direct his/her behavior. . . .

Myth 7: Parents Spank Only Rarely or Only for Serious Problems

Contrary to this myth, parents who spank tend to use this method of discipline for almost any misbehavior. Many do not even give the child a warning.

They spank before trying other things. And some advocates of spanking recommend this. At any supermarket or other public place, one can see examples of a child doing something wrong, such as taking a can of food off the shelf. The parent then slaps the child's hand and puts the can back, sometimes without saying anything to the child. John Rosemond, the author of *Parent Power,* says, "For me spanking is a first resort. I seldom spank, but when I decide . . . I do it and that's the end of it.". . .

The high frequency of spanking also shows up among the 4,375 parents in the National Family Violence Surveys that my colleague Richard Gelles and I conducted in 1988 and again in 1990. Over 90 percent of those who had toddlers at home used some form of corporal punishment during the preceding 12 months. The typical parent told us of about 15 instances in which they had hit the child during the previous twelve months. That is surely a minimum estimate because spanking a child is such a routine and unremarkable event that many instances are forgotten. Other studies, such as the one completed by John Newson and Elizabeth Newson in 1963, report even more chronic reliance on corporal punishment. Daily spanking is not at all uncommon.

Myth 8: By the Time a Child Is a Teenager, Parents Have Stopped

Parents of children in their early teens are also heavy users of corporal punishment, although at that age it is more likely to be a slap on the face than on the behind. Over half of the parents of 13-year-old children in our two national surveys hit the child in the previous 12 months. The percentage drops each year as children get older, but even at age 17, one out of five parents is still using corporal punishment.

Of the parents of teenagers who told us about using corporal punishment, 84 percent did it more than once in the previous 12 months. For boys, the average was seven times and for girls, five times. These are also minimum figures because we interviewed the mother in half the families and the father in the other half. The number of times would be greater if we had information on what the non-interviewed parent did.

Myth 9: If Parents Do Not Spank They Will Verbally Abuse Their Child

The evidence from research is exactly the opposite. The National Family Violence Surveys included information on verbal abuse by over 4,000 parents. The parents who did the least spanking also engaged in the least verbal aggression.

It has to be pointed out that non-spanking parents are an exceptional minority. They are defying the cultural prescription which says that a good parent should spank if necessary. The depth of their involvement with their children probably results from the same underlying characteristics that led them to reject spanking. There is a danger that if more ordinary parents are told to never spank, they might replace spanking by ignoring misbehavior or by verbal attacks. Consequently, a campaign to end spanking must also stress the importance of not ignoring misbehavior and of avoiding verbal attacks as well as physical attacks.

Myth 10: It Is Unrealistic to Expect Parents to Never Spank

It is no more (and no less) unrealistic to expect parents to never hit a child than to expect that husbands should never hit their wives, or that no one should go through a stop sign, or that supervisors should never hit employees. Despite the legal prohibition, some husbands hit their wives, just as some drivers go through stop signs and some supervisors hit an employee.

If we were to prohibit spanking, as is the law in Sweden, there would be parents who nevertheless continue to spank, but that is no more reason to not have such a law than the fact that some husbands continue to hit their wives more than a century after the courts stopped recognizing the common law right of a husband to "physically chastise an errant wife.". . .

The Myth of Effectiveness

There are a number of reasons why almost everyone overestimates the effectiveness of spanking, but a central reason is what has been called "selective inattention." Selective inattention occurs when people do not pay attention to or remember the times when spanking fails to work because it contradicts what they believe to be true, i.e., that spanking always works, thus providing the "evidence" that spanking always works. Conversely, if someone knows that the parents do *not* spank, it is assumed that the child must be spoiled, wild, etc. So there is a tendency to overlook the good behavior of the child, and to attribute the inevitable instances of misbehavior to the lack of spanking, thus providing the "evidence" that parents who don't spank "when necessary" have spoiled children. These all-too-human errors in information processing create the perception that spanking is much more effective than it really is and are probably the main reason for the persistence of the effectiveness myth. The reality is that although all children misbehave, the behavior of non-spanked children, although far from perfect—they are after all, children—is on the average better than the behavior of children whose parents spank.

> *"Non-spanking parents tend to . . . . [d]o more explaining and reasoning."*

The selective inattention raises the question of why the "necessity" of spanking is such a deeply held belief. Why do most Americans have a vested interest in defending spanking? The following are some of the possible reasons.

Almost all have been spanked as children, so it is part of their normal life experience.

Even if someone is suffering from one of the harmful side effects such as depression, they may not realize that having been spanked may be one of the reasons for their depression and they can continue to believe that spanking is harmless.

Almost all parents use spanking on toddlers. Consequently, if someone who is or has been a parent accepts the idea that spanking is wrong, it implies that they have been a bad parent, at least in that respect. That is difficult to admit.

Almost everyone has been hit by their parents. Consequently, to say that this was wrong is to condemn one's own parents. That is also something that few people are comfortable doing.

These beliefs and attitudes have been crystallized as part of American culture and the American view of what a good parent owes to a child. There is abundant evidence that people tend to misperceive things that are contrary to basic tenets of their culture and beliefs.

Most spanking occurs when parents are frustrated and angry. In that context parents tend to get emotional release and satisfaction from spanking, which is confused with effectiveness in changing the child's behavior.

There is almost always a "kernel of truth" behind most myths and stereotypes. The belief in the efficacy of spanking is no exception. The truth is that some parents who do not spank also do not attempt to correct misbehavior. As explained earlier, children of these extremely permissive or neglectful parents do tend to be out of control. However, such parents are a minority of non-spanking parents. Their children tend to be difficult to deal with, or sometimes even to be in the same room with, and these few instances are burned into memory.

Cultural Family Traditions Can Be Abusive

by Ruth Rosen

About the author: *Ruth Rosen teaches history at the University of California at Davis, and has written* The Lost Sisterhood: Prostitution in America.

Are genital mutilation, forced prostitution, marital rape, murder of raped daughters, deaths resulting from dowry disputes merely customs, or do they constitute violations of human rights? Spurred by the spread of global feminism, some activists are seeking to redefine the hidden injuries of sex as violations of women's human rights.

Redefining Women's Rights

Before the women's movement, many such cruelties were not defined as crimes. During the last two decades, however, feminists in the United States and elsewhere named the sexual crimes women had once suffered in silence. Wife-battering, rape, incest, sexual harassment, sexual slavery, to name but a few, are no longer protected by archaic laws. Still, such crimes continue to be called, and regarded, as "women's issues." As a result, they are trivialized as cultural problems.

Charlotte Bunch, the director of the Douglass College Center for Global Issues and Women's Leadership, has taken a leading role in persuading human-rights organizations to reconsider sexual crimes and violence against women as human-rights abuses. Bunch notes that the typical victim of human-rights abuses is portrayed as a male dissident tortured or imprisoned by the state. Women, she observes, suffer equally egregious crimes, but most often at the hands of relatives in their own homes.

The American legal system's emphasis on civil and political rights is not sufficiently elastic to create a broader definition of human rights. Instead, feminists like Bunch look to the Universal Declaration of Human Rights, adopted Dec. 10, 1948, by the United Nations. Although gender is not specifically addressed, the declaration defines bodily integrity, along with shelter, food and

Ruth Rosen, "Women's Rights Are the Same as Human Rights," *Los Angeles Times*, April 8, 1991. Reprinted by permission of the author.

work, as a basic human right. Still, most human-rights groups dismiss sexual crimes as matters of culture.

But as Bunch warns, gender-specific crimes are not only unpleasant, they also maim and kill women. Consider, for example:

• In the United States, a rape is committed every six minutes and battery is the leading cause of injury to adult women.
• In places as diverse as Bangladesh, Canada, Kenya and Thailand, 50% of female homicides are committed by family members.
• In India, eight out of 10 wives are victims of violence from domestic battery or dowry-related abuses. In the worst cases, dowry disputes result in death.
• Amniocentesis used for sex selection leads to the abortion of more female than male fetuses, as high as 99% in Bombay.
• During childhood, the World Health Organization reports, girls are fed less, breast-fed for shorter periods of time, brought to doctors less often and suffer from malnutrition more often than boys.
• In adulthood, untold numbers of women suffer serious health complications from illegal abortions and genital mutilation.

Use the language of human rights and what seemed to be customs begin to look like human-rights abuses. Slavery (forced prostitution), sexual terrorism (rape), imprisonment (confinement to the home) and torture (systematic battery) are considered major human-rights violations.

Violations Against Women Must Be Recognized

Why bother to redefine women's rights as human rights? Because they provide moral touchstones against which we can measure a society's treatment of any individual or group. As the democratic opposition demonstrated in Eastern Europe and the Soviet Union, the demand for human rights challenges arbitrary violence and coercion and creates a framework for a more democratic society.

The language of human rights also has immediate political consequences. When an Indian woman escapes an arranged marriage or a raped Bangladesh girl is threatened with death by male relatives, they are usually refused political asylum by Western nations. These are customs, they are told, not human-rights violations.

"Women . . . suffer equally egregious crimes [as men], but most often at the hands of relatives in their own homes."

In 1979, the U.N. Convention on the Elimination of All Forms of Discrimination Against Women began addressing violations of women's political and legal rights. As of 1990, 104 nations—the United States is *not* among them—have ratified the convention. Amnesty International publicizes violations of women prisoners. The next step, however, is to recognize that women, unlike men, suffer more often at the hands of relatives and other citizens than from state-sanctioned violence. The tactics used to publicize the torture and imprisonment of men—reports and letters to heads of state—do not meet the needs of women. Activists must publicize and challenge the laws and customs that violate women's most fundamental human rights.

To expand our idea of human rights is to challenge the cultural relativism that currently protects sexual crimes and violence against women's bodily integrity. Human-rights activists must find the courage to call a custom a crime. Slavery, we should remember, was once a legally supportable and culturally acceptable institution.

Chapter 2

Is the Prevalence of Family Violence Exaggerated?

Chapter Preface

In 1994, U.S. Department of Justice statistics revealed that 57 percent of all children under age twelve who were murdered throughout U.S. major cities were killed by their parents. And the National Coalition Against Domestic Violence (NCADV) reports that "every 15 seconds a woman is battered in the United States by her husband, boyfriend, or live-in partner."

Responding to statistics such as these, researchers Donileen R. Loseke and Richard J. Gelles write, "Family violence challenges deeply held cultural ideals. In a society such as ours, where homes and families are often idealized as havens and people protecting us from the heartless world of dangerous strangers, how can it be that more people are injured by loved ones than by strangers?"

Yet whether or not the prevalence of family violence exists at such alarmingly high rates remains a topic of debate. Professionals, advocates, and government administrators struggle to understand and identify its extent amidst disputes over how to define and measure the problem.

Those challenging the "epidemic" proportions reported in the media say the research is shoddy at best, and intentionally misrepresented at worst. "We are barraged with horrendous figures," writes reporter Cathy Young. She argues that inaccuracies result from faulty research methods such as projecting data from nonrepresentative samples upon larger populations and inadequately screening the cases reported. "The 'mental health' establishment is long on claims and short on evidence," says senior Hoover Institution fellow Thomas Sowell. Instead of activists dedicated to the welfare of children, he sees "promoters of child abuse hysteria" and "zealots" who are willing to present a distorted picture in order to further their own political agendas.

Nonetheless, the U.S. Department of Justice—the major source of data on family violence—has been accused of underestimating the scope of the problem. Critics charge that many people are reluctant to report abuse—either because the problem has for so long been considered taboo or because they fear retribution from their abusers—and that the agency has failed to account for these victims. In contrast, a U.S. Senate Judiciary Committee that documented one million attacks on women by their mates during 1991 estimated three times that number—three million—went unreported. Insisting that statistics on family violence are deceivingly low because of such vast underreporting, some activists claim that doubts expressed by some in the media over the magnitude of abuse will further discourage an already hesitant population from speaking out. "Silence is precisely what the abuser needed and demanded. And still does," notes writer Elizabeth M. Matz.

"Reliable figures on the scope of the problem are elusive," writes reporter Charles S. Clark in the *Los Angeles Times*. And, whether they believe existing data are too low or too high, most commentators tend to agree. Authors debate the prevalence of family violence in the following chapter.

Claims of Child Abuse Are Often Unsubstantiated

by Elena Neuman

About the author: *Elena Neuman is a writer for* Insight, *a politically conservative news magazine.*

Somewhere between 2 million and 3 million allegations of child abuse and neglect tie up the nation's hot lines every year. Of that number, 60 percent are deemed false and dropped. Of the remaining 40 percent that lead to investigations, about half (involving nearly 700,000 families) eventually are dismissed, but not before children have been strip-searched, interrogated by a stream of social workers, police officers and prosecutors, psychologically tested and sometimes placed in foster care. Such actions usually occur without search warrants, parental consent, court hearings or official charges—and often solely on the basis of the anonymous telephone call.

Not Worth the Risk

Those who defend these practices point to tragic cases of child abuse and neglect each year in which, if not for the emergency powers granted to child protective services workers, children would be further tormented or even killed. The case of Lisa Steinberg, the 6-year-old beaten to death by her guardian in New York, proved to many that the system is not sufficiently vigilant and led to calls for more funding to hire additional social workers.

In fact, recent studies show that the number of child maltreatment fatalities is on the rise; in 1993, an estimated 1,299 children died from abuse or neglect—a 50 percent increase since 1985. Child protective services knew about the circumstances in 42 percent of the cases before death occurred.

"Sure, there are loads of frivolous calls being made into the hot lines, but so what?" says David Liederman, executive director of the Child Welfare League of America, based in Washington. "If there's any kind of thought that there could be something going on, and if the social workers don't follow the prescribed procedures and a child dies, then what happens? Is it worth the risk?"

Innocent Families Suffer

Many Americans think not, but others—especially those who find themselves swallowed up by an incomprehensible child welfare bureaucracy—complain that the nation's child protection agencies are out of control. They believe that a national hysteria about child abuse, particularly child sexual abuse, traumatizes innocent families. Lives are turned upside down on a moment's notice; reputations are sullied by an accusation. Children are ripped from loving homes. "This has been framed as an issue of children's rights vs. parents' rights, as if a false allegation only hurts parents," says Richard Wexler, an assistant professor at Pennsylvania State University and author of *Wounded Innocents: The Real Victims of the War Against Child Abuse*. "But the problem with this system is not that it hurts parents—although it does. The problem is that it hurts children. There are at least 200,000 children in foster care right now who could safely be in their own homes if the proper services were provided.". . .

Constitutional Rights Are Threatened

Laws regarding the civil liberties extended to those accused of child abuse vary state by state. In Illinois, for example, a district court ruled (and an appeals court upheld) that child protection service workers are entitled to strip-search children at will. "The life of even one child is too great a price to pay," pronounced District Judge John Nordberg.

Not only is the Fourth Amendment's protection against unlawful searches and seizures suspended in many states; so too are the Fifth Amendment's protection against self-incrimination, the Sixth Amendment's safekeeping of the right to counsel and several other fundamental elements of due process. People accused of child abuse are not even read the Miranda warning mandatory in criminal cases, because child abuse cases are considered administrative proceedings.

Rules of evidence regarding hearsay also are not applied to child abuse and neglect cases, many of which rest entirely on the testimony of an impressionable child or an anonymous caller. Perhaps most pernicious is the assumption of guilt as it pertains to alleged child abusers. "The child protection system is probably the greatest threat to the individual liberty of your everyday, normal, law-abiding citizen," says Nelson Farber, . . . who has litigated many child abuse claims later proved false. "If a

> *"Lives are turned upside down on a moment's notice. . . . Children are ripped from loving homes."*

kid's interrogated and says, 'Daddy bathes me,' then to a caseworker that means Daddy abuses her. If the kid says, 'Daddy doesn't bathe me,' then they think, 'Why doesn't Daddy ever bathe her?—the mother must have known something about Daddy.' So they've got you in this catch-22. It's positively kafkaesque.". . .

Advocates of child protection services, on the other hand, say that cases [in which families are disrupted by unjustifiable investigations] are extraordinarily rare. "I find it hard to believe that large numbers of innocent families are being hurt," says Liederman. "We have a system where there's triage going on every single day, where there are so many reports of abuse and neglect that the public agencies cannot keep up with the investigations. Does that lead to the conclusion that they have any time to waste on frivolous charges?"

Overreporting Brings Shoddy Investigations

They may not. But laws in every state require caseworkers to investigate each and every allegation of child maltreatment. And the number of abuse reports is ballooning at a rate of 6 percent a year, primarily as a result of mandatory reporting laws for teachers, health care professionals and child care workers, as well as from an enhanced cultural awareness about abuse. As overworked caseworkers scramble to keep up with their investigations, the logical results are shoddy investigating, hasty interviewing and uninformed recommendations.

> *"The child protection system is probably the greatest threat to the individual liberty of your everyday, normal, law-abiding citizen."*

"There's no question that there's a problem with vast overreporting," says Douglas J. Besharov, a resident scholar specializing in child welfare issues at Washington's American Enterprise Institute and author of a monograph titled *Defending Child Abuse and Neglect Cases: Representing Parents in Civil Proceedings.* "When social workers get the cases, even they say that many of the cases are a waste of their time. Even they toss them out."

Accurate figures are hard to come by in assessing the number of innocent families who wrestle with child protection services each year, primarily because agency records are shielded under a cloak of confidentiality and only the few cases that get to court are open to public scrutiny. (Many innocent families "plea bargain," admitting their "guilt" to caseworkers just to get their kids back. These cases do not go to trial.) Data from a 1993 survey released in April 1994 by the National Committee to Prevent Child Abuse found that of the 2.9 million children reported to child protective services in 1993 as alleged victims of child maltreatment, nearly 1 million cases were substantiated.

Definitions of Abuse Are Inadequate

Different groups draw different conclusions from this data. Child welfare advocates believe that the large number of unsubstantiated cases are instances of abuse that caseworkers couldn't prove. They also say that thousands of cases go unreported. Advocates for falsely accused parents say that the label "substantiated" is a misnomer—and that many substantiated cases turn out to be false as well. Moreover, as many as half of all substantiated cases actually are "at risk" cases in which the "potential" for abuse has been determined. A federal research effort known as the *Study of National Incidence and Prevalence of Child Abuse and Neglect: 1988* found that 27 to 61 percent of the cases substantiated by child protection services did not qualify as maltreatment under the study's definitions. (It also found that 9 to 12 percent of the cases declared unfounded by child protection services did fit the study's definitions of maltreatment.)

Nevertheless, anecdotal evidence of systemic abuse abounds. A San Diego grand jury spent a year investigating the county's child welfare system after a congressman filed a complaint on behalf of five constituents. From 1991 to 1992, the jury witnessed hundreds of confidential juvenile court hearings and interviewed more than 250 social workers, psychologists, lawyers and caseworkers who spoke candidly on the condition of confidentiality. . . .

"In too many cases, child protection services cannot distinguish real abuse from fabrication, abuse from neglect and neglect from poverty or cultural differences," the grand jury concluded in its report, *Families in Crisis*. It found that social workers have "nearly unlimited power" and that the department appears "incapable of policing itself." It also revealed widespread miscarriages of justice by police officers who fail to conduct independent investigations and juvenile courts that rely heavily on caseworker reports. . . . Says deputy foreman Carol Hopkins, . . . "This is happening across the country."

Agencies Invade Homes Nationwide

Dana Mack, an affiliate scholar at the Institute for American Values in New York, agrees. While researching her book on the modern American family—interviewing focus groups gathered through databases at market research organizations—she stumbled upon the problem of invasive child protection. "These were people with no ax to grind," says Mack. "I never once initiated the subject [of false allegations of child abuse]. But in every single focus group that I have done, somebody brought up an incident. They talked about invasions by child welfare agencies into their lives and about how they're afraid to discipline their children."

Victims of Child Abuse Laws, a national support and advocacy organization for families who say they have been falsely accused, maintains that during the 10 years following its founding, almost 70,000 people used the organization's information and referral services. The group's newsletter has a circulation of 110,000 and VOCAL chapters have been established in each of the 50 states and Canada.

"Many innocent families 'plea bargain,' admitting their 'guilt' to caseworkers just to get their kids back."

In the fall of 1991 after a conference at Harvard University, a group of professionals formed the National Coalition for Child Protection Reform. "Our hope is to turn the public monologue about child abuse into a dialogue," says Elizabeth Vorenberg, NCCPR president and former assistant commissioner of public welfare in Massachusetts. "It's not politically correct to be on the side of the parents in matters of this kind. You get called 'pro-abuse' and ridiculous things like that. But we believe that a system can be created that keeps far more children out of our destructive system of foster care and protects more children from harm at the hands of their parents."

The System Needs Reform

Those who are most critical of the system seem optimistic that reform is possible. Vorenberg's group advocates the expansion of family preservation programs, which recently received increased federal funding under the Family Preservation Act of 1993. Such programs send supportive caseworkers to families in crisis who otherwise would have their children placed in foster care. (In the 20 years since the first Family Preservation program was initiated, 88 percent of the at-risk children who went through the program remained in their homes a year later.) Moreover, family preservation is less expensive than foster care. In Michigan, for example, costs averaged $4,059 per child in 1991, compared with $13,021 for a child in foster care.

> *"27 to 61 percent of the cases substantiated by child protection services did not qualify as maltreatment."*

The American Enterprise Institute's Besharov, however, cautions against increases in family preservation programs. "If the problem is overreporting, then the solution isn't more government intervention," he says. Besharov recommends establishing a rational screening system on child protection hot lines and reforming mandatory reporting laws that grant immunity to anyone reporting alleged abuse and make educators and health care workers liable for not reporting it. Such laws became ubiquitous after 1974, when the Child Abuse Prevention and Treatment Act offered federal grants to child protective agencies in states with mandatory reporting laws.

Penn State's Wexler says he would eliminate anonymous reporting altogether; child abuse hot line callers should be required to give their names and addresses. That way, a repeat caller could be detected and even charged with malicious reporting. Malicious reports, Wexler says, are a particular problem in poor neighborhoods where they sometimes are used as weapons in disputes. Even children have been known to report parents after being disciplined or punished.

Wexler also would narrow the definitions of neglect and abuse, which sometimes are so broad as to verge on the ridiculous. In Illinois, neglect constitutes failure to provide "the proper or necessary support for a child's well-being." In Mississippi, a child is neglected if he is "without proper care, custody, supervision or support." In South Dakota, neglect occurs when a "child's environment is injurious to his welfare." Says Wexler: "Virtually any parent could be charged with child neglect under these definitions."

Other critics say that child protection caseworkers should be required to secure search warrants in investigations. "Every place in the country has a system where there's a judge on duty 24 hours a day to get calls for warrants," says Judge Ralph Adam Fine of the Wisconsin Court of Appeals, formerly of the state juvenile court. "They do it over the phone. It can be done in 20 minutes if need be. But at least you have someone who's detached, disinterested and neutral who can balance the various factors and implement the Fourth Amendment.". . .

Child Testimony Is Flawed

But some think deeper, attitudinal changes are needed to reform a system that errs on the side of the child. According to Stephen Ceci, professor of developmental psychology at Cornell University, children are impressionable and can speak in half-truths, exaggerate or just plain fantasize. In four recent studies, Ceci found that children interviewed in certain ways may invent substantial falsehoods.

In one study, a researcher asked a 4-year-old if he had been to the hospital because his finger had been caught in a mousetrap. The child responded, accurately, that he had not been to the hospital (in fact, there had been no incident with a mousetrap, either). The next week, when the researcher asked the same question, the child "remembered" crying when his finger was caught. By the 11th week, the boy had created an elaborate account of how his brother had pushed his finger into the mousetrap. No less than 56 percent of the children interviewed in this manner reported at least one false event as a truth. So definite were they and so descriptive were their accounts that professionals who saw videotapes of the children's testimony were convinced the events had happened.

Children who testify about familial abuse typically undergo hours of interrogation by caseworkers and prosecutors, as well as therapy sessions with psychologists who encourage them to reveal their secrets. "Most people say that if a child eventually admits something, then that something must have happened," says Ceci, considered a moderate by most experts in the acrimonious specialty of child

> *"It's not politically correct to be on the side of the parents. . . . You get called 'pro-abuse' and ridiculous things like that."*

suggestibility. "For those of us who do research in this area, however, that's not a foregone conclusion. You can, in fact, bring individuals—both children and adults—to false beliefs."

Reclaiming Parental Rights

The Institute for American Values' Mack says that changes in attitudes toward parenting also must precede policy reforms. The family is under attack from many different sources, including the "therapeutic state," says Mack. "To change the system, we have to really change our attitudes toward government intervention—the idea that government interference in family life is beneficial. We have to restore some confidence in the ability of parents to raise their children."

Jeff Bell, founder of Of the People, an organization fighting to add assurances of parents' rights to every state constitution, depicts the problem of false allegations as a clash between parents and social workers, bureaucrats and educators. "I think it's an ideological movement being pushed by the therapeutic elites who really don't think that parents do a very good job in general, and that more and more intervention needs to be made in the name of protecting children and limiting the role of parents."

Modest change already is under way. "I think the past two years have seen a loss of patience with the [child protective] system on the part of families all across the nation," says David Wagner, director of legal policy at the Family Research Council. "Five years ago nobody talked about these issues. But now we're starting to see not only articles about false allegations, but also some reform action."

In Missouri, a reform bill was introduced in the state legislature to require state operators (such as ambulance dispatchers) to screen calls to the child abuse hot line. The Virginia legislature has debated whether to hold hearings before placing a person's name on the state child abuse and neglect registry. And a federal appeals court in New York ruled in March 1994 that the standard of evidence used by the state to place a suspect's name on the state register posed an "unacceptably high risk of error." The court declared the current system "unacceptable."

But there also have been a number of failed reforms. A California bill that would have demanded a trial to terminate parental rights failed. So did another California measure that would have lifted child protection workers' unqualified immunity from prosecution. . . .

Change is coming slowly. . . . "I really feel mistreated and frustrated," says Betty Jordan, whose name was listed on the Virginia child abuse and neglect registry. "Social workers are not making the judgment calls that they need to be making, yet they have almost unlimited power. And parents are being second-guessed. The way we choose to raise our children is be-

> *"Some think . . . changes are needed to reform a system that errs on the side of the child."*

ing questioned right and left. I know better than the state whether my child has the maturity to handle being home for one hour by himself. People are afraid to discipline their children in public for fear of being reported. The rules have changed. It's so confusing now."

Violence Against Women Is Often Falsely Reported

by Frank S. Zepezauer

About the author: *Frank S. Zepezauer writes and teaches in Sunnyvale, California.*

Male sexual misconduct—rape, incest, stalking, sexual harassment, child molestation, pornography trafficking—has, according to some observers, become a problem so big that it demands a big solution, not only the reform of our legal system but of our entire society. Yet the increasingly heated debate over this crisis has focused primarily on how these misbehaviors are defined and how often they occur. The estimated numbers keep mounting. We hear that perhaps 31 million women are suffering from some form of rape, 41 million from harassment, 58 million from child sexual abuse, and all 125 million of them—from toddlers to grandmothers—from a toxic "rape culture" that suffocates the feminine spirit.

Not Every Allegation Is True

Much less discussed is how often an allegation of male sexual misconduct is false. The question seldom enters the debate because, presumably, it had long ago been settled. Pennsylvania State Law Professor Philip Jenkins, in a review of the "feminist jurisprudence" which leads the sex crisis counterattack, reports that in response to the question its proponents have established an "unchallengeable orthodoxy." It is that "women did not lie about such victimization, never lied, not out of personal malice, not from mental instability or derangement."

Jenkins is not the first to cite this will to believe. Wendy Kaminer reported that "it is a primary article of faith among many feminists that women don't lie about rape, ever; they lack the dishonesty gene.". . .

Believing the self-proclaimed victim of sexual misconduct has thus evolved from ideological conviction to legal doctrine and, in some jurisdictions, into law. California now requires that jurors be explicitly told that a rape conviction

Excerpted from "Believe Her! The Woman Never Lies Myth" by Frank S. Zepezauer, *Issues in Child Abuse Accusations*, vol. 6, no. 2, Spring 1994. Reprinted with permission.

can be based on the accuser's testimony alone, without corroboration. Canada is proposing that a man accused of rape must demonstrate that he received the willing consent of a sexual partner.

These new rules rest on the assumption that women do not lie because they have no motive to lie. Consequently, as Jenkins states, the question of the "victim's credibility" has now become "crucial."

Is that credibility warranted, particularly as feminist jurisprudence would want it established, as nearly automatic? Not if we consult recent history. And if we do, we will find that we do indeed face a sexual misconduct crisis, but not the one radical feminists now insist is ubiquitous in our society. . . .

Children Become Pawns

Expanding definitions of sexual misconduct, rapidly increasing accusations, intensely politicized publicity campaigns, and significantly high percentages of false allegations [have] appeared in . . . the agencies which deal with the sexual molestation of children. With this kind of sexual misconduct the credibility of a third party, the child, becomes a factor, and we hear, in addition to appeals to "believe the woman," an appeal to "believe the child." We are now learning that children can be manipulated into supplying dramatic testimony of sexual abuse and that in most cases the accusation originates not with the child but with the mother. Thus the question of credibility once again focuses on women. As one lawyer put it, "For a lot of these people 'believe the child' is just code. What they really mean is, 'believe the woman, no questions asked.'"

To keep this issue in perspective, note three significant facts. The first is that of the 2,700,000 cases of child abuse reported every year less than 10% involve serious physical abuse and only 8% involve alleged sexual abuse. The second is that, contrary to the male victimizer/female victim paradigm of feminist ideology, at least as many boys as girls are victimized by child abuse, if not more. The third is that the majority of child abusers are women, that the most dangerous environment for a child is a home formed by a single mother and her boyfriend, and the safest is formed by a married mother and a husband who is the child's biological father. These assertions are themselves widely disputed.

> *"These new rules rest on the assumption that women do not lie. . . . Is that credibility warranted?"*

However, one of the most extensive studies on the subject, by Murray Strauss and Richard Gelles, reports that for physical abuse, the rate is higher for mothers than for fathers: 17.7% for mothers vs. 10.1% for fathers. They found that preteen boys are slightly more likely to be abused than their sisters but that the pattern changes after puberty. Strauss and Gelles, however, also refer to some contravening studies that show higher rates for fathers. . . .

Thomas Fleming cites a Canadian study that concluded that preschoolers were 40 times as likely to be abused in broken and illegitimate families as compared to those in intact two-parent families.

In many cases allegations of child sexual abuse occur in a nasty divorce made nastier by a custody fight. It is now so common that it has received scholarly attention and its own acronym, S.A.I.D. (Sexual Allegations in Divorce). The consensus is that in "S.A.I.D. syndrome" cases the number of such allegations increased so rapidly—up from 7 to 30% in the eighties—that one scholarly team called it an "explosion." Others, noting how often the guilt of the accused was assumed, used the word "hysteria" and searched for analogies in the Salem and the McCarthy witch hunts.

> *"The lowest assessment of false allegation was 35%, the highest 82%, averaging at 66%."*

Another consensus is being reached: that the majority of these allegations are false. Melvin Guyer, Professor of Psychology at the University of Michigan, reports that "in highly contested custody cases where the allegation is made, a number of researchers have found the allegations to be false or unsubstantiated in anywhere from 60 to 80% of those cases." Another investigative team stated that of 200 cases they studied "about three-fourths have ultimately been adjudicated as no abuse." Some studies have come in with a lower but still significant estimate. For example, a 1988 study by the Association of Family and Conciliation Courts said that sexual molestation charges in divorces are probably false one-third of the time.

Allegations of child abuse, both divorce related and in general, are flying out so frequently that those who believe themselves victimized by false charges have organized a nationwide support group, VOCAL (Victims of Child Abuse Laws), which now includes 80 local chapters. This group refers its members to both informal and professional counsel, sends out a newsletter, and offers access to a rapidly expanding data base. In 1989, its summary of relevant statistics cited 23 studies which reported findings on both sexual and non-sexual child abuse. Among these, the lowest assessment of false allegation was 35%, the highest 82%, averaging at 66%. . . .

Why Women Lie

Reasonable doubts about a woman's veracity . . . do not necessarily mean that she has deliberately lied. She may, for example, have suffered from confusion, a problem now proliferating as the definition for sex crimes becomes increasingly complicated and inclusive, leaving all parties struggling with questions about definition and propriety. Or she may have been affected by emotional instability or mental illness, which one study reported was a factor in 75% of false allegation in divorce cases. In some cases a woman or her defenders might exaggerate a misdemeanor into a felony. . . .

In addition, there has been a tendency to emphasize what a victim felt rather than what happened. Thus, a woman can truthfully say she felt raped, abused or harassed by behavior which is actually non-criminal. Moreover, the woman's feelings are often influenced by outside parties with whom she has confided—friends, family members, social workers, therapists, clergymen, rape counselors, lawyers, political activists—any of whom can interpret her emotion as a sign of felonious abuse. . . .

By the same token, among the divorcing wives who file sexual molestation charges against their husbands are some who have been coached by self-serving lawyers. Columnist Barbara Amiel stated that "a lawyer is coming close to negligence if he does not advise a client that in child custody cases and property disputes, the mere mention of a child abuse allegation is a significant asset."

Swept Up by Passion

In *The Morning After*, Katie Roiphe reported still another cause of false allegations: political passions generated by activities such as the "Take Back the Night" marches. She tells about "Mindy" who so wanted to be a "part of this blanket warmth, this woman-centered nonhierarchical empowered notion" that she was "willing to lie." A similar story was told by a Stanford University professor whose daughter was, he claimed, behind a conspiracy to murder him. He testified that he had had a good relationship with her until she attended an anti-rape rally. "She appeared to have gotten swept up . . . and was experiencing great emotional distress."

These mitigating circumstances have often softened the judgment of authorities who confront women guilty of misrepresentation. . . . [Law professor Anita Hill testified at the 1991 Senate confirmation hearings for U.S. Supreme Court Justice Clarence Thomas, alleging that he had sexually harassed her during a period when she was in his employ.] Whether Anita Hill lied about Clarence Thomas still cannot be determined, but David Brock demonstrated that in several other matters she had indeed lied. . . .

> *"Questionable allegations multiply because the accuser has far more to gain than lose."*

Such disclosures should encourage skepticism toward the now widely held belief that, in accusations of sexual misconduct, women never lie. The same skepticism should be activated when we hear its supporting explanation: that filing such a charge is so painful that only a truthful woman would proceed. That belief, although equally strong, is equally suspect. The research that revealed how many sexual misconduct allegations are false has also revealed how often these unfounded accusations are strongly motivated.

The clearest example of compelling motive can be found in the Sexual Allegation in Divorce (S.A.I.D.) syndrome. In such cases questionable allegations multiply because the accuser has far more to gain than to lose. Simply charging a divorcing spouse with child molestation—or wife battering or spousal rape—can turn a hot but evenly balanced custody battle into a rout. In many cases, the accused husband must vacate what had been the "family" home and submit to prolonged alienation from his children. He also finds himself ensnared by both the criminal justice and the social service bureaucracies whose conflicting rules of evidence can deny him the presumption of innocence. In a process that only a Franz Kafka can describe, he must then devote his resources to defending himself rather than pursuing the original divorce litigation.

> *"Many of the investigators eventually mention the influence of ideological feminism."*

Even then he may find himself in jail or in court ordered therapy while his accuser has won *de facto* custody not only of the children but of the house. Should he eventually win vindication, a process which can literally take years, he may enjoy at best a hollow victory which leaves him financially and emotionally drained, nursing a permanently injured reputation and functioning as an "absent" father with a sparse schedule of controlled visits. It is no wonder, then, that to express the reality, commentators have sometimes used dramatic language, such as "the ultimate weapon" or the "atom bomb."

The impressive results that are so often easily achieved with false allegations in custody disputes suggest the kind of temptations women may feel in other situations. Among those found to have lied about rape or sexual harassment, for example, a number of motivations have been identified. The McDowell report [a focused study of the false allegation question undertaken by a team headed by Charles P. McDowell of the U.S. Air Force Special Studies Division], listed those they uncovered in declining order of appearance. "Spite or revenge" and "to compensate for feelings of guilt or shame" accounted for 40% of such allegations. A small percentage were attributed to "mental/emotional disorder or attempted extortion." In all cases, then, the falsely alleging woman had any of several strong motives to lie. But, as with the S.A.I.D. syndrome, the most common motive was anger, an emotion which prompts more than a few embattled women to reach for "the ultimate weapon."

Although money gained through extortion ranked low among the motives for false rape allegations, it appears to rank higher when sexual harassment claims prove to be unfounded. A casual survey of some of the suits that have been filed suggests why. In the eighties, successful claims often brought damages in the $50,000 to $100,000 range. . . .

A Feminist Political Agenda

But where extortion does appear, the motivation may be political as well as monetary, not only in particular cases but in the growth of the entire sexual misconduct crisis. Whether it is rape or sexual harassment or divorce-related child molestation or recovered incest memory, many of the investigators eventually mention the influence of ideological feminism. . . . Norman Podhoretz, who wrote about "Rape in Feminist Eyes," attributes the current over-publicized obsession with rape to "the influence of man-hating elements within the (women's) movement (which) has grown so powerful as to have swept all before it." As far back as 1985 John Sullivan attributed the overheated denial of false accusation to attempts to defend the "feminist theory of rape." And Philip Jenkins, who reported the trend toward automatically-assumed female credibility, stated that it was part of a larger campaign to establish "feminist jurisprudence."

Whatever their motivations in particular cases, there is little doubt that ideological feminists have achieved significant political gains from publicizing the sexual misconduct crisis. The real Anita Hill may or may not have been lying, but the Hill/Thomas affair propelled sexual harassment into a hot issue that rapidly generated a subindustry of scholars, consultants, and bureaucrats, prompted a "Year of the Woman" campaign that helped several women into congress in 1992, and revived a flagging women's movement.

The same spectacular results may follow from the Tailhook Scandal, which, like Hill/Thomas, is raising serious questions about motive and credibility. [Twelve lawsuits have been filed by Naval Lt. Paula Coughlin and other women attending the 1991 Tailhook Convention in Las Vegas, alleging sexual assault by their male colleagues.] Whether Paula Coughlin's testimony will become as clouded as Anita Hill's, her whistle-blowing has already scuttled the careers of a still growing number of naval officers, not to mention the Secretary of the Navy himself, intensified in-service anti-sexual harassment campaigns, reinforced an already strong feminist presence in the armed forces, and helped soften the military's granitic opposition to women in combat. These incidents also helped to power a "Violence Against Women" bill through congress which will channel still more millions of government money into women's programs, not to mention winning congressional validation of feminist jurisprudence. That's a lot of political gain achieved by the words of a few women who suffered little more than an affront to their sensibilities.

> *"False allegations . . . have deprived a rapidly growing number of men and women of their reputations, their fortunes, their children."*

A Crisis of Perception

This growing gap—between the anguish suffered by the victims of traditionally defined sex crimes and what is suffered by victims of ideologically-defined crimes—suggests that the crisis we face is not the result of a sexual misconduct epidemic but of the crisis mentality itself, an ever more hysterical vision of a "rape culture." It has a foundation in reality. In what has become a ritual disclaimer, those who have exposed the surprising number of false allegations of sexual misconduct have also admitted the appalling number of genuine accusations. And those who have attacked the incompetence, self-interest, and zealotry that has denied the extent of false allegation have also recognized the courage and energy that has exposed the problem of honest allegation begging vainly for belief. They have therefore applauded the effort to seek for this long ignored injustice both social and legal remediation.

But that effort, carried too far and exploited too often, has generated another gap: between our awareness of the now highly visible victims of sexual misconduct and the almost invisible victims of false allegation. The lesser known victims have their own stories to tell, enough to reveal another long ignored injustice that demands remediation. False allegations of sexual misconduct have deprived a rapidly growing number of men and women of their reputations, their fortunes, their children, their livelihood, and their freedom; have wasted the time and money of countless tax-supported agencies; have destroyed not only individuals but entire families and communities; and have left some so desperate that they have taken their lives.

For that reason, in the current revision of our sexual misconduct code, we must retain as a guiding premise the realization that women can lie because we know that, for several reasons, more than a few women have lied, more often than researchers into false allegation had expected, far more often than "rape culture" ideologues have admitted . . . too often, in any event, to be ignored by our jurisprudence, feminist or otherwise.

The Prevalence of Child Sexual Abuse Is Exaggerated

by Arnold Beichman

About the author: *Arnold Beichman is a research fellow at the Hoover Institution and a columnist for the* Washington Times.

During Joseph Stalin's collectivization genocide in the early 1930s, a 14-year-old boy named Pavlik Morozov became a communist martyr. Young Pavlik denounced his own father to the local authorities as a grain hoarder, a great crime in Stalin's war against the kulak. Pavlik's father was, of course, shot. In revenge, the villagers killed Pavlik.

According to Robert Conquest's biography of Stalin, the children of later "enemies of the people" were "invariably required to denounce and renounce their parents in public sessions at their schools."

Is it possible that in this age of denouncing and renouncing parents, teachers, foster parents and grandparents as alleged sex deviants, Pavlik is alive and well in the United States? Is it possible that the most stabilizing force in a democratic society, the family, is now endangered by what might be a witch-hunt against parents and relatives who are being charged with often unprovable allegations of sexual abuse of children? In Russia, the son exposed his father as a grain hoarder. In America, the child exposes his parent as a sex marauder.

The Vanishing Family

Karl Marx wrote in *The Communist Manifesto* that "the bourgeois family will vanish as a matter of course with the vanishing of capital." He was wrong. It may be that radical changes in the culture are doing the job. Defined as a counterrevolutionary force, the family has long been a target not only of Marxists but of radical egalitarians. Harvard Professor John Rawls, a philosophical exponent of equality over liberty, has written that "the principle of fair opportunity can be only imperfectly carried out, at least as long as the institution of the family exists."

I am not suggesting that Marxists, radical feminists or radical egalitarians have engineered a diabolical plot against the family by fomenting a panic about sexual abuse. But we are awash in surveys of dubious provenance that are interpreted to mean that parents can't be trusted near children.

Honestly now, do all fathers or stepfathers commit incest with their daughters or stepdaughters? Do all children tell the truth and all parents lie? Children are encouraged to "divorce" their parents, to sue them for damages. The mere accusation against parents is the indictment and the guilty verdict. . . .

Newsweek's cover story April 19, 1993, dealt with the case of an elderly couple, Ray and Shirley Souza, who were convicted of sexually abusing two of their grandchildren. Most of the evidence, says *Newsweek*, "comes from the confusing testimony of two small girls." The case against them "is haunted with ambiguities."

"Mandated" Becomes Fraudulent

No one can argue that there is no sexual abuse of children, sometimes by strangers, sometimes by relatives. But somehow it all seemed under control until Congress in 1974 passed the Child Abuse Prevention and Treatment Act. The number of cases of alleged abuse skyrocketed.

The law funds programs to fight child abuse, but there is a catch. In order to qualify for the money, states must have "mandated reporting," which requires anyone suspecting child abuse to report the child victim to local authorities. Under mandated reporting, asserts *Newsweek*, nearly 3 million children were reported as suspected victims in 1992. Fewer than half of those complaints were found to deserve further investigation.

In 1991, the *Public Interest* published an article by Professor Neil Gilbert of the University of California, Berkeley, titled "The Phantom Epidemic of Sexual Assault." Much of the research on sexual assaults, said Gilbert, "is only part of the radical feminist effort to impose new norms governing intimacy between the sexes."

> *"We are awash in surveys of dubious provenance that are interpreted to mean that parents can't be trusted near children."*

He cited an incredible discrepancy in statistical surveys about sexual assaults against women. One table concluded that one of every 1,000 women is victimized, while another survey said one of every two women is molested before reaching her mid-20s.

Gilbert said such a discrepancy arose from different definitions used by the researchers. One survey included as victims "of incestuous or extrafamilial sexual abuse before age 18" children who merely received "unwanted kisses and hugs" or children who had not been touched at all but had encountered an exhibitionist.

"If unwanted hugs and kisses," writes Gilbert, "are equated with the sexual abuse of children, we have all been victims."

The sex abuse epidemic can reach rather unforeseeable extremes. Canadian Press recently reported a case before the Supreme Court of British Columbia in which a mother, being sued along with her husband by their son for psychological abuse, argued in her defense that she had been abused by her father. And if the father is alive, he could argue that he had been abused by his parents and so on—back, back, back in infinite regress to Adam and Eve.

The Ministry of Women's Equality of British Columbia's semisocialist government recently passed amendments to what it calls the Limitation Act. According to Minister Penny Priddy: "This legislation recognizes the reality that victims may have suppressed memories of abuse, or live in fear of abusers, until the opportunity to bring legal action has passed. This will allow a survivor of childhood sexual abuse to take legal action regardless of the length of time that has passed since the abuse took place."

Whew! Is it time to ask whether the criminal code is the only way to deal with the mostly unprovable—beyond a reasonable doubt—cases of child maltreatment? Especially when the accusations go back to events that occurred decades earlier? The future of the family as a social unit based on trust and love is at stake.

Repressed Memories of Childhood Sexual Abuse Are Dubious

by Michael D. Yapko

About the author: *Michael D. Yapko, a recognized expert in memory and hypnosis, practices marriage and family counseling in San Diego, California. His books include* Trancework: An Introduction to the Practice of Clinical Hypnosis, Hypnosis and the Treatment of Depression, *and* Suggestions of Abuse: True and False Memories of Childhood Sexual Trauma *from which this viewpoint is excerpted.*

Long-term memory is the dimension of memory that allows us to retain information over time. Long-term memory is the largest component of human memory, holding information ranging from a minute ago to decades ago. Long-term memory is fundamental to life, allowing us the continuity of our experience. You don't have to relearn your name and address every day, or how to do the routine things you do. Continuity of information allows for evolution, progression, mastery. Information must be rehearsed and given meaningful associations in order to be available in long-term memory.

A key point to note here is that *not everything is stored in long-term memory.* . . .

Memory Isn't Foolproof

Memory retrieval is a process vulnerable to many influences. The common experience of "going blank" at exam time when asked to recall material you know that you know gives an indication of how your level of emotional distress and your mood can affect memory retrieval. High levels of emotionalism can distort and block memories, decreasing their accuracy and availability.

Another factor affecting memory retrieval is the length of time that has elapsed since the memory's formation. A memory doesn't just sit passively in the recesses of your mind waiting to be pulled out in pristine form at just the right moment. As time passes, new information and new experiences add to and take away from our interpretations of memories of past experiences. The "good old days" can seem better and better, or, conversely, the "bad old days" can seem worse and worse, as your life continues and new perceptions mingle with old ones. In general, the passage of time leads us to embellish or diminish memories, distorting them in one way or another. Remember: Memory is a representation of an experience; it is not the experience itself.

> *"The methods used to retrieve memory . . . [can] alter its face completely."*

Other factors have been identified that influence the accuracy of memory, including (1) the person's motivation to notice, interpret, and remember; (2) the expectations that lead one to "see only what one expects to see," and not what is really there; (3) the methods used to retrieve memory, which can suggest additions or deletions to a remembered experience that alter its face completely (a point especially relevant to the process of recovering repressed memories); (4) the relationship with an outside memory investigator, which may increase or decrease responsiveness to prompts; and (5) the person's personality and reactions to memory gaps that may exist (one person may accept them as gaps, while another may have a need to fill them in, even with misinformation, as in a process called "confabulation").

In sum, memory is a process that involves many variables, each of which has the potential to enhance or disrupt the storage and retrieval of accurate memories. . . .

The Beginnings of Memory

In a therapeutic process commonly called "rebirthing," a woman named Gloria is encouraged to reexperience what her therapist tells her must have been a traumatic birth. The therapist leads Gloria to believe that her symptoms are directly derived from the way her birth occurred, deducing that her problem in creating or maintaining intimate relationships arose from inadequate bonding with her mother in the earliest moments of life.

Gloria accepts the therapist's invitation to close her eyes and relax, and soon she is comfortably detached from the rest of the world and deeply absorbed in her own internal experiences. The therapist suggests she go back, way back in time, all the way to the darkness, warmth, and weightlessness of being in her mother's womb. Soon Gloria gradually shifts into a fetal position, and there is a look of blissful comfort on her face, though she says nothing.

The therapist prepares her for the shock to come—squeezing painfully through her mother's birth canal, the bright lights of the delivery room, the cold air against her sensitive skin, the feel of cool air rushing into her lungs, and the slap on her behind. Soon Gloria is crying. She begins to scream, "I don't want to go. I'm not ready to go!" The therapist encourages her to express her rage at being born, which Gloria forcefully does. She is told to listen to the conversation in the delivery room, and for a moment she is quiet, straining to hear. She says she hears someone saying to her mother, "Congratulations, you have a beautiful baby girl." Her eyes fill with tears and she whispers her mother's answer: "She was an accident. How can I be a mother?" Gloria cries intensely, and the therapist gently asks, "You were an accident?" Gloria says, "I never knew that before. My mother never wanted me. I was never meant to be." The therapist touches her lightly in a kind and supportive way and says, "Now you know why you have never been able to feel connected to anyone."

Memories from within the womb? Remembering conversations and feelings from the first moments of life? Let's complicate matters a bit. Let's say Gloria then asks her mother if she was a planned, wanted baby and her mother truthfully tells her she was not. Does that prove she "remembered" accurately? Or did she merely bring to life in the rebirthing process something that she had long sensed but simply could not face before? That is what a good therapy can often do—help people face what a part of them has known all along but couldn't deal with. But that is not to be confused with remembering actual events or conversations from so far back.

When does memory begin? What is the youngest age from which an adult may have a clear and direct recollection of an event? What is *your* earliest memory, and how old were you when the event occurred? Your earliest memory is most probably very much like a snapshot—an image without continuity.

A great deal of research has been done on this topic, which is of obvious importance to our view of reports of abuse from infancy. For example, can

> *"There is no reliable means for distinguishing truth from fiction."*

a single memory ostensibly occurring at the age of six months be considered reliable? The research indicates overwhelmingly that the answer is no. Study after study indicates that memories occurring before the age of two or three are most uncommon, and must be considered questionable—that is, they are likely to be the products of suggestion (arising from seeing old photographs and hearing family stories), confabulation, or simple misremembering. You must bear in mind that this is not an absolute phenomenon. Parts of an early childhood memory may be wrong while other parts may be reasonably accurate.

Further studies show that the majority of people have little in the way of detailed memory for as much as the first five to seven years of life. How much do *you* remember of your day-to-day life as a four-year-old? Whatever you do remember of your childhood is likely to be vague and impressionistic images of significant but disconnected events. And, just as described earlier, they can be laced with inaccurate information. . . .

Separating Truth From Fiction

Therapists are just as likely as any other group to twist facts to fit beliefs. They have devised a plausible means for maintaining the belief that memories from the earliest hours and days of life are recoverable with enough accuracy to justify believing them—the so-called "body memory." Since most therapists are agreed the infant mind is not yet sufficiently developed to organize and store memories, they postulate that memories are stored in the body. Years later, when cognitive development permits an understanding of what these body memories mean, particularly when a "helpful" therapist is there to interpret them, the individual can now translate his or her body memories into direct knowledge of having been abused. What exactly is a body memory? Can someone store sensory impressions on a purely physical level for later recall and accurate interpretation? As in the rebirthing process described earlier, can an infant or even a fetus "record" conversations as sound sequences that later, when language has been learned, can be understood as meaningful conversation?

> *"Detailed memories of experiences you have never actually had can come from countless sources."*

These are unprovable and not entirely plausible hypotheses set forth by therapists who want or need to believe in the innate wisdom of the infant mind and body. The facts about memory are twisted to fit the theory that all experiences are memorable and retrievable. Such ideas are hardly objective, and may be potentially dangerous when they are offered as "evidence" that abuse occurred. . . .

Many therapists continue to maintain the rigid but unfounded belief that memories of all experiences *must* be in there somewhere in one form or another. If such therapists didn't believe the things that they believe, they would have to admit that a lot of the therapy they practice is based on mere speculation, even utter nonsense. This thought is much too threatening and so leads many therapists into the very "denial" they accuse those with a healthy skepticism of being in. Denial is just as likely to occur in therapists as in their clients. . . .

True or False?

Virtually all of the experts I have interviewed agreed that there is no reliable means for distinguishing truth from fiction. Continued questioning only yields more details, plausible but unverifiable. Lie detectors measure only the degree of believing, not truthfulness. We can only speculate about motives. Finding out that the parts of the person's memory that *can* be verified (like what grade school he or she went to) are accurate doesn't mean the whole memory is accurate. Likewise, finding out that part of the memory is wrong doesn't mean the whole memory is wrong.

It is precisely because it is often nearly impossible to prove or disprove someone's memory that the role of therapists is so critical. Their suggestions of past lives, birth traumas, primal screams, body memories, infantile images, and so forth, are all potentially powerful influences on the quality of clients' memories. . . . It bears repeating that memory is a process of reconstruction, assimilating information from multiple sources ranging from old movies to our own self-deceptions and illusions. It is imperative that caution and good judgment be exercised by therapists and clients alike in doing any work involving distant or presumably repressed memories.

Memory necessarily involves processes of perception. You simply cannot remember life events that did not first pass through your senses, singly or in combination. In the same way that you can be fooled by visual illusions (seen any good magicians lately?), or illusions in *any* of your sensory modalities, for that matter, you can be fooled by illusions of memory. . . .

Memory is a process of reconstruction, not simply of remembering. Missing details are slowly filled in with plausible guesses that often aren't even recognized by us as guesses. This is the process of "confabulation.". . .

The false memories that arise in response to suggestions of . . . a birth trauma or a repressed memory of abuse are genuinely believed by the rememberer. That is what makes accusers so convincing. And just as they typically cannot prove the truth of their memories, typically no one else can disprove them, either. This is the basis of faith, not science. As soon as someone asks me, "Well, isn't reincarnation possible? Couldn't these memories be true?" I have to concede that, yes, it's theoretically possible. And it's theoretically possible that Martians are in the next room controlling my blood pressure. Theoretical possibilities are not evidence.

False Memories Come From Many Places

Detailed memories of experiences you have never actually had can come from countless sources, with your imagination being the primary one. Any imaginative writer creates characters, their backgrounds, and challenging situations for them to live through. . . .

People can and do develop a "believed-in imagination" that serves as an endless supplier of "facts" and details that can sound remarkably plausible, yet have no truth to them. If you watch enough television, see enough movies, read enough books, and talk to enough people, you end up with plenty of details for whatever stories you wish to create.

People typically do not intentionally lie about a newfound belief that they have been abused, and the terms "false memories" and "suggested memories" do not in any way imply deliberate deception. People confabulate for all sorts of innocent reasons, most commonly: (1) out of a need to define an identity, (2) out of hostility toward the accused for perceived injustices unrelated to abuse, (3) out of delusional beliefs created for entirely idiosyncratic reasons, or (4) as a result of outside influences that lead the individual to misinterpret or misunderstand his or

> *"At their most devastating, accusations of abuse can tear families apart and ruin individual lives."*

her past experiences. Therapy is perhaps the most common of these outside influences. . . .

The Paradox of Repressed Memory

Despite the lack of intention, at their most devastating, accusations of abuse can tear families apart and ruin individual lives, all on the basis of presumably repressed memories. Repression is a highly controversial concept within the mental health profession. At one end of the repression continuum is David Holmes, a University of Kansas psychologist who reviewed six decades' worth of research and concluded that there was no evidence to support the notion of repression at all. At the other end of the continuum is Renee Fredrickson, a psychologist and the author of *Repressed Memories*. Fredrickson makes no distinction between repression and forgetting, apparently considering all absence of memory to be psychologically motivated or repressed. Regarding repression and trauma, she writes:

> *"To assume . . . that a memory gap is most likely associated with a sexual trauma is an arbitrary belief system."*

> The traumatic and the trivial are the two kinds of information your mind represses. . . . Trauma is any shock, wound, or bodily injury that may either be remembered or repressed, depending on your needs, your age, and the nature of the trauma. Some of your childhood traumas may be remembered with incredible clarity, while others are so frightening or incomprehensible that your conscious mind buries the memory in your unconscious. . . . Although all forms of abuse can result in repressed memories, sexual abuse is particularly susceptible to memory repression.

The assumption is that traumatized individuals go through a process called "dissociation," a defensive splitting off of awareness from the horrific aspects of the trauma. It is as if they removed themselves psychologically from the traumatic experience as it occurred, retaining no conscious memory for what took place. Dissociation, repression, suppression, and denial are all ways for an individual to avoid consciously dealing with painful realities, but the questions about these mechanisms are many and to date they have gone largely unanswered.

Fredrickson's assumption that repression is a product of need, age, and the nature of the trauma is too simplistic to be entirely true. All sorts of traumas happen to all kinds of people at all ages, and everyone has the same need to avoid pain. Why some people repress memories and others do not, and even how often repression occurs, is still largely unknown. To assume, as Fredrickson does, that repression and forgetting are the same, and that a memory gap is most likely associated with a sexual trauma, is an arbitrary belief system that would be highly suspect in a therapist for its potential to unduly influence clients.

There is no scientific evidence whether memories which surface after years of being repressed are authentic or inauthentic. It is a legitimate concern to wonder how we can objectively tell when repression is in force in a client's life. Symptoms alone are not evidence. . . .

Repression, because it is poorly understood and subject to conflicting interpretations, muddies our understanding of trauma and its effects on survivors. If a therapist sees repression as inevitable where trauma is concerned, then there is no need to seek truly objective evidence that confirms or disproves the belief. The confirmation bias [a tendency to look selectively for evidence that supports what you already believe] can be so great that therapists literally believe that the "evidence" for repression is greatest from the person who least suspects it. In other words, if you were directly asked whether or not you were abused, and you said, "No," the therapist with a confirmation bias would feel justified in saying, "Well, you have the symptoms of someone who has been abused, and since you don't think you were, you must be repressing the memories of abuse."

Do you see the bind in which the client is placed? How can you remember what you are repressing, or know what you don't know? And if you must always leave open the possibility you were abused, then how do you ever safely conclude you weren't? . . .

The Extent of Repression

It is unknown just what percentage of people are repressing memories of abuse, since you cannot directly ask, "Are you repressing memories of abuse?" Repression is associated with trauma in a statistically significant number of cases, but it is not possible to obtain exact figures. Consider one example, reported in the *New York Times* in July 1992. A Rhode Island man who had been sexually abused as a child by a priest repressed the memories until he was well into adulthood. Aware of an underlying feeling of "mental pain" despite a successful life, he lay on a bed and tried to understand why. First came an idea he'd been betrayed, and later came the memory of the priest who abused him at the age of twelve. He then confronted the priest who, thankfully, admitted that the molestations did, in fact, occur. Subsequently, no fewer than fifty others then came forward to accuse the same priest of abusing them similarly. Only the accuser and two others claimed to have repressed memories of the abuse; the others remembered and simply had not discussed it with anyone.

In one study involving a twenty-year follow-up of 100 children who had been treated in a hospital setting for sexual abuse, Linda Meyer Williams, of the Family Violence Research Laboratory at the University of New Hampshire, found that one in three did not spontaneously remember the abusive experiences that had been documented in their hospital records. In

> *"The range of reports of repression is currently too broad to be meaningful."*

another study, researchers reported that 60 percent of their sample of 468 clients with a reported history of sexual abuse in childhood had been unable to remember the abuse at some point in their lives.

In still another study, one not involving sexual abuse, 14 percent of people hospitalized after an accident had forgotten their hospitalization only six months later. Is this evidence of repression?

Since what constitutes abuse is ambiguously defined, and the boundaries separating repression from simple forgetting are not clearly drawn, it is apparent that the range of reports of repression is currently too broad to be meaningful. Furthermore, it is clear that not all traumas lead to repression, for some people remember quite clearly and have never forgotten what happened to them. In fact, the majority of abuse survivors are like Oprah Winfrey, who always knew she was abused but apparently never spoke to anyone about it.

What causes repression and who represses memories of trauma? Clearly, it is not the nature of the trauma that determines the repression, since one can find some people who repress every kind of trauma and others who live in distress with the constant memory of it. Is it a particular personality type prone to repression? This is one of the very important questions that is as yet unanswered.

Physicians Underreport Child Abuse

by Janice Somerville

About the author: *Janice Somerville writes for* American Medical News, *a weekly publication of the American Medical Association intended as a forum for issues affecting physicians and their practices.*

She believed she had no choice. The electricity bill was overdue again, and the electric company had threatened to shut off the power in her home. But she had no one to take care of her 4-year-old son. Reluctantly, she locked the door, and left.

He cried all morning. A neighbor called the police, who took the child away. After three years in dozens of foster homes, where he was beaten and neglected, the boy was finally returned to his heartbroken mother.

Benjamin Wolf, an attorney for the American Civil Liberties Union of Illinois, which won a lawsuit against the state's Department of Children and Family Services, said the boy's story is far too common. "Children are taken from their parents, often because they don't have a home or enough to eat, and begin a bleak, lonely, painful life in foster care."

Physicians Believe Protective Services Harm

Many physicians agree, and some decide they would rather break the law than report a suspected case of child abuse. Filing a report would violate informed consent and the Hippocratic oath to do no harm they say.

Since 1967, all 50 states have required physicians to report suspected cases of child abuse and neglect. The laws apply to all doctors; even those treating adults who confess to abusing children must file a report.

Frequently, however, child protection services simply remove children from their families—or do nothing. Physicians often are unable to get any follow-up.

Children under the care of child protection services are warehoused in overcrowded mental institutions and shelters, bounced from foster home to foster home and denied medical care and education, critics say. Some are beaten and sexually abused.

"The promise implicit in the child abuse reporting laws is an empty promise for many children," said Eli H. Newberger, MD, a leading pediatrician in the field.

Abused children in Illinois "have escaped one dysfunctional family for another," concluded a court-appointed panelist in a case against the state's Department of Children and Family Services early in 1991.

Most critics of the system agree child protection agencies are grossly underfunded and overworked. Since the standards for abuse were broadened, and awareness of child abuse has grown, the agencies have been deluged with calls. The number of reported cases rose by 200% in the 1980s. Yet their funding—and ability to properly review such cases—has not grown proportionately.

> *"Many physicians . . . would rather break the law than report a suspected case of child abuse."*

A federal report released in mid-September 1991 described the National Center for Child Abuse and Neglect, which operates under the Department of Health and Human Services, as "an agency that, given its inadequate support, has had unrealistic expectations placed on it as the volume and complexity of child maltreatment reports have increased."

The advisory board also said the lack of a national child protection policy has fostered a response that is "fragmented, inadequate, and often misdirected." Moreover, "maltreated children themselves . . . are often left in unsafe homes or placed in foster homes equally as dysfunctional as their natural homes."

David Lloyd, a spokesman for NCCAN, said that while the federal response could be improved, the blame for the nation's failure is far-reaching. "All too many families are failing, and all too many of the informal structures we have to support families are failing. The formal CPS system, which is the responsibility of the states, also is failing."

He also said the deficiencies of the child welfare system make a poor rationale for not reporting child abuse. "We've had far more children die because their abuse was not identified and reported than have died because they were placed in foster care.

"The question," he said, "is whether the physician is fully trained to investigate all aspects of the family to make such a decision, and whether the physician is in a position to provide the social services that CPS should provide if the report were made."

Clearly, he said, few, if any, are. Lloyd also disagreed with physicians who say they have failed to report because the reporting laws are vague, as indicated by a Rand Corp. study. "The statutes are generally clear as far as requiring reasonable belief and providing immunity for erroneous reports made in good faith.

"We may need to see states and counties increase efforts in training docs and other health care providers in understanding how to identify suspected cases, how to make reports, what the investigation process is like, and how to get feedback from the CPS agency."

The crisis in child protection services is not the only reason physicians fail to report, although it is the most problematic.

Some physicians find reporting inconvenient, begrudging not only the hours they might have to spend in court testifying but also the time to make the initial call or write a report.

Others break the law, ironically, because they don't like courtrooms. Some are afraid to confront the suspected abuser, and some are afraid of losing patients.

Others worry about liability, although the laws offer immunity if the report is made without malice. Such immunity clauses, however, do not cover circumstances sufficient to overcome a presumption of good faith, such as when a physician overlooked hemophilia as the cause of a child's bleeding problems.

Such "selfish" reasons, however, are confined to about 3% of physicians who failed to report, according to the Rand study.

Like many others, the study found that the reporting laws are frequently violated. More than 40% of the mandated reporters surveyed said they had decided not to report a suspected case of child abuse or neglect.

The top reason for failing to report, insufficient evidence, was cited by 60% of those who had ever decided not to report. The next most common reason, that the neglect was not serious enough, was cited by one-third. Gail Zellman, PhD, director of the study, said reporters often break laws for these reasons because the statutes are unclear about what constitutes "abuse and neglect" and "reasonable suspicion."

Nineteen percent said they did not report because they believed a report would disrupt treatment and because they could help the child better than child protection services; 16% cited the poor quality of the services.

A major problem not addressed in the study is that physicians often refuse to believe that people they've known for years could be abusive, experts say. This is particularly true for middle- and upper-class families, because of the widespread belief that the only child abusers are poor minorities. Statistics seem to support this idea, but Dr. Newberger charges that is only because of gross underreporting of abusive white, wealthier families.

> *"Physicians often refuse to believe that people they've known for years could be abusive."*

"They don't believe it occurs in their practices," said Richard D. Krugman, MD, of the C. Henry Kempe National Center for the Prevention and Treatment of Child Abuse and Neglect.

Failure to Report Leaves Children at Risk

Education can overcome many of these reasons for failure to report, experts agree, but reform of both the reporting system and the child protection system are needed to overcome the dilemma faced by physicians who believe it is unethical to report.

"The child protection system in the United States is fragmented, underfunded, overworked, episodic and unable to generate any information that would let us know that children are, in fact, being protected. Some physicians have deliberately followed a pattern of civil disobedience and do not report child abuse because of their belief that above all they should 'do no harm.'

"In my view, such an approach leaves physicians, and more importantly children, at serious risk," Dr. Krugman wrote in the May 1991 issue of the *American Journal of Diseases of Children*.

> *"Her stepfather said she hurt herself. . . . Two weeks later, she bled to death from a blunt trauma to her abdomen."*

Dr. Krugman said the answer, for physicians, is not to stop reporting but to work within the community to improve the local child protection agency. Physicians also should focus on prevention, he said. . . .

Zellman at Rand offered another solution. She suggested creating a new category of reporters—registered reporters—who could rely on their expertise to decide whether to report. "Physicians who are well trained in child abuse and who have a good understanding of the laws could screen cases, rather than flooding the system with reports it lacks the ability to review."

David L. Chadwick, MD, director of the Center for Child Protection at San Diego's Children's Hospital, blamed much of the problem on a lack of training and education in all fields dealing with child abuse. Mistakes are made on all sides too often, he says.

"There are children I know of who've been wrongly taken from their homes because the doctor failed to properly diagnose their bleeding problems. And there are even more tragic cases, like the 3-year-old with a fractured tibia who told the nurse that her daddy had done it to her. Her stepfather said she hurt herself while he was twirling her around by her ankles. The juvenile court judge returned her home, deciding the two related well and that it wasn't physical abuse.

"Two weeks later, she bled to death from a blunt trauma to her abdomen. The moral is that everyone must be very careful and very well trained and the work must be multidisciplinary.". . .

If physicians are not willing to go to court and back up their diagnoses, or if they're unsure of themselves, they should refer such cases, he said.

"People have to get excited about children and make sure they're protected."

Reporting of Child Abuse– Related Deaths Is Inadequate

by Michael J. Durfee, George A. Gellert, and Deanne Tilton-Durfee

About the authors: *Michael J. Durfee coordinates Los Angeles County's child abuse prevention program. George A. Gellert serves as deputy health officer for the Orange County Health Care Agency in California. Deanne Tilton-Durfee is the vice chairperson for the U.S. Advisory Board on Child Abuse and Neglect, president emeritus and legislative chairperson of the California Consortium for the Prevention of Child Abuse, and the executive director of the Los Angeles County Interagency Council on Child Abuse and Neglect.*

Over 1000 American children die each year of intentional injuries at the hands of a caretaker. Most are infants or young toddlers. No single health, social service, law enforcement, or judicial system exists to track and comprehensively assess the circumstances of child deaths. This viewpoint describes the expanding national implementation of interagency multidisciplinary child death review teams in response to the critical need for systematic evaluation and case management of suspicious child deaths.

The Magnitude of the Problem

It is difficult to estimate the incidence of fatal child abuse using traditional data systems. Available statistics reflect varied levels of competence in detection, evaluation, and recording of child deaths and variation in definitions used by different agencies. The National Committee for Prevention of Child Abuse, which annually surveys all states, reported a national incidence of 1383 child abuse fatalities for 1991. The National Committee for Prevention of Child Abuse survey does not utilize a rigorous case definition and excludes cases not known to social service departments or other child abuse agencies. The Centers for Disease Control uses vital statistics and Federal Bureau of Investigation *Uniform Crime Reports* to arrive at an annual national figure of about 2000

Excerpted from "Origins and Clinical Relevance of Child Death Review Teams" by Michael J. Durfee, George A. Gellert, and Deanne Tilton-Durfee, *JAMA* 267 (no. 23, June 17, 1992):3172-75. Copyright 1992, American Medical Association. Reprinted with permission.

child fatalities from abuse or neglect. In Los Angeles County, California, 14 years of multiagency child death review suggests that the numbers will increase as abuse-related fatalities are more accurately identified and reported.

Unique Factors in Child Death

Death scene investigators evaluating adult victims may follow protocols fairly objectively. First responders to an imminent or actual child death scene, however, may be swept up in an intense focus on providing life support for the victim and emotional support for the victim's family. Even when it becomes apparent at the hospital that the circumstances of death are suspicious, delays may occur before an investigator returns to the scene of the event, or investigators may visit only the hospital and request that the medical staff interpret the death.

Criminal investigation of a child death caused by a caretaker is unique for investigators, since the perpetrator is legally responsible for the child and has continuous access to the victim. This contrasts with the majority of adult homicides where the victim and perpetrator are not cohabiting at the time the injury causing death is perpetrated. Child deaths may also result from the neglect of children by caretakers who are expected to provide for the child victim's biological needs. The concept of not feeding, protecting, or otherwise providing for the unique needs of a young child may be difficult to comprehend for a homicide detective with no child abuse training.

Most suspicious child deaths occur among very young children. Studies of "fatal child abuse" or of "homicide by caretaker" indicate that 50% of the victims are under 1 year of age. These young victims may have no previous records or only medical records that are not frequently accessed as part of the death investigation. Autopsies of young children require a specialized understanding of pediatrics, pathology, child abuse, and forensic investigation. Few jurisdictions have such experts. Autopsies may be conducted by physicians with no formal pathology training, much less specialization in forensic pathology. Radiological and laboratory equipment for clinical or forensic tests may make a diagnosis possible, but these tests may be unavailable locally or may not be ordered to reduce costs.

The above factors contribute to inappropriate surveillance, potential underreporting, misclassification, and mismanagement of child deaths. Case management is further confounded by problems in interagency communications. An extreme example of a case lost in multiple systems involved a 10-month-old infant whose family had 52 agency contacts before the child was eventually beaten to death. Contacts included law enforcement, child protective services, hospital emergency departments, public health nurses, and a psychiatric emergency

> *"The numbers will increase as abuse-related fatalities are more accurately identified and reported."*

team. Most individual agency actions appeared reasonable, but no single agency had a comprehensive and collective record of contacts with the family.

Improved Reporting Helps the Living

Child abuse prevention and intervention are relatively new phenomena. "Child abuse" was not indexed in *Index Medicus* [a monthly bibliographic listing of references from over 3000 international medical journals] until 1965 and "infanticide" was not indexed until 1970. Much of the limited medical literature on fatal child abuse has been published since 1989. The preponderance of medical and other data are available only from uncirculated sources.

Los Angeles County began the nation's first interagency child death review team involving criminal justice and health and human service professionals in 1978. This team evolved from the experience of clinical teams conducting "death review" rounds on internal medicine wards. Weekly review of all adult deaths on a busy hospital service demonstrated the educational

> *"An extreme example . . . involved a[n] infant whose family had 52 agency contacts before the child was eventually beaten to death."*

benefits of a systematic review of death as a way to improve services to the living. . . .

Child protective services provides records from previous contacts with the victim's family and coordinates efforts to protect surviving siblings. Medical professionals access and interpret clinical records of trauma or physical neglect, educate the team on pertinent medical issues, and may assist in referrals for direct health care evaluation and services for surviving family members. Public health specialists may provide vital records and can develop epidemiological risk profiles of families for early detection and prevention of child death and serious injury.

Other team members can include representatives from mental health agencies, fire department emergency medical personnel, probation and parole departments, substance abuse treatment providers, local school and preschool educators, sudden infant death syndrome experts, and state or local child advocates. Private hospitals may participate if they are actively involved with child abuse prevention or have involvement in a case under review. . . .

Increased Accuracy Reveals Higher Death Toll

Seven child death cases chosen from a systematic team review from 1981 through 1983 that were designated as natural or accidental in causation were modified at a coroner's inquest to "death at the hands of another." Several of these cases resulted in criminal actions and referrals of surviving siblings for protective services. Another case reviewed by the team was reclassified from homicide to natural death.

The multiagency team process is more vigorous than the single agency process, more capable of clearly identifying a case that is suspicious, and more able to deal with special challenges, such as the difficulty of identifying the perpetrator out of multiple caretakers, separating out physical findings that confuse the determination of cause of death, or distinguishing sudden infant death syndrome from suffocation. The results are more focused, more complete, and the process is more accountable. Outcome reports from the team add to that accountability.

> *"Seven child death cases . . . designated as natural or accidental . . . were modified at a coroner's inquest to 'death at the hands of another.'"*

Child death review also creates an opportunity for a systematic review of agency actions (and inactions). This has been particularly important with respect to improving and integrating interagency communications, and allowing agencies the opportunity to address deficits in their own systems. Surviving siblings can be identified and referred for protection, evaluation, and service. Health professionals with previous contacts with the child or family can improve their clinical judgment and case management skills by learning retrospectively from the follow-up information obtained through child death review.

Small case numbers in rural counties and the ability of the involved agencies to focus extensively on each case offer an opportunity for some teams to develop specifically targeted local preventive actions for childhood injury. Such action may involve various multiagency prevention programs, including child safety seats for automobiles, drowning prevention, and suicide prevention.

Law enforcement, child protective services, coroner's investigators, and public health nursing team members all conduct home visits and investigations. These professionals thereby possess outreach capability for families that are beyond the coverage of mainstream community medical systems. Team education allows such professionals to become a resource for detecting and referring medical and social problems that predispose a family to violence. High-risk problems that may be detected include pregnancies involving maternal substance abuse, pregnant women exposed to domestic violence, failure-to-thrive infants, and homes lacking basic child safety measures.

Special Populations

Other special populations would benefit from review, including spousal homicides with surviving children, child siblings as perpetrators, children killing parents, and homicides of disabled adults and the dependent elderly by family members. The team process may be extended to live children with the addition of children with severe nonfatal injuries.

Child and adolescent suicides with a history of prior child abuse represents another potential population for multiagency review and management. In Los

Angeles County, 28% of all suicides under the age of 18 years in 1989 were found to have a history of previous child protective services. The incidence of previous child abuse was inversely related to age (85% of 14-year-olds). This has resulted in the formation of a multiagency task force to address child and adolescent suicide.

The Los Angeles County coroner investigates approximately 40 fetal deaths annually from a countywide total of over 1000 fetal deaths per year. Most of the coroner's cases appear to result from maternal substance abuse, usually cocaine. Several fetal deaths each year result from homicide or assault of a pregnant woman. Fetal deaths traditionally receive intervention only at the hospital. Team intervention with fetal deaths from maternal substance abuse may include a public health nurse referral to help the mother and other family members prevent such behavior in the future. Fetal deaths from assaults on the mother may be followed by criminal justice investigation and prosecution. . . .

Medical team members have special value as liaisons with other health care providers who cared for the child before the incident that caused death. Occasionally, previous caretakers will have noted injuries or family problems that may assist in defining a pattern of abusive behavior. Previous caretakers may also have failed to report suspected child abuse or neglect and may benefit from peer support and consultation.

Future Goals

The US Advisory Board on Child Abuse and Neglect has made specific recommendations to the Secretary of Health and Human Services about the development of child death review teams. . . . The task for the 1990s will be to build a national network of teams and to integrate that network with health care providers to establish a prevention system for families and children before they are injured or killed.

Child death review began initially as a method to address suspected child abuse or neglect fatalities. Many teams have expanded this focus to address all coroners' cases including suicide, accidental deaths, and natural deaths. Prevention of child abuse fatalities involves early detection of families at risk and coordinated multiagency intervention directed at those risk factors. Factors that elevate risk in a particular locality can be identified through the study of past child deaths. The team process facilitates more competent and predictable intervention through agencies that have learned to work together more effectively.

The interagency child death review team is clearly an idea whose time has come. Child death review teams have grown rapidly since 1989 with little or no external funding and limited national leadership. Federal and state funding and support of child death review teams would greatly facilitate the expansion of review across the nation. A national data registry could quantify and demonstrate the impact on detection, management, and prevention of fatal child abuse on an ongoing basis.

Violence Against Women Is Underreported

by The Jacobs Institute of Women's Health

About the author: The Jacobs Institute of Women's Health was founded to study women's health issues and their treatment within existing medical and social systems.

It has been estimated that more than 2.5 million females experience some form of violence each year, and that nearly two of every three of these females are attacked by a relative or person known to them. The Centers for Disease Control and Prevention notes that one national survey found that 34% of adults in the United States had witnessed a man beating his wife or girlfriend, and that 14% of women report that they have experienced violence from a husband or boyfriend.

Underreporting Skews Estimates

Violence can take many forms. . . . This viewpoint focuses on physical violence, mainly because there are national data available on the topic. There is considerable variability in estimates of violence against women. The information presented in this viewpoint is based on nationally reported data. These data may provide conservative estimates, because they rely on reported events.

More than 1 million women seek medical assistance each year for injuries caused by battering. It is estimated that 22–35% of women treated in hospital emergency departments have injuries or symptoms associated with physical abuse. However, few emergency departments have policies that specifically set forth protocols for identifying and treating victims of domestic violence.

Estimates of the extent of violence against women come from two major sources. The Federal Bureau of Investigation compiles Uniform Crime Reports consisting of crimes reported to authorities. These reports underestimate the scope of violence against women, because about half of the women fail to report crimes. Reasons given by these women for not reporting the violent incident include feeling that it was a private or personal matter or that the offense

Reprinted with permission from the Jacobs Institute of Women's Health from *The Women's Health Data Book*, 2nd ed., J.A. Horton, editor, *Women's Health Issues*, vol. 5, pp. 122-27.

was minor, and fear of reprisal from the offender or his family or friends.

The other major source of data is the U.S. Department of Justice's National Crime Victimization Survey (NCVS), which conducts in-person and telephone interviews on an ongoing basis. In this survey, a nationally representative sample of households is used to determine recent crimes experienced by the respondents or members of their household 12 years of age or older. These data are used to estimate the full extent of crime by comparing them with official reports of crimes. Between 1987 and 1991, this survey may have underestimated violent crimes, particularly rape, because it did not ask respondents direct questions about sexual assault and the relationship between the victim and the offender. Questions on the NCVS that deal with issues of family violence have been redesigned, and beginning in 1993, the survey asks direct questions about this kind of violence.

In the early 1970s, a study was undertaken to estimate the magnitude of underreporting in the NCVS. A reverse record check of police files found that two-thirds of rape victims who had reported the rape to police also told the survey interviewer about the crime. Only 54% of the rapes that had been perpetrated by persons who were known to the victim were reported to interviewers; in contrast, 84% of the rapes that had been committed by strangers were reported. . . .

Although a great deal of attention has been given to the issue of violence in the American family, available data are limited and provide only conservative estimates of the problem. Victims of violence may suffer long-term effects, and there appears to be a transgenerational effect that projects the impact of violent crimes in the future. It is clear that additional efforts are needed to determine the scope of the problem and to propose ways to eliminate it. . . .

> *"Reasons given by these women for not reporting the violent incident include . . . fear of reprisal from the offender or his family or friends."*

Rape by Intimates

According to NCVS data, nearly 133,000 women were victims of rape or attempted rape each year between 1987 and 1991. These data showed that women were more likely to be raped by someone they knew (55% of the reported rapes) than by a stranger (44% of the rapes). It was estimated that only 53% of all attempted or completed rapes, however, were reported to police. Only 15% of those who reported the crime said that they did so to prevent it from happening again, and more than half (56%) of the victims wanted the offender to be punished. Of the rape victims who did not report the assault to police, 28% made the decision because they felt it was a private or personal matter that they could take care of themselves, about 17% feared reprisals by the offender or his family or friends, and a somewhat smaller proportion (15%)

Table 1. Percentage of females reporting rapes to police, reasons for reporting or not reporting, and nature of victim-offender relationship, 1987–1991

| Reporting to police | % of female victims of rape | | |
	Total	Non-stranger	Stranger
Rape reported to police	53	53	55
Most important reason for reporting			
To stop or prevent further rapes to victim or someone else	15	17	11
To punish offender	56	52	65
Other reason or not ascertained	29	31	24
Most important reason for not reporting			
Private or personal matter	28	35	13
Police couldn't do anything	4	1*	11
Police wouldn't do anything	11	11	11
Afraid of reprisal from offender	17	18	15
Other reason or not ascertained	40	35	50

*Estimate is based on 10 or fewer cases.
Source: Bachman R. *Violence Against Women: a National Crime Victimization Survey Report*. Washington, DC: Bureau of Justice Statistics, 1994:11.

felt that the police would be ineffective or insensitive (Table 1). However, the reasons for reporting or not reporting rape depended on the relationship between the victim and the offender. . . .

Regardless of whether the victim was raped by a stranger or someone known to her, 60% of the women received medical care and 30% of the women were injured seriously enough to be hospitalized.

Marital Rape

Marital, or spousal, rape has become a crime only in recent years and is one of the least-researched aspects of rape. Estimates of its prevalence are limited to a few studies. One study estimated that 14% of women who had ever been married had been raped by husbands or former husbands. Another study found that force or the threat of force was used against 10% of women. The prevalence of marital rape is reported to be higher in battered women. Women who report marital rape are said to have severe and long-lasting psychologic trauma that is perhaps more severe than that of women raped by strangers and that requires intensive psychiatric intervention. . . .

Battering

Approximately 2 million women are severely assaulted each year by male partners. Estimates of the prevalence of physical abuse by a husband against his wife are often based on the use of the Conflict Tactics Scale, which relies on self-reports of any level of physical force. When estimates of violence are limited to more serious levels on the Conflict Tactics Scale, such as the use of a weapon, abuse appears to occur at a lower rate of about 4%. This may be misleading, however, as women can be severely injured and even killed by being thrown, punched, kicked, or choked.

Although considerable research efforts have been directed at identifying the specific demographic factors associated with battering of women, accurate data are difficult to obtain. It is clear, however, that battering of women occurs at all levels of society. Battering appears to be more common at lower socioeconomic levels, but this may be simply a reflection of the availability of resources to middle- and upper-class families to keep their

> *"Marital, or spousal, rape has become a crime only in recent years and is one of the least-researched aspects of rape."*

problems with violence from coming to public attention. In a careful review of the literature, it was noted that the only variable that has been related to the severity and/or frequency of wife abuse is the abuser's own experiences of abuse as a child.

Battering may be the major cause of injury to women in the United States. Extensive research conducted at Yale University indicates that battering accounts for almost one in every five visits to emergency rooms by women. In one urban center, only 5% of the victims of domestic violence seen in the emergency room were identified as such in the medical report of the visit. One reason for this may be because both patient care providers and the victims of battering themselves are often reluctant to discuss the topic of physical abuse.

Abuse does not stop during pregnancy. Studies report that the prevalence of physical abuse during pregnancy ranges from 8% to 17%. The proportion of battered women who report that the abuse continues during pregnancy may be as high as 36%. In another study, 8% of pregnant women reported being abused during the current pregnancy.

Homicide

Women are most often murdered by their spouse, their boyfriend, or a member of their household. It is estimated that one of every six homicides involves a family member. About half of these murders are committed by spouses, and women are 1.3 times more likely than men to be the victims. The Federal Bureau of Investigation's Uniform Crime Reports shows that 28% of all female victims of murders in 1989 were believed to have been killed by their husband or boyfriend.

When women commit murder, their victim is five times more likely to be their spouse, an intimate acquaintance, or a member of their family than a stranger. In some cases, women who are the victim of chronic abuse eventually become violent toward the abuser. Frequently, women who kill their spouses have been the victims of spiraling levels of abuse of increasing frequency and severity. In most cases of spouse homicide, the police previously had responded as many as five times to incidents of family violence.

Repressed Memories of Sexual Abuse Are Valid

by Donald Barstow

About the author: *Donald Barstow is affiliated with Renewed Hope Counseling Service in Oklahoma City.*

The term "false memory syndrome" is used to denote several different concepts: (1) iatrogenic memories, (2) suggested memories, including by hypnosis, (3) confabulation, (4) fabricated or fictitious memories, and (5) distorted memories. The term is also used to connote the creation or invention of memories of events that never occurred. In view of the serious ramifications this postulate can have on the issue of childhood sexual abuse, it is imperative that the concept be carefully examined.

What Memory Is

Memory is defined by Webster (7th New Collegiate Dictionary) as "the store of things learned and retained as evidenced by recall and recognition." L. Squires and N. Butter define memory as "a store of information, as well as the processes involved in accessing that store." M. Adler also stated that "we do not remember objects we have never perceived or events in our lives, such as emotions or desires, that we have not experienced." Thus, a person can only have memories of actual experiences. If you have never visited the British Museum, you can have no memory of such a visit. It follows logically, from the above definition, that there can be no such entity as "false memory syndrome" since a person either has an experience or does not; either has a memory or does not.

By definition, neither a therapist, hypnotist, nor any other person can create and implant a memory in another person's mind of something that person has not experienced; nor can the person himself do so. It is possible, however, for therapists and others to add information regarding a memory, that is to say, to graft information into an already existent memory. This will result in the production of an altered memory that is formed by the input of new information

Donald Barstow, "A Critical Examination of the 'False Memory Syndrome,'" *Family Violence & Sexual Assault Bulletin*, vol. 9, no. 4, 1993; © 1993 Family Violence & Sexual Assault Institute. Reprinted by permission.

provided by the therapist. This altered memory comes from the fusion of two EVENTS in the person's experience. There is no creation of a false memory, i.e., the client does not (and cannot) "remember" something that has never been a part of his/her experience. Therefore, even if a person could be convinced that something happened to him/her that did not actually happen, all we can say is that the person has been deceived about the facts. A false memory of who, what, why, when, where, and how often has NOT been created.

> *"[No one] can create and implant a memory in another person's mind of something that person has not experienced; nor can the person himself do so."*

There is some distortion involved in any perception. No two people will provide a police officer with exactly the same details regarding an automobile accident. But the witnesses are not charged by the police with obstructing justice because of these EXPECTED, NATURALLY occurring discrepancies. To the contrary, two exactly matching descriptions are viewed suspiciously by investigating officers. Normal discrepancies in the memory of details cannot be used as evidence for the "false memory syndrome."

How Memory Happens

Three steps must occur in order for a person to have a memory. First, the individual must experience an event. Second, the event must be retained, and third, the person must be able to retrieve the event. Proponents of the "false memory syndrome" concept would apparently have us believe that a memory can be "created" without following this procedure.

Since memory is a physiological process which produces changes in the microneuroanatomy of the brain, there can be no such entity as "false memory" since a false memory would not produce a neuroanatomical response. Consequently nothing would be "recorded" that could be recalled at a later date.

It is also important to note that accepting a statement of fact creates a memory of the *fact*, but not a memory *about* the fact. For example, one may believe the *fact* that Washington crossed the Delaware River, but one has no *memory* of the crossing.

The Fallacy of False Memory "Syndrome"

We also need to determine the meaning of the term "syndrome." According to researchers B. Kozier, G. Erb and R. Olivieri, this word refers to "a group of signs and symptoms resulting from a single cause and constituting a typical clinical picture." Thus all legitimate syndromes are composed of both signs and symptoms. A symptom is defined by the same source as "subjective data that only the person himself can give, such as thoughts and feelings." A sign is defined as "evidence of a disease or body dysfunction that can be observed and described by others." Where is the list of symptoms or complaints of patients suffering from "false memory syndrome"? Where is the list of signs that can be observed by health care personnel that characterize this condition and distinguish it from all other syndromes? Where is the description of the disease process, the diagnostic information, and the recommended treatment approach? It is obvious that if these questions cannot be scientifically answered, no such syndrome exists.

At times, mention has been made of fictitious accounts of childhood sexual abuse. Fiction is something created by the imagination or feigned. It is a conscious and deliberate act. For a certainty, fictitious accounts exist, but this is not a false memory; it is willful and purposeful behavior. A fabricated memory of abuse does not result in a memory of actual abuse, but only a memory that one has fabricated a fictitious account of abuse.

Altered vs. False

What about confabulation? This is a condition in which a patient fills in memory gaps, but does so from his/her fund of life experiences. A cobbler will not confabulate memories of performing neurosurgery, nor will a television repairman confabulate memories of constructing an atomic device. E. Loftus made the comment that "it is difficult to tell whether clients who produce repressed memories are responding to the wishes, expectations, and more or less subtle suggestions of therapists whose interests and approval they are seeking." While it may be difficult to determine the accuracy of all details of the memory, by definition a repressed memory is a real memory. It is true that some individuals are highly suggestible, particularly those under hypnosis or in severe distress, and that clever individuals can induce some additions to the already present memory. But this is not a false memory; it is nothing more than an alteration of a real memory.

Loftus continues by stating that one therapist questions clients by asking: "Your symptoms sound to me like you have been abused when you were a child. What can you tell me about that?" She insinuates that this innocuous question can plant the seed of a false memory. However, suppose that I visit a physician with complaints of bloody diarrhea, tenesmus, and abdominal pain. Based on knowledge and experience, s/he may suspect I am suffering from amebiasis. A competent doctor might say: "It sounds to me like you might have amebic dysentery. What can you tell me about travel abroad?" Will I suddenly "produce" a false memory of travel through Central America with a stop in Jucuapa, El Salvador, where I picture myself drinking out of a local creek? Hardly. Such a question does not serve as a catalyst for false memory production; it merely raises a possibility which is con-

> *"A fabricated memory of abuse does not result in a memory of actual abuse, but only a memory that one has fabricated . . . abuse."*

firmed or denied based on the client's memory. This is neither poor practice nor intimidation by the therapist.

Loftus cites the case of a woman from Oregon whose therapist is convinced that she is the victim of abuse. The client tried and tried to trigger memories without success. This anecdote conflicts with the position the author seems to support. The therapist was unable to convince the client, or induce a false memory, because THERE WAS NO MEMORY. She concludes by stating that fabricated memories of abuse are destructive, and indeed they are. However, fabrication is one thing, and false memories are quite another.

"By definition a repressed memory is a real memory."

It is important to always distinguish between what "false memory" denotes, and what some individuals desire it to connote. Distorted, fabricated, and suggested memories, including confabulation, are not false memories as the proponents of "false memory syndrome" would have us believe. By false memory, they seem to imply that a client can have a memory of an event that never transpired, that a therapist can suggest a memory, and the client will accommodate by creating one. But instead of describing the definition and dynamics of a false memory, they write about changes, modifications, distortions, and fabrications of memories brought by suggestion and hypnosis. This is a mixing of apples and oranges. False accusations and false memories are decidedly different concepts. This author readily admits that memories can be altered in details which have little significance, but is scientifically unconvinced of the existence of this unicorn named "false memory."

Experience—Not Belief—Creates Memory

It must be emphasized that beliefs, no matter how sincere, or how cleverly implanted, do not create memories. Believing that Alexander the Great had a horse named Bucephalus does not create a memory of the size, color, weight, appearance, or training of the horse. Neither does believing a lie about sexual abuse create a memory of that abuse. It is also to be noted that the principle defense mechanisms marshalled by victims of abuse are minimization, denial and repression. Survivors fight against the pain of recovered memories that reveal abuse by a loved significant other.

So then, if the term "false memory syndrome" refers to false statements about memory, it is evident that all memories are false memories since all memories contain some distortion and therefore are rarely, if ever, 100% accurate. In this case, the term would lose all significance since everyone would have to agree that ALL memories fall within the "syndrome." On the other hand, if the term is used to designate memories of events that never occurred (analogous to matter originating in a vacuum), proponents have failed to demonstrate the legitimacy of the concept.

113

In closing, consider this final illustration. Imagine being in a foxhole in Vietnam with a buddy. Mortar, machine gun, and rifle fire are all around. Imagine the terror you would feel. Try to make your body break out in a cold sweat. Make your heart race, your muscles shake, your bladder empty itself involuntarily. Can you feel all the physical and emotional responses inherent in such an experience? Not unless you were there. Likewise, victims who retrieve memories of childhood sexual abuse would be unable to voluntarily produce these same physiological signs and symptoms if they had not had the experiences. So-called "false memories" do not produce post-traumatic stress disorder. So-called "false memories" do not result in the intensity of signs and symptoms that occur during therapy. It is therefore interesting to note Adler's comment on repressed memories:

> On this view of things which have been put out of mind because we find them unpleasant to contemplate, things which are repressed in order to avoid conflict, are not forgotten when they cannot be consciously remembered. Nor are they below the threshold of recall in the sense that retention of them has been so weakened by time that no effort at recollection can revive them. On the contrary, they may be capable of quite vivid revival when the emotional obstacles to recollection are removed. Freud applies his theory of the "obliviscence of the disagreeable" to such everyday occurrences as the forgetting of familiar names as well as the repression of memories connected with the emotional trauma of early life.

It appears that while advocates of the "false memory syndrome" acknowledge the existence of the mechanism of repression, and seem not to question the validity of repressed memories in other areas of emotional illness, they pursue with ardor the belief that all retrieved memories of childhood sexual abuse are highly suspect. While not impugning their integrity or sincerity, many are alarmed that their writings will exert a negative impact on the legitimacy of childhood

> *"Distorted, fabricated, and suggested memories . . . are not false memories as the proponents of 'false memory syndrome' would have us believe."*

sexual abuse as a major social and public health issue facing this country. There is also concern that this position could very well revictimize the victims of sexual abuse by strengthening the confusion, minimization, denial, and repression that characterize survivors' resistance to recovered memories of abuse. And many worry that uninformed individuals may be induced to deny the prevalence of this societal cancer, minimize the impact on victims, and suppress efforts to protect vulnerable children. Many also fear that "false memory syndrome" publicity will impede appropriate legal prosecution and conviction of perpetrators. These would be tragic consequences indeed! It is up to us to see that this never happens.

Chapter 3

Who Are the Victims of Family Violence?

Chapter Preface

During the predawn hours one Sunday morning in 1991, a man lay beside a blood-splattered nightstand. His wife had phoned the police earlier, when it was still what might be considered evening. Michelle Chapman, arrested five years before for stabbing her husband, Thomas, was a woman who knew her potential for violence. "Come get him and take him away before I kill him!" she had told the emergency operator. But instead, the officers who came advised her to spend the night at a neighbor's apartment. They left after a few minutes, without bothering to check on Tom. Apparently Michelle did not appear dangerous to them. Within an hour of their departure, Tom was dead.

"The sexual stereotype that men are always the batterers and women are always the victims misrepresents reality," writes associate editor Gordon Grilz in the *Prison Mirror*. National surveys conducted in 1975, 1985, and 1992 by prominent family violence researchers Murray Straus, Richard Gelles, and Glenda Kantor produced findings that appear to back him up: the women in the studies initiated approximately half of physically abusive incidents between couples. Two Canadian research teams—Roger Bland and Helen Orn (1986); Merlin Brinkerhoff and Eugen Lupri (1988)—conducted surveys in Alberta, Canada, that yielded similar results.

Those who question the significance of these findings counter that, regardless of who initiates the conflict, Straus, Gelles, and Kantor's studies demonstrate beyond doubt that women sustain the most serious injuries. Citing FBI figures, these advocates point out that in 1992 alone, 1,432 women were killed by male partners while only 623 men were killed by female partners. The disparity between men and women as victims shows up again in U.S. Department of Justice records: an annual average of 572,032 cases are reported by women; for men the number is 48,983.

Men's advocates explain that these gross imbalances result in part from men being much more hesitant than women to report abuse. "We're taught to take it like a man," explains Alvin Baraff, a clinical psychologist with MensCenter Counseling in Washington, D.C. He tells of a male patient who did venture a call to the police. Their response: "Why can't you control your wife?" Reporter Deborah Hastings, in an article devoted to the experience of male victims in domestic violence, writes that "men who claim such abuse are deemed wimps and laughed at."

Still, the argument persists that despite such realities, domestic abuse victims remain overwhelmingly female, and that diverting attention from this fact demonstrates yet again the sexism that has underlain society's failure to treat violence against women as a serious crime throughout history. "We're a long way from even equality," says Christine Littleton, who teaches courses on women and law at UCLA, "let alone some form of disadvantage to men."

Gender is one of the demographic characteristics studied by social scientists in their search for a more fully developed profile of those comprising the population at risk for family violence. The following chapter presents the differing answers to the question: Who are the victims of family violence?

Women Are Victims More Often Than Men

by FAIR (Fairness & Accuracy in Reporting)

About the author: *FAIR is a politically liberal media watch group concerned with correcting perceived bias and imbalance in the news.*

Husbands are battered as much as wives in the United States? John Leo, syndicated *U.S. News & World Report* columnist, is sure of it. "There's no doubt about it," Leo said as a guest on CNN's *Crossfire*. "It was established in 1980 by a female researcher."

When co-host Michael Kinsley asked him if it seemed plausible that women were as violent as men, Leo dismissed the question. "We don't have to cogitate this," he said. "The evidence is in. All these studies have established this."

Claims of Gender Parity Among Batterers

Leo is not alone in insisting on parity between battered men and battered women. Domestic violence "is not either the man's fault or the woman's," Judith Sherven and James Sniechowski wrote in an *Los Angeles Times* op-ed. "Both the male and the female are bound in their dance of mutual destructiveness."

"Why do we protest domestic violence against women and not even know about violence against men?" men's advocate Warren Farrell wrote in a *USA Today* column, arguing that women's violence is as bad as men's—if not worse.

Alan Dershowitz . . . used his syndicated column to argue that spousal murder is "primarily a psychological issue of pervasive familial violence on all sides, generated by the passions of family interaction."

Misinterpreted Data

All these claims and suggestions about "battered men" being as pervasive and serious a problem as battered women are based on studies that are either discredited or taken out of context.

One of Leo's major sources is Richard Gelles, who with Murray Straus did surveys on family violence. Leo may like Gelles' work, but Gelles doesn't like

FAIR, "Battered Men? Battered Facts," *EXTRA! Update*, October 1994. Reprinted with permission.

Leo's: "He takes enough factual statements and twists them so he gets it to come out the way he wants," Gelles said.

The Gelles/Straus numbers that Leo and others seize on are based on simply asking people whether they have ever hit, pushed, slapped, etc., their partners. They do not reflect the context of family violence. They do not indicate whether violence was used as aggression or in self-defense, or whether violence caused or was intended to cause injury. Using such numbers without qualification results in bizarre conclusions: that children's violence against parents is a much more serious problem than parents' violence against children, for example.

Gelles put his research in perspective in a Long Island, New York, *Newsday* op-ed: "In the majority of these cases, the women act in response to physical or psychological provocations or threats. Most use violence as a defensive reaction to violence."

Ignoring the Facts

Those who equate domestic violence against men with that against women either ignore or dismiss the results of the federal Bureau of Justice Statistics, which found that 92 percent of those who report being assaulted by an intimate partner are female. They also brush off reports from emergency rooms, where 90 percent of the victims of domestic violence are women.

But statistics are not the strong point of these battered men advocates. Dershowitz claims that a Bureau of Justice Statistics study shows that "women kill almost as often as men do in the context of family murders." The study actually found that men committed 66 percent of family murders, so apparently for Dershowitz "almost as often" means the same thing as "about half as often."

> *"Research that looks at violence in a meaningful way shows that [men] are a tiny fraction of the number of battered women—perhaps 5 percent."*

Sherven and Sniechowski, in their op-ed, claim that "half of spousal murders are committed by wives, a statistic that has been stable over time." In fact, according to 1991 figures from the FBI, which has the most comprehensive murder statistics, 71 percent of people murdered by their spouses are women.

While it is true that some men are battered, research that looks at violence in a meaningful way shows that they are a tiny fraction of the number of battered women—perhaps 5 percent. These men are not helped by pundits who use overhyped, out-of-context numbers to argue that battering is no one's fault in particular—with the implication that nothing in particular needs to be done about it.

Women Are Not Victims More Often Than Men

by Wendy McElroy

About the author: *Wendy McElroy is a contributing editor to the libertarian magazine* Liberty, *and author of two books,* Freedom, Feminism and the State *and* XXX: A Woman's Right to Pornography.

The April 9, 1995, march on Washington to protest violence against women was yet another attempt to politicize the crimes of rape and domestic assault. Boosted by fresh funding from 1994's Omnibus Crime Act, feminist advocacy groups are pushing the images of women as victims and men as beasts. Gloria Steinem declares that "the most dangerous situation for a woman is . . . [to be with] a husband or lover in the isolation of their own home." A massive billboard campaign proclaims: "One woman is battered every 15 seconds.". . .

Gender-Based Guilt

Yet according to the 1993 National Crime Victimization Survey, conducted by the U.S. Bureau of Justice Statistics, sexual assaults on women *declined* 20 per cent from 1992 to 1993. And the same survey that found that a woman is beaten every 15 seconds also found that a man is battered every *14* seconds. This research indicates that 54 per cent of all "severe" domestic violence is committed by women. It's strange that we rarely hear *these* statistics.

In the current climate of hysteria, those who question the conventional wisdom are denounced as enemies of women. Radical feminists are using the issues of domestic violence and rape to create a new jurisprudence that assesses guilt and imposes punishment based on gender. In *Feminism Unmodified*, University of Michigan law professor Catharine MacKinnon argues that "some of the same reasons children are granted some specific legal avenues of redress . . . also hold true . . . for women." Lenore Walker, director of the Domestic Violence Institute and the leading exponent of "battered woman syndrome," explains the political underpinnings of violence against women: "A feminist political gender analysis has reframed the problem of violence against women as one of misuse of power by men who have been socialized into believing they have the right to control the women in their lives, even through violent means."

A Sexist Hate Crime

The Violence Against Women Act (VAWA), which Congress approved in 1994 as part of the Omnibus Crime Act, advances the radical-feminist goal of redistributing power from the ruling class (men) to the oppressed class (women). VAWA defines "gender-motivated crimes" as federal civil-rights violations, converting domestic violence and rape into "hate crimes." The law recognizes men and women as antagonistic classes to be governed by different standards of law.

VAWA allows not only criminal prosecution but also civil suits for "the recovery of compensatory and punitive damages, injunctive and declaratory relief, and such other relief as a court may deem appropriate." Just as "crimes motivated by race" can be tried under federal civil-rights statutes, so too can "crimes motivated by gender." In effect, a man can be tried (and punished) twice for the same crime. . . .

The success of "battered woman syndrome" as a defense in murder cases also illustrates how standards of justice have been warped by the politicization of violence against women. Traditionally, a plea of self-defense required imminent danger without the possibility of escape. Today, courts are acquitting women who kill abusive husbands in their sleep.

Women Batter Men

Such deviations from traditional legal standards are driven largely by the perception that domestic violence is something that men do to women. As we have seen, this is a myth. The research cited above is far from an isolated case. In 1975 and 1985, sociologists Murray A. Straus and Richard J. Gelles conducted what may be the best available studies of family violence. They found that men were as likely as women were to be victims of domestic violence (though women are more likely to be seriously injured). Indeed, in the decade between the two studies, the rate of violence by men against women dropped, while the rate of violence by women against men rose. To counter the charge of "gender bias," Straus reran the 1985 numbers using only the responses of women—and came up with the same results.

> *"The same survey that found that a woman is beaten every 15 seconds also found that a man is battered every 14 seconds."*

Other studies also indicate that men are victims of violence more often than women. In 1994, according to the Justice Department, 55.5 per cent of domestic murder victims were men. That July, the 13th World Congress of Sociology reported that in 1992 American husbands assaulted wives at a rate of 4.6 per cent, while wives assaulted husbands at a rate of 9.5 per cent. The 1993 National Crime Victimization Survey found that women were 40 per cent less likely to be victims of violent crime than men.

Feminist Dogma Maims Research

Dogmatic attitudes have crippled honest research into domestic violence. In 1988 R. L. McNeely, a professor at the University of Wisconsin's School of Social Welfare, and a graduate student, Gloria Robinson-Simpson, published an article noting that men are the victims of domestic violence about half the time. According to the *Washington Post*, a women's organization threatened to use its potent influence in Washington to have McNeely's research funding pulled. In 1978, when Suzanne Steinmetz published an article on the "battered husband syndrome," distressed feminists called anonymously and threatened to hurt her children.

Such zealots are aided by others who unthinkingly accept propaganda as fact. In October ("National Domestic Violence Awareness Month") of 1994, when members of Congress rushed to express their support for battered women, accuracy was lost in the stampede. Representative Olympia Snowe (R., Me.) declared, "Domestic violence . . . is the leading cause of injury to women aged 15 to 44, according to recent research by the Surgeon General and the American Medical Association." The study to which Representative Snowe was alluding actually found that violence *in general* was the leading cause of injury to women in a single black West Philadelphia slum. In only 12 per cent of the cases was the perpetrator identified as the woman's husband or lover. Representative Eva Clayton (D., N.C.) claimed that "in one year more than four thousand women have been killed by their husband or partner." Imagine how surprised the FBI must be: its Uniform Crime Statistics place the number somewhere between 1,200 and 1,400.

> *"Men are not monsters. . . . They should not be made to stand before a legal system that presumes their guilt."*

The FBI, of course, is not using the expansive feminist definition of domestic violence. In its 1994 "Fact Sheet," the San Francisco–based Family Violence Prevention Fund describes "domestic violence" as "the actual or threatened physical, sexual, psychological, or economic abuse of an individual by someone with whom they have or have had an intimate relationship."

Feminists are also pushing a redefinition of rape. In 1991 Canada passed a "no means no" rape law, which reversed the burden of proof and narrowed the definition of consent. Under this law, sex is rape whenever a man fails to "take reasonable steps" to make sure he has the woman's consent. Even if the woman yells "Yes!" repeatedly during coitus, the sex act could be considered rape if she is in a "diminished state"—say, drunk or on drugs. . . .

Rape allegations can have a disastrous impact on the accused man. In the summer of 1994 the *New York Times* reported that a male student at Pomona College in California had been denied his diploma because a woman decided to denounce a sex act that had occurred two years earlier. She claimed rape based not on the use or threat of force but on the lack of explicit consent.

This sort of injustice is the inevitable consequence of treating men as a separate and antagonistic class, rather than as individuals who share the same humanity as women. Men are not monsters. They are our fathers, brothers, sons, husbands, and lovers. They should not be made to stand before a legal system that presumes their guilt. Feminists must resist the temptation to wield power as unjustly as men have in the past.

Professional Women Are Often Victims of Domestic Violence

by Hillary Johnson

About the author: *Hillary Johnson is a frequent contributor to* Working Woman *magazine.*

For most people, the phrase "domestic violence" summons a stereotypical scene: police pounding on the door of a ramshackle house; a man loudly, perhaps drunkenly, declaring his innocence; a woman crying. But for a vast number of middle- or upper-class women, many of them professionals, domestic violence is a secret, usually silent affair. They are prisoners of their world, but for many reasons they feel compelled to don a mask of normalcy. In spite of their bruises and scars, they may not even admit that they are victims. And until they fully acknowledge what is happening to them—a process that can take years—the very last thing they want to do is make their situation public.

Battering Crosses Class Lines

Definitive statistics on these white-collar victims are hard to come by, especially because shame or fear of reprisal makes them reluctant to report the crime. The Justice Department's 1994 National Crime Victimization Survey (NCVS) found that only about half the women who suffered domestic abuse between 1987 and 1991 reported it to the police. As incredible as it may seem, *Family Violence: Crime and Justice*, a 1989 book that reviewed the research on the subject, projected that one-fifth to one-third of all women could be assaulted by an intimate at some point. And the perception that most victims are poor and uneducated is clearly distorted. The NCVS found less than a 10% difference in the rate of family violence between those with household incomes of less than $10,000 and those earning more than $50,000. "Women of means are just as trapped as women on welfare," says Carol Arthur, the director of the Domestic Abuse Project in Minneapolis, Minnesota, a nonprofit program that aids victims. "The stories and issues are all the same. There are just different barriers to leaving the relationship."

Perhaps the greatest myth about white-collar domestic violence is that its victims should be able to arrange smooth, bloodless departures because, unlike poor women, they are blessed with financial and social resources. "The irony is how hard it can be even for women who earn more than the men they're involved with to leave," says Sharon Rice Vaughn, who co-founded one of the first battered-women's shelters in the country in 1972 in St. Paul, Minnesota. "It is particularly hard for professional, highly paid women to believe that battering is happening to

> *"The perception that most victims are poor and uneducated is clearly distorted."*

them." One TV reporter was blind to the warning signs in her own relationship even though she had covered a number of domestic-violence cases. "I was in denial that I could be an abused woman because I'm smart, I'm professional, I know a lot of cops," she says. "And there was this constant self-questioning—is it really as bad as I think it is?" Experts say the confusion is compounded by a *Gaslight* [a movie by Alfred Hitchcock in which a husband schemes to convince his wife that she is going insane] effect created by the sporadic, random nature of the abuse; the victim wonders whether she really is being brutalized or whether the attacks are somehow her fault. The effect is even more potent when there's a strong desire to keep the relationship intact. "It's about *wanting* it to be a one-time thing," notes a domestic-abuse counselor.

Women's Success Breeds Targets

In addition, professional women are trapped by a fear of exposure. "That's the abuser's secret emotional blackmail," says Rice Vaughn. "If you have a reputation, your reputation will be ruined." In fact, women who earn more or are more successful than their partners can be more vulnerable targets than women of like status to their husbands', according to Evan Stark, co-director of the Domestic Violence Training Project in New Haven, Connecticut, 40% of whose clients are middle- and upper-class victims of domestic abuse. "Those men are compensating by resorting to socially condoned male dominance," explains Rice Vaughn. "It becomes their form of revenge. It's as though she is being blamed for his failures—if she weren't so successful, he wouldn't be seen as less successful."

Lorraine Holmes, an attorney in Homestead, Florida, represents mainly women who have been battered or otherwise abused by their husbands. Holmes herself lived with an abusive man in South Florida for four years beginning in 1984 while attempting to build her law career. She was the wage earner, he the househusband who assured her he would soon "make it big" in the music business. "I always counsel women to make an escape plan," says Holmes. "If it means saving only $3 to $4 a week from the household money, *do* it." Her own plan involved confronting her former husband—although she knew the result would be injury to herself—during an 18-month trial "pro-arrest period" in greater Miami. She arranged a two-week absence from work, then informed her husband of her intent to divorce him. "He dragged me across the floor, threw me into a wall and threatened to kill me. I had handprint bruises on my arms and an abrasion on my face, but I don't remember whether it was from him hitting me or slamming me into the wall."

Afterward, Holmes slipped away to a neighbor's and called the police. Her husband spent three nights in jail, giving Holmes time to get a protection order and, she adds, a gun. Her husband violated the order by contacting her by telephone. Now, despite her flourishing practice, even the Florida Bar has access only to a post office–box number. And although it has been over two years since she last heard from her ex-husband, she continues to live in fear. "I still believe he's capable of homicide," she says.

Subtle Manipulation

How did Holmes get involved with a violent man, and why did it take her four years to leave? Certainly, little about her suggests someone easily intimidated or willing to suffer abuse. During the 1970s, Holmes, who graduated in the top 7% of her law class, spent most of her time fighting for feminist causes. And her husband-to-be, like many abusers, showed no predilection toward violence throughout a five-month courtship; indeed, Holmes found him particularly seductive and charming. "He was the only man I had ever gone out with who was as smart as I was," Holmes says. "His sweet-talking got me hooked on the relationship. He had already started the crazy-making—convincing me I had no memory, that my recollections of conversations were wrong—but it was done very subtly. Despite one prior incident of abuse, I married him in May 1985."

Aside from the subtle manipulation, there were no warning signs that he was capable of severe physical violence. The first blow enraged Holmes: "I told him to get out of my life." Her reaction was typical of many women, says Evan Stark, "who have grown up with a certain level of entitlement—they're incensed. And at first they think they can control or change it. But with these manipulative men, you can be in a relationship for a *long* time before you get it together to leave." Stark points out that in many white-collar households, the violence is not just sporadic but rare; rather, the abuser depends on "coercive strategies—the use of intimidation and threats—to gain and keep control." Holmes allowed her husband to return when he convinced her that the violence had been a fluke. "When people like me, who are

> *"I was in denial that I could be an abused woman because I'm smart, I'm professional."*

125

out to change the world, get into a relationship with someone who is so clearly disturbed, the crusading part of our personality comes out—we're going to fix that, too," she says.

Nevertheless, her husband steadily escalated the psychological harassment and abuse. "Batterers use the same techniques as terrorists," Holmes says. "Isolation, threats and random violence. I never knew whether I was coming home to a cooked meal and a bubble bath or to accusations and intimidating behavior, which may or may not have resulted in physical violence, like the meal being thrown in my face or him jabbing at my gut with a two-by-four."

> *"Many professional women suffer years of torment because they are isolated in their experience . . . [and] can be loath to seek help from women's shelters."*

Holmes wanted out by the end of the second year of marriage, but like many in her situation, she was demoralized and discouraged, as well she might have been: Statistics indicate that women who leave their abusive partners are at a 75% greater risk of being killed by their abusers than those who stay. "I've followed the news and seen a lot of domestic-homicide reports in Miami," says Holmes. "No one cared . . . —they were back-paged. I would just get up the courage to leave, and then I would read about another murder." Holmes's salvation came when she began meeting other victims of domestic assault at a counseling service offered by Dade County. "Most of these women had gotten free, and they were able to help me objectively assess the risk of mortality."

Suburban Isolation

Although Holmes and some other women interviewed for this article sought help through public agencies, many professional women suffer years of torment because they are isolated in their experience. Unlike poor women, who may have used other public services, professional, middle-class women can be loath to seek help from women's shelters. If they look for help, it is typically in the private offices of marriage counselors. But "marriage counseling assumes you're on a level playing field with your abuser," says Susan Neis, director of Cornerstone, an organization providing services to domestic-abuse victims in four affluent suburbs of Minneapolis. "You aren't."

Professional women usually have a great deal to lose by severing ties with their abusers, often including an expensive home in an exclusive neighborhood, their social standing in the community, their financial security and a superior education for their children. Because so much is riding on the perpetuation of their marriage, they may lack supporters—even among their own families. . . . Says Carol Arthur, . . . "I have heard women weigh their safety with what they would give up. If the violence happens only three or four times a year, they barter."

There is also the problem of a legal system that one victim characterizes as an "abuser's haven." Women trying to divorce wealthy, established husbands typically find themselves ensnarled in court battles for years. Finally, the fact remains that when a man is intent upon killing his wife, there is no sure way to prevent it. One distinguished judge whose husband was arrested for assaulting her says, "I have not even tried to get a divorce, because I believe it would be fatal." She stipulated that she could not, under any circumstances, be identified. "Absence of malice," she says, in a reference to the libel defense, "won't help me when I'm dead."

Killing Their Careers

Aside from the physical and emotional toll, domestic violence can exert a crushing weight on a career. Holmes was just starting out in an elite Miami firm when her husband began his terrorist tactics. "He would physically restrain me from going to work," Holmes says. Once, stark naked, he pursued her out the front door and into the yard in order to pull her back inside. "Eventually," Holmes recalls, "I was barely out of the house before I would begin to be afraid of what would face me when I got home. It blew my concentration at work. In the corporate world, and

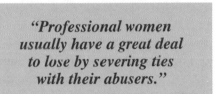

"Professional women usually have a great deal to lose by severing ties with their abusers."

certainly in the legal world, you're expected to perform at 120% no matter what. Toward the end, people were rewriting my briefs. I was told that I couldn't put together a cogent sentence."

Holmes discovered as well that a frank admission of an abusive relationship can deter prospective employers from hiring women. When she explained the gaps in her job history to employers, "they immediately assumed that if I was so weak as to allow myself to be abused, I would be a weak litigator," she says. It was one reason Holmes launched a solo practice.

Jeanne Raffesberger, a Wisconsinite, was an ambitious technical analyst in the insurance industry. Throughout a 15-year marriage, her husband repeatedly threatened her life with knives and, twice, with a .357 Magnum revolver. But, as with many working women married to abusers, it was the day-to-day psychological harassment that damaged her most. "He would call me stupid, tell me I was a miserable failure," she says. Some days her husband would prevent her from going to work by taking her car keys from her. Whenever she began to make progress in her career, he would demand that she quit her job, stay home and clean house—eight hours a day. At 2 P.M. she would fill the sinks and tubs with hot water and Pine Sol. When her husband arrived home later to the wafting aroma of pine, he was reassured that she had fulfilled her wifely duty to him. Nevertheless, within days he would order her to "get off her ass" and find work. "It was a gradual, incremental slide into total chaos," she remembers. She abandoned her career. . . .

The Powerful Abuser

For professional women married to abusers who are also power brokers out to preserve their reputations, the road to freedom can be virtually endless—and carpeted with broken glass. Money offers these men a way to perpetuate the psychic pain through the courts; the more money, the more tools the abuser holds and the longer the battle rages.

Jenny Barry's marriage to Tom Barry followed a brief, intense courtship that left Jenny's friends envious of her seemingly remarkable fortune: Barry was a well-known retailer in a large southern city whose chain of clothing stores had made him a millionaire (the couple's names and identifying details have been changed). Jenny was a successful sculptor who had already had three one-woman shows in prominent local galleries. Not long after the wedding, Barry threw her against a wall when she asked him to hang up her coat.

"I moved out and told him I wouldn't come back until he got help," Jenny recalls. After two weeks, Barry's assurances that he would never again harm her lured her back. The next time, he tried to choke her. She spent eight days with a friend in Seattle. "He was like a time bomb—I never knew when he was going to blow—but afterward there was always great remorse." She didn't think of herself as a battered woman. After all, she was living in a million-dollar house with a very rich husband. And Barry's assaults were infrequent enough to keep her off guard. "I wasn't brutally beaten every week," Jenny recalls. "I was living with a bully." The chronic fear, she says, killed her creativity, and her career as an artist "came to a dead stop."

> *"The more money, the more tools the abuser holds and the longer the battle rages."*

Eight years into the marriage, when she learned that Barry was still in contact with a former lover and had lied to her about it, Jenny sought a divorce. She didn't mention the physical abuse in her petition; she had simply come to accept that as a fact of the marriage. As the process began, Barry was allowed visitation with their 5-year-old daughter every other weekend. After one visit, the little girl revealed that Barry had touched her in what Jenny thought was a sexual way. Jenny's attorney suggested a physical exam; a pediatrician found that the child's injuries "could be consistent with an occurrence of sexual abuse." Barry denied the charges. The court found that "inappropriate sexual contact" had occurred, but awarded Barry continued shared custody since it did not appear to the court to be "part of a pattern of behavior" and there was "no future threat of abuse." In addition, the judge sealed the divorce records.

A Victim of the System

Jenny had borrowed $30,000 from her mother for legal fees and living expenses. Eventually her attorneys' fees topped $150,000, and she had to start representing herself. During the proceedings, she was told that she could remain in the house, but, she recalls, "Tom drained the equity by taking out loans against it for his businesses. The house went into foreclosure, and my daughter and I were given 48 hours to leave." The house was sold to one of Barry's business associates. In the end, Barry, who had declared liabilities exactly equal to his almost $4 million in assets, was awarded sole rights to all the businesses, plus all interest in pending projects and deals. Jenny was awarded a 1983 Volkswagen, their furniture and alimony of $2,500 a month for 10 years. Recently, she declared bankruptcy. Her daughter, now 11, continues to visit her father every other weekend.

"First I was abused by Tom," Jenny says. "Then my daughter was abused by Tom. And then we were abused by the system."

Florida attorney Holmes calls these protracted legal frays "wars of attrition." "When the cash runs out, the attorneys withdraw," she says, leaving the woman the loser because she is usually unable to stand toe-to-toe with her abuser financially. "These guys are very slick at hiding assets. They've often done it throughout the marriage." Like Jenny Barry, some women resort to representing themselves, but, Holmes continues, "a *pro se* litigant stands virtually no chance of winning. I have never withdrawn from a domestic case when the money runs out, by the way, but I hand out a sheet to my clients telling them to expect that he will spend every penny on attorneys rather than give it to them or the children."

Some observers consider the plight of women who are victimized by such men qualitatively worse than that of women whose husbands, however brutal, lack the financial toolbox to manipulate the judicial system. "Society goes after the little guy," notes one victim, "but the big guys are clever, and they won't give up until they destroy you."

Leaving for the Children

Most abused women experience a moment when they resolve to get out of the relationship at any cost. For Ann, an oncology nurse in the Northeast (her name, profession and location have been changed for her protection), that point came when her then 3-year-old son witnessed her husband hitting her in the throat and throwing her across a room. When her husband left the house afterward, she called a service for battered women at her mother's urging. "The feedback I got was, 'This will not get better.' I thought, 'I cannot have my son grow up thinking this is OK.' A moving van arrived six days later, and I was gone."

> *"Society goes after the little guy . . . but the big guys are clever, and they won't give up until they destroy you."*

Ann and her son moved several states away, to her hometown. That was in 1991. Her husband, a computer expert, dragged the divorce proceedings on for two and a half years, unsuccessfully seeking sole custody of the child. A few months before a judge was to rule on alimony and child-support payments, he changed his $50,000-plus job to a half-time, half-salary, no-benefits position, a not-uncommon tactic that reduced Ann's anticipated support payments by about half.

For Ann, however, money was not the central issue. "The fear that he would manipulate the legal system in such a way that I would lose my child was almost incapacitating at times," she says. Ultimately, a judge ruled that the two would share legal custody. Then, 18 months ago, Ann's former husband moved within two miles of her house, ratcheting up her fear level by several notches. Unfortunately, there exists no safe, neutral place where Ann can deliver her son to him under protection. She keeps her doors locked and her curtains drawn, and she uses caller ID. "When the doorbell rings, I have a physical response," she says. "When a car drives by, I look."Acknowledging that she is in danger every time she must take her son to her ex-husband, she says, "Prove that to the judge! No one believes you, because these guys have beautiful masks. There's nothing I would like more than to have legal justice in this situation, but this guy's too smart." After a moment. she adds, "It's the slow murder of the soul that goes on—and what judge is going to hear that? I sense that I could be in legal battles over my son until he's 18. He's 7 now.". . .

> *"Any advantages women of means may have over poor and blue-collar women are minimal."*

The Price of Freedom

Like Ann, Jeanne Raffesberger was able to summon the courage to file for divorce only when, while beating her, her husband began beating their two young sons as well. Although there had been violence before, she, like numerous other women in her situation, did not identify herself as a battered woman until then. Afterward, her husband packed his workout bag and left for the gym. Raffesberger took her children and headed for a women's shelter. "I would live in a box under a bridge, I would panhandle, I would eat dog food—but I wouldn't live there anymore," she says.

The state prosecuted her husband only for child abuse. Meanwhile, Raffesberger hid from him, taking an apartment, buying her own car and getting an unlisted phone number. Released after serving 30 days in a work program, her husband was allowed supervised visits with his children and, eventually, unsupervised visits. "There was no way to facilitate a safe exchange," Raffesberger says, "and he found out where I lived."

Like many women who know their abusers well, she sensed one day that her husband was in an explosive phase, but she was more concerned with her children's safety than with her own. Later that evening, frantic because her husband had failed to return one of their sons, Raffesberger called a state representative she'd become friends with to ask for advice. While she was on the phone, the front door crashed open and her husband began shooting. Raffesberger ran into her backyard and scaled a seven-foot wooden fence. Just as she reached the top, a bullet grazed her arm and she fell to the other side. Her husband then fired through the fence. A second bullet entered her back, near her spine, shattering five ribs. He used his last bullet on himself, putting the gun to his chest and killing himself. The first squad car on the scene was driven by the policeman who just an hour earlier had spoken with Raffesberger's husband regarding the whereabouts of the son.

Raffesberger has recovered from her physical wounds. Like others whose lives have been profoundly altered by domestic violence, she has chosen to devote her future to working on behalf of other victims. Already her testimony before the Minnesota Legislature has influenced a provision in the new federal crime bill that, if enforced, will prohibit the sale of firearms to a man with a valid protection order against him. Raffesberger plans to enter graduate school in the fall of 1995 to study public policy.

Although domestic violence discriminates along gender lines rather than class lines, professional women have one advantage over poor women: their job skills and education. It is precisely because they have independent incomes, says Stark, that some white-collar women are able to extricate themselves.

Still, any advantages women of means may have over poor and blue-collar women are minimal, says Carol Arthur. "White-collar women are like all other women in terms of getting sucked into the psychological and emotional abuse that traps them," she says. "All the messages we got growing up taught us to define ourselves in terms of our relationships." In the end, having the emotional strength to leave that notion behind is what really sets one woman apart from another.

Immigrant Women Are More Often Victims of Family Violence

by Milyoung Cho

About the author: *Milyoung Cho is a freelance writer based in San Francisco.*

The FBI estimates that a woman is beaten, raped, or abused by her husband every seventeen seconds. In San Francisco, according to a 1991 study of over 400 undocumented women conducted by the Coalition for Immigrant and Refugee Rights and Services, 25% of the Filipinas and 35% of the Latinas surveyed were married to wife-batterers. . . .

So far, the struggle against domestic violence has been focused on the arenas of legal advocacy, policy change and battered women support services. These alternatives, unfortunately, depend mostly on professional staff, leaving community people largely out of the picture.

Not that it would be easy to develop grassroots leaders comfortable speaking out against the abuse in their own homes or communities. The shame and guilt surrounding victims of domestic abuse can be extremely isolating. In addition, cultural taboos against exposing "private" family matters reinforce isolation, and women's dependence on their husbands—for a livelihood or legal status— also pose serious obstacles to fighting abuse at any level.

Escaping the Marriage Prison

The 1986 Marriage Fraud Act forced all individuals applying for permanent residency through their spouse to be interviewed two times with their spouse, the first at the time of applying, the second two years later. This law effectively "trapped women who married in good faith, when they became battered, in a marriage prison for two years," explained Becky Masaki, executive director of the Asian Women's Shelter in San Francisco. "It forced people in 'real marriages' into a two year waiting period. Within a two year period, domestic violence frequently escalates severely."

Excerpted from "Waking Up from a Domestic Nightmare" by Milyoung Cho, *Third Force*, May/June 1994. Reprinted with the permission of the Center for Third World Organizing, Oakland, California.

A national campaign led by immigrant and battered women's rights groups successfully led to the passage of a policy granting a waiver to immigrant women applying for residency who are caught in a violent marriage during the two-year waiting period. Passed in November 1990, the new law, contained in the Violence Against Women Act, lifted the second-year joint interview requirement for a woman able to prove that she is battered by her spouse. This waiver allowed battered women to leave their relationships and maintain their right to be considered for permanent residency.

According to Masaki, "These new conditions helped out countless numbers of women. It created a window of opportunity for a lot of women to save their lives. Since the new law was enacted, when I would get a woman caller who was afraid for her life, with the violence getting worse, I could tell her to make an appointment with the Asian Law Caucus, to get her documentation down and file for a waiver."

The Right to Self-Petition

However, as Leni Marin, senior program specialist and coordinator of the Battered Immigrant Women's Rights Project (BIWRP) at the Family Violence Prevention Fund in San Francisco, pointed out, the problem is that the majority of undocumented women haven't been allowed by their spouses to petition for immigration status.

"Those who haven't gone to first base are left out in the cold because husbands refuse or withdraw petitions or threaten their wives with deportation when the women run to a shelter."

The Immigration and Nationality Act permits U.S. citizens and permanent residents to file petitions for their spouses to obtain legal permanent residency. The undocumented spouse, however, is not permitted to petition for her own status. The citizen or resident spouse may also revoke the petition at any time prior to the issuance of permanent residency to their spouse. If the citizen/resident is willing to petition for his spouse, the spouse may be on her way to being legalized, but if the citizen/resident is a batterer, it is highly likely that he will refuse to do this.

> *"Seventy-seven percent of undocumented and recently documented Latina women . . . in the Washington, D.C. metropolitan area are battered by their husbands."*

Immigration Policy Makes Women Vulnerable

Seventy-seven percent of undocumented and recently documented Latina women who are married to U.S. citizens or permanent residents in the Washington, D.C. metropolitan area are battered by their husbands, according to an ongoing survey conducted by AYUDA [the Spanish word for "help"], Inc. of Washington, D.C. In 69 percent of these cases, the citizen or resident husband never filed a visa petition on behalf of his undocumented spouse, and in cases where petitions were filed eventually, the husbands delayed filing for a period of time ranging from 1.5 to 9 years.

> *"When a woman who has no papers . . . is raped, beaten and emotionally abused by her spouse, . . . it is likely that existing service programs will turn her away."*

BIWRP is at the forefront of a national coalition effort pushing a right to self-petition provision entitled "Protection for Immigrant Women," which falls under the Violence Against Women Act. "Some laws foster battering," Marin explained, "because they don't allow [an undocumented person] to petition on her own behalf. She has to depend on a citizen or permanent resident spouse. The woman depends on him because he is the only one who can change her status. It is another tool to exert power and control. If a woman has a valid marriage, even within the scope of the existing immigration law, she shouldn't be dependent on her spouse because he'll use this as a tool. We have to remove this tool because it is entrapping her in horrible conditions."

The Violence Against Women Act, which was passed by the House on November 20, 1993, contains the "Protection for Immigrant Women" provision. The Senate's version of the bill, however, does not contain the provision. "Without this law," argues a coalition of women's rights groups, "there is a group of citizens and permanent resident spouses who are immunized from criminal prosecution for any crime against their spouses and children because the batterer can always get the victim deported."

Women's groups that might not otherwise actively support immigrant issues are backing this particular effort because, as Marin put it, "it can be seen as a woman's bill rather than an immigrant bill. We therefore see public officials with anti-immigrant track records, such as Senator Barbara Boxer, as main proponents." Marin, however, continued to explain that although many "will view this as a women's rights issue, the staunch anti-immigrant will see this as an immigrants' rights issue, and as another way to open the flood gates [to immigration] through claiming 'fraudulent cases' of batterings."

Nowhere to Go

When a woman who has no papers legitimizing her presence in this country is raped, beaten and emotionally abused by her spouse, she may escape the household and seek support, but it is likely that existing service programs will turn her away. They may not have the language capacity to communicate with her, or they may simply be full. Community, family and religious groups may tell her to go back to her husband, that it is necessary to make some sacrifices for the family.

As Masaki explained, "A lot of service providers are shutting their doors [because of] the anti-immigrant climate. They are afraid of taking in undocumented women. So where do [the women] go?

"It is an overwhelming situation that they don't even want to take on. But it's not acceptable to not take it on just because there are too many barriers. . . . We can't just give up on a whole segment of the population, give up on our sisters, even under the harsh climate against immigrants."

Efforts from within immigrant communities of color have responded to the lack of outreach and needs-specific services for battered immigrant women of color. Maria Olea, coordinator and one of the founders of Mujeres Unidas y Activas [United and Active Women] in San Francisco, described the effectiveness of her group's approach in terms of working to empower battered Latinas: "Maybe because we are from the base, we are not experts, we are undocumented, we know how life is, we live in the Mission [a low-income district of San Francisco], they have our home phone numbers, we never say, 'Sorry, we are closed.' Sometimes we cry with them, are happy when they resolve a problem. We work more closely. Most think Mujeres Unidas is like a family."

A central struggle for Mujeres Unidas y Activas is to inform the community: "Every day we have to fight with the media because they give wrong information. Our community doesn't know which is law, which laws passed or not. We don't know this country. Undocumented women can't go to school. There is sensationalism in the Spanish media too. It's really hard, our work. We have to go in different ways: information and education, empower people and advocate.". . .

Preventive Measures Are Needed

From initiatives to change U.S. policy to rallying the United Nations to recognize violence against women as a human rights violation, the reality is that changes in domestic and international policy have limited effect on domestic violence. For example, the Protection for Immigrant Women bill will not protect women who are battered by husbands if they too are undocumented, or lesbians or gay men who are battered by their same sex partners. The particular focus on, for example, women who are married "legitimately" may serve only to further marginalize women who are married "illegitimately."

New strategies are surfacing to try to change community behavior and attitudes toward domestic violence. Leti Volpp, ex-board member of the Asian Women's Center in New York City, commented: "Groups like Mujeres Unidas or the Filipinas Advisory

"We have to sever our ties with the community, hide from the community, to protect ourselves."

Committee to the Asian Women's Shelter, which is spearheading community education about domestic violence in the Filipino community, are all too rare as groups with many members who have directly experienced some of the kinds of abuse we are talking about. What's happening now in terms of the kinds of tactics used to fight domestic violence is important and necessary, but we have to start doing more community-based work as well."

Cynthia Toliver, director of community education at Casa de Las Madres [Mothers' House], which provides shelter and advocacy for battered women and their children in the English and Spanish speaking communities in San Francisco, stressed the importance of community education: "If we could do everything, we wouldn't need a shelter. Through community education we would put out the information with the focus being other than on (service) intervention."

Unfortunately, the nature of shelter services that serve primarily to hide women from their abusers add to the aura of secrecy and shame that already surrounds this issue. Blanca Ramirez, former director of the south Bronx People for Change and a volunteer organizer of Women of the South Bronx points out, "women who have to leave their homes because of abuse end up having to live in secrecy to recuperate. We have to sever our ties with the community, hide from the community, to protect ourselves. Then only advocates can fight for us. Instead of removing the victimizer, we remove ourselves."

The Elderly Are Vulnerable to Abuse and Neglect

by Suzanne Fields

About the author: *Suzanne Fields is a syndicated columnist for the* Washington Times *newspaper.*

An elegant, dignified widow, who lived alone when she was still in her 80s, began to change her behavior around the age of 83. She was always meticulously dressed, but suddenly she began answering the door barefoot.

When someone told her about an engagement of one of her granddaughters she was thrilled to hear it. But she was thrilled to hear it over and over and over again because she forgot all about it five, 10, 15 minutes later.

It was strange how her memory of her childhood was as clear as the crystal she still set on the table. But the short-term memory was gone.

This woman was lucky. Grandchildren would visit and look at the family albums with her, while she entertained them with stories of their parents when they were young. Her adult children arranged to have a woman care for her when she was alone, making sure that she was comfortable and well-groomed. She lived with the mementos of her life until she died in her own bed.

"Granny Dumping"

Many older people are not so lucky. Their illness often becomes more severe, their memory more impaired, their behavior more belligerent and their family finances too diminished to hire a caretaker.

That's why an ugly phrase has entered the sociological lexicon. It's called "granny dumping."

In the spring of 1992, our attention was riveted to the story of John Kingery, 82, who has Alzheimer's disease and who was abandoned, presumably by his daughter, at a dog-racing track in Coeur d'Alene, Idaho, holding a box of adult diapers and grasping a Teddy Bear as though it was his security blanket. He told attendants at the races that he didn't know who he was.

He wore the bewildered expression of a lost child, though he was actually the

Suzanne Fields, "Twilight Years in the Twilight Zone," *Conservative Chronicle*, April 22, 1992. Reprinted with permission.

equivalent of a baby left by a mother on the church steps, in hopes that some-one would find a good home for him.

But a granny or gramps who is dumped lacks the promise and potential of an abandoned baby. Hospitals and nursing homes have waiting lists for sufferers of Alzheimer's disease, and few want to adopt an elderly person with a deterio-rating illness that is often accompanied by eccentric, even dangerous behavior.

Rita Hayworth, one of the first celebrity victims of Alzheimer's disease, had wealth and a loving child to place a cool cloth on her brow, comb her hair, and dab her favorite perfume on her wrists. Many of the elderly are not so fortunate.

> *"John Kingery, 82, who has Alzheimer's disease . . . was abandoned, presumably by his daughter, at a dog-racing track."*

In the year 2020 we will have a population of 15 million over 85 years old, five times the number to-day. It's likely that 12 million Americans will suffer from Alzheimer's disease.

Many "middle-aged children," or members of the "sandwiched generation," who are squeezed by emotional and financial overload from children and aging parents, are sometimes unable to cope with their burdens and society offers them scant relief.

While it is unfathomable for most of us to conceive of abandoning a parent, the American College of Emergency Physicians estimates that up to 70,000 el-derly parents were abandoned in 1991 by relatives. True stories sound like opening scenes from a horror movie.

A woman with silver hair tied back in a bun is left in a hospital driveway, her pocketbook empty of identification or money. Another old woman checks into a motel where a relative pays the fee for the first night, and says he'll be back the next day. He never returns. A granny in a wheelchair is quickly rolled into an emergency room and all the doctors can see are the taillights of a car disappearing down the road. In many states it's illegal to dump a dog, but not a parent.

Senator Bill Bradley, Democrat of New Jersey, introduced a bill [the Family Caregivers Support Act, which failed to pass,] to help certain families pay for adult day care, to ease the pressure on them. We need a national debate to seek other solutions for an increasing problem. The twilight years must not become the taillight years.

The Elderly's Vulnerability to Abuse Is Exaggerated

by Joseph P. Shapiro

About the author: *Joseph P. Shapiro is a journalist and contributor to* U.S. News & World Report, *a weekly newsmagazine.*

Elder abuse did not exist in the public mind until 1979. That year, a group of Boston researchers used a federal grant to test their hypothesis that something akin to child abuse was prevalent among the elderly. Their study argued that the problem did exist, and it set off alarms about mistreated elders, bruised and battered by stressed-out or uncaring children—a view driven home by shock-value congressional hearings run by the late Representative Claude Pepper in 1981.

All this led to the creation of an extensive legal system of reporting, investigation and even sometimes the involuntary institutionalization of a threatened aged person. Today, more than 140,000 cases of suspected abuse are reported yearly. Yet there are now troubling questions: Was it counterproductive to start from the child-abuse model? Did that reinforce unhelpful stereotypes about the elderly, setting back, rather than aiding, efforts to wipe out abuse?

Common Myths About Elder Abuse

Older people—like children—are highly vulnerable to abuse. Perhaps nothing has hurt anti-abuse efforts more than this almost automatic assumption. To write elder-abuse laws, states simply copied existing child-abuse statutes. Today, 43 states require doctors and other social-service professionals to report to state authorities a bruise, a fracture or anything else that suggests abuse. This may make sense with children who cannot speak up for themselves. But it strips the elderly of the confidentiality between doctor and patient—not to mention the ability to make their own decisions—that is afforded all other adults. States have spent millions of dollars to investigate such reports, regardless of the subject's wishes. Sometimes abuse is caught. More often, critics complain, the result is little more than perfunctory paperwork. Far more efficient, says Hofstra University law professor John Regan, would be spending money on solid preventive programs, such as helping family members with in-home care or even psychological counseling.

Unlike children, most elderly Americans are independent (40 percent live on their own), financially secure (they have a median household net worth of $60,300, nearly twice the national average) and capable of taking care of themselves. Cornell University gerontologist Karl Pillemer argues that elder abuse has more in common with spousal abuse than with child abuse.

Elder abuse is rising at alarming rates. Those driving the elder-abuse issue regularly contend there are some 2 million reportable cases of abuse each year, up from 1 million in 1982. The figure comes from a distortion of the research by Pillemer, who concluded that no more than 1.1 million older Americans have been abused—ever. In fact, even Pillemer himself says there are no sure numbers—which suggests that it makes more sense to

> *"Unlike children, most elderly Americans are independent, . . . financially secure . . . and capable of taking care of themselves."*

be cautious rather than alarmist when examining the problem. Although it is logical that abuse will become a more urgent problem in a rapidly graying America, it is not clear that abuse is occurring with greater frequency. More likely, with rising awareness by health-care workers and the public, is that more cases are being reported.

More Misconceptions

Physical abuse is most common. Most elder-abuse laws—following the child-abuse model—focus on physical, psychological and sexual abuse, as well as neglect. But new research suggests the elderly are more probably victims of financial exploitation. Pillemer found financial abuse was the primary problem in 50 percent of cases in Canada, although it is much tougher to detect: A forged check is far harder to spot than a black eye. Contrary to popular perception that the elderly are victimized most often by door-to-door con men and get-rich-quick schemers, the typical abuser is frequently a somewhat distant relative or an acquaintance. Spouses are rarely involved, since most money and property are jointly held.

Stressed care givers are the most likely abusers. The first wave of research suggested that it was usually well-meaning family members who hit older relatives when care giving became difficult, say in the case of a person with dementia. This echoed theories that child abuse resulted from stress on the parents. New studies, however, debunk this. According to Rosalie Wolf of the National Committee for the Prevention of Elder Abuse, abusers of older people tend to be relatives or acquaintances with their own histories of problems such as mental illness and alcoholism. Douglas Kaplan, the public guardian for Yolo County, California, says a growing group of offenders is children and relatives who take money to support drug habits.

The Rights of the Elderly

So far, the national ferment over elder abuse has not adequately addressed the painful questions that plague many families. For instance, when is it appropriate to intervene to protect an older person from the ravages of old age? And how can the rights of the elderly be most strongly preserved even as that intervention is considered? Five years ago, the Associated Press ran a seminal series of articles that showed almost anyone could get guardianship over a troubled aging person. In some states, the aged had virtually no standing in guardianship decisions and sometimes lost the right to vote, drive a car, control finances and make other basic decisions. Since then, recommendations by the American Bar Association prompted almost every state to tighten control of guardianship decisions.

But courts often cannot afford to hire the investigators needed to make the new laws work. Irene Rausch, a private guardian in Pinellas County, Florida, notes that the probate court there has only one investigator to check on 3,000 wards. To Denver Probate Judge Field Benton—whose court is so strapped that he no longer can hire a bailiff—the solution came from the American Association of Retired Persons, which recruited its members as volunteer monitors in that city, as well as in Houston and Atlanta. The need for better monitoring becomes more pressing, notes Michael Casasanto, former president of the National Guardianship Association, as guardians grapple with such newly complicated decisions as when to withdraw life-support machines from the terminally ill.

One highly publicized case that illustrates why elder abuse is rarely as black and white as child abuse was front-page news in Boston for months. The stories focused on Kevin Fitzgerald, a rising-star politician with a reputation as a reformer, and his relationship with an elderly constituent named Mary Guzelian. Fitzgerald, a state legislator, and his aide Patricia McDermott met Guzelian in 1981, when she sought their help to avoid eviction from her apartment. At the apartment, they found general filth—plus 11 plastic bags stuffed with cash.

> "Although . . . abuse will become a more urgent problem in a rapidly graying America, it is not clear that abuse is occurring with greater frequency."

Within 16 days, a court appointed McDermott conservator—with power to make decisions for Guzelian—and a will was drafted. Fitzgerald and McDermott helped her buy a new apartment; Guzelian eschewed it, choosing instead to live on the streets and beg for money. When she was struck and killed by a taxi in 1985, Fitzgerald and McDermott inherited her $500,000 estate.

State and federal investigators are examining whether there was any impropriety in the case. Fitzgerald, saying he did nothing wrong, nonetheless recently resigned his job as state House majority whip, hours after a legislative ethics committee recommended stripping him of the post for violating a rule against accepting gifts from a constituent. But the case is not clear-cut. Just as the law recognized Guzelian's choice to live in alleys, it gave her the right to will her money to anyone she was capable of choosing, as long as there was no "undue influence" on her decision making.

The Guzelian case, complicated by questions of mental competency, self-determination and money, presents all the issues that the debate over elder abuse ought to have addressed in the 1980s. The plaint of Donna Reulbach of the Massachusetts Executive Office of Elder Affairs about another case—one in which an 88-year-old woman accidentally set fire to her trash-cluttered apartment and died—also applies to the Guzelian affair. "We can't force people to take services," says Reulbach. That, of course, is the precise reason why protecting older Americans is different, and often far more difficult, than protecting children.

Rates of Family Homicide Are Highest Among African Americans

by Peggy S. Plass

About the author: *Peggy S. Plass is a lecturer at the University of Virginia's Department of Sociology.*

The high incidence of violence between family members has become increasingly well documented in the last decade so that it is now generally recognized that a large number of individuals in the United States will experience some sort of violence at the hands of family members at some time in their lives. At the most extreme end of the continuum of this violence, the Federal Bureau of Investigation (FBI) reported that 14% of the 20,045 homicide victims in the United States in 1990 were murdered by members of their own families. As is the case with all types of homicide, African Americans are victimized by lethal violence at the hands of family members at rates that are many times higher than those for other racial groups in the United States. This viewpoint will present a descriptive analysis of this special subset of family murders, namely, those that occurred among African Americans.

Inattention to Violence Within the African American Community

There are a number of reasons for an examination of family homicides occurring specifically among African Americans. First, although the inordinately high rate of homicide among African Americans has been observed and documented for many decades, there has been what criminologist Darnell Hawkins calls "a lack of systematic detailed analysis of the phenomena, including attention to intra-group distribution and patterning of the crime among blacks." A descriptive analysis of patterns of homicide rates for African Americans disaggregated on the basis of victim/offender relationship provides much-needed attention to just such "intra-group distribution and patterning of the crime.". . .

Furthermore, the choice of family as the specific relationship category in

Excerpted from "African American Family Homicide" by Peggy S. Plass, *Journal of Black Studies* 23 (no. 4, June 1993):515-35; © 1993 by Sage Publications, Inc. Reprinted by permission of Sage Publications, Inc.

which to examine patterns of African American homicide is also quite important, in that it has been noted that research regarding the incidence of family violence among African Americans has also been inadequate. For example, J. Asbury notes with regard to the treatment of women of color in the mainstream spouse abuse literature that it

> typically addresses the issue of (race) in one of three ways: by failing to mention the race of the women included . . . by acknowledging that only European-American women are included . . . or by including some women of other ethnic groups but not in proportions comparable to their numbers in the national population.

Given this inadequate attention to the issue of patterns of violence among African Americans, coupled with the overall inordinately high levels of homicide among this group in the United States, examination of patterns of family homicide victimization among African Americans is an important undertaking and a step toward better understanding the etiology of such events. . . .

The data presented here were taken from the Comparative Homicide File (CHF), which is itself derived from the Supplemental Homicide Reports (SHR) collected annually by the FBI. The SHR contains detailed information on both victims and perpetrators in each homicide event that occurs in America in a given year. . . .

A Disparity in Patterns

African American men have very slightly higher victimization rates at the hands of partners than do African American women. This pattern is sharply different from that found by other researchers for partner homicide in the White population, where women are about twice as likely to be victims of partner homicide as are men. Why is it that among African Americans victimization rates for the two genders are nearly equal, with males actually having a slightly higher rate? Although no certain conclusions can be drawn from these descriptive data, it is possible to hypothesize as to what the meaning of this significant divergence in the patterns of partner homicide for Whites and African Americans might be.

> *"African Americans are victimized by lethal violence at the hands of family members at rates . . . many times higher than those for other racial groups."*

A logical place to start in thinking about explanations for the quite disparate patterns for the involvement of African Americans and Whites in family homicide is with an examination of why women kill their husbands. There is much evidence that would seem to suggest that women kill their husbands after they have been abused by them, often for a period of many years. This explanation seems to hold equal weight for women of both races. Although no studies focusing exclusively on African American women who killed their husbands could be located, women

of color are included in many studies. The murder of a battering husband becomes, for many women, the only means of escape from an abusive relationship, especially in light of the fact that those men who are the most severe (and
dangerous) batterers are also those who are least likely to "allow" their wives to
leave or divorce them. Thus the
women who kill their husbands may
be seen as a subset of all battered
wives—that is, those who have either
found no other means of escape from
these relationships and/or those who
feel sufficiently threatened by the violence of their partners that they find
an equally (or more) violent response

*"African American women,
on the average, have
lower income . . . [which]
may prove a definite
deterrent to . . . leav[ing]
a violent relationship."*

is their only alternative. A key question, then, may be why might it be more difficult for African American women to leave battering relationships than it is for
White women? Or, alternatively, why might African American women be more
likely to "choose" homicide as a response to battering than are White women?

It is quite possible that economics play an important role in keeping women
of either race from leaving a dangerous marriage. The family violence literature
has often cited economic dependency as a tie that tends to hold battered women
in violent marriages. In addition, families who experience economic stress are
at higher risk for the experience of violence as well. African American women,
on the average, have lower income than do White men or women or African
American men. The difficulty of making it without the support of two incomes
may prove a definite deterrent to many African American women in attempts to
leave a violent relationship before it comes to the stage of lethal interaction. . . .

African American Women Have Fewer Options

This dynamic is complicated for African American women by what some family
sociologists have referred to as a marriage pool disparity. The age differential between men and women (with the number of women exceeding that of men) begins
at an earlier age level for African Americans than it does for Whites. The result is
a marked shortage of potential marriage partners for African American women,
beginning in the early 20s, the period during which Americans are most likely to
marry. This marriage pool disparity for African American women is further complicated by the fact that other social factors remove even more of the available
African American men from the ranks of potential marital partners. R. Staples, for
example, suggests that higher percentages of African American than White men
are homosexual, imprisoned, or enlisted in the armed forces. African American
men, particularly the most successful and well-educated African American men,
are also more often involved in interracial marriages than are African American
women. The end result of this is that African American women have much more
limited options in the search for a marital partner than do White women. . . .

It is quite possible, then, that given the relative shortage of African American men, African American women may feel more pressure to "hold onto" a mate once they have found one. Even a battering relationship may seem attractive in light of the limited options for permanent relationships. The sex ratio, then, may itself be seen as a factor that would make African American women less likely to be able or willing to leave battering relationships. Thus White women may be more likely to leave a battering relationship before the violence escalates to the lethal stage than are African American women.

It is also important to consider reasons why the violence occurring in African American marriages more often turns lethal for African American men than for African American women. One relevant question here is why homicide may be more likely to be the only escape hatch for African American women than it is for White women. There is evidence that community support systems and other homicide safeguards may be less available to African American women than they are to White women. Use of the police to mediate domestic disputes is less common among African Americans. Asbury suggests that African American women are reluctant to call in the police, to have their husbands arrested and jailed, because of (correctly) perceived racial injustice in the criminal justice system. The unwillingness of African American women to make use of this perceived White-dominated system of social control may increase the likelihood of the occurrence of homicide.

African American women are also less likely to make use of grassroots community organizations such as shelters for battered women than are White women. Asbury writes that African American women tend to see the shelter movement as something run by and for White women. A. Browne and K. Williams found that the presence of a battered women's shelter in a community, although having no effect on the rates at which women were victims of partner homicide, did have a negative relationship on the rate at which men are killed by their wives. The reluctance or inability of African American women to use this resource, then, may be a contributing factor in the rate at which they kill their husbands.

> *"African American women are reluctant to call in the police . . . because of (correctly) perceived racial injustice in the criminal justice system."*

The greater degree of reluctance or inability of African American women than White women to dissolve a battering marriage is not a fully sufficient explanation for the divergent patterns of partner homicide for the two races, especially given the fact that in general, divorce is a more common occurrence in African American families than in White ones. Although it may be that this appearance of greater willingness and ability to divorce is common among African American couples in general, although those in violent relationships are indeed less likely to dissolve relationships for all the reasons cited above, it is also possible, even probable, that there are other factors and alternative explanations. One of these may be found in the consideration of the perceived dangerousness of African American men. J. Boudouris attributed his finding of higher rates of homicide offense among African American wives to the greater risk of assault faced by African American women at the hands of African American men. Likewise, Browne found the level of violence perpetrated by husbands, and the partners' perception of how

> *"Racism ... can in itself be seen as a factor in increasing the rate of homicide."*

dangerous these men were, was a key factor in differentiating between women who killed their battering husbands and those who successfully left these relationships without any lethal interaction. It is possible that African American men are so much more violent and so much more often violent in their marriages than are White men that African American women are more likely to perceive the violence that occurs as life threatening and, therefore, are more willing or likely to respond with killing their husbands in self-defense. . . .

"Child-Abusing" Discipline

African American sons are much more likely to be killed by their parents than are daughters, with the victimization rate for males murdered by a parent being almost 2 times that for females. Put another way, 64% of all African American children killed by a parent are sons, with 36% of the victims being daughters.

The fact that sons are so much more likely to be killed than are daughters may be a reflection of the greater degree of violence perpetrated by males. They may well be seen as more of a threat, especially as they reach adolescence or beyond and may actually be more of a threat to their parents. Lacking other resources for controlling their children, parents may be more likely to use violence—even ultimately lethal violence—to control the behavior of their more aggressive sons.

Controlling children is quite important from the perspective of many African American families. Given the many dangers that face African American children, especially males, the ability to discipline children may well be seen as a matter of life or death itself. Given the high rates of drug abuse, imprisonment, gang membership, assault, homicides, and other dangerous life experiences that threaten children (especially males), African American parents may feel compelled to use sometimes extreme measures in attempts to keep their children out of trouble. This desperation to discipline or control children may sometimes result in lethal events. R. Lassiter suggests that history itself plays a role in contributing to what she calls "child-abusing discipline" in African American families. The difficulties of dealing with life under slavery and later in a racist White society have made for a system of harsh child-rearing practices among African Americans. Parents feel that they must be tough with their children at home if these children are to be enabled to survive the harsh White world. Thus the racism of the larger society and the historical and present-day discrimination experienced by African Americans in the United States can in itself be seen as a factor in increasing the rate of homicide perpetrated against African American children (especially males) by their parents.

Turning to the gender of perpetrators, African American children are somewhat more likely to be killed by a father than a mother. Fifty-two percent of African American women and 60% of African American men killed by a parent were murdered by a father. . . . The fact that such a great percentage of African American children grow up in single-parent homes makes the greater risk for homicide at the hands of fathers surprising. It is likely that the higher level of violence and aggressiveness found among African American men in other contexts may also be responsible for the trends of child homicide victimization found here. . . .

The Need for Better Data

Disaggregation of African American homicide rates, especially on the basis of important criterion variables such as victim/offender relationship, is an important step in understanding the nature of lethal interactions in this community. . . .

Having access to data on all homicide events from the United States (as opposed to a regional or single city sample), which the CHF allows, provides for a high level of confidence that the patterns revealed here are characteristic of the ways in which African Americans experience homicide at the hands of family members in the United States. Finally, disaggregation of the homicide rate can lead to asking better and more fruitful questions about African American homicide victimization. Knowing more about how homicides occur within this group (as opposed to simple comparing of overall African American victimization with that of the general population) can lead to better efforts at explanation, to better understanding, and ultimately to better ability to prevent such tragedy.

Gays Are Often Victims of Domestic Violence

by Patrick Letellier

About the author: *Patrick Letellier counsels victims of domestic violence, including gay men, and serves on the advisory committee to the Gay Men's Domestic Violence Project at The Community United Against Violence in San Francisco. He is the coauthor of the book* Men Who Beat the Men Who Love Them.

Domestic violence has long been understood as the abuse of women by their male partners. When examining heterosexual relationships, this view is indeed accurate: 95% of heterosexual spouse abuse victims are women. So rampant is this abuse of women by their male partners that battering is now the leading cause of injury to women in the United States. The epidemic of domestic violence in the United States is not, however, exclusively a heterosexual phenomenon. Lesbians and gay men are also being assaulted and injured by their intimate partners at startlingly high rates and many are turning to the medical system for help.

Experts estimate that between 25–30% of all gay men and lesbians in intimate relationships are victims of domestic abuse. Recent research also indicates that lesbian and gay male domestic violence is just as serious and/or lethal as heterosexual battering. A 1993 homicide study in San Francisco revealed that both of the identified lesbians and four of the six identified gay men murdered in 1991–92 were killed by their intimate partners. The purpose of this viewpoint is to assist medical professionals and paraprofessionals in accurately identifying and effectively treating battered gay men they encounter. It is necessary to state from the outset that there is virtually no empirical research on gay male battering. Thus many of the concepts discussed in this viewpoint are based on the author's clinical work with this population as well as personal experience as a victim of gay domestic violence.

Challenging Assumptions

Not all gay relationships are violent. One widespread misconception about gay men is that they are emotionally unstable and, as a result, are unable to

Excerpted from "Identifying and Treating Battered Gay Men" by Patrick Letellier, *San Francisco Medicine*, April 1994. Reprinted by permission of the author and the San Francisco Medical Society.

form lasting and meaningful intimate relationships or their relationships will be plagued by violence and/or sexual promiscuity. This homophobic assumption is easily refuted by current research demonstrating that gay men are as psychologically healthy as their heterosexual counterparts, that they couple at approximately the same rate and that they experience the same level of relationship satisfaction. Experts believe that domestic violence in gay male relationships occurs at the same rate as it occurs in heterosexual relationships.

> *"Lesbian and gay male domestic violence is just as serious and/or lethal as heterosexual battering."*

Gay domestic violence is not sexual behavior. A second misconception about gay domestic violence is that the battering is not violence at all, but rather part of sadomasochistic sexual behavior that is actually wanted and enjoyed by the victim. This misconception serves to deny the seriousness of gay domestic violence and blame the victim for its occurrence by inappropriately sexualizing the violence. It is imperative that physicians remember that battering is a violent and criminal act, not a "relationship problem" or sexual behavior that "went too far." Battering is coercion, abuse and violence that is non-*consensual*.

It is also important to recognize that many battered gay men are sexually assaulted by their partners and, as a result, are at high risk for HIV infection. Gay men with injuries caused by sexual assaults should be handled under the same guidelines and with the same sensitivity as other rape victims. Additionally, medical personnel should not assume that all gay men understand what behaviors constitute safe sex. Battered gay men are likely to be isolated from the community and thus removed from accurate information about HIV. This may be particularly true of low-income gay men or gay men of color, given that most safe-sex information targets white, middle-class gay men.

Gay domestic violence is not "mutual combat." It is often assumed in gay domestic violence that because both partners are the same gender and may be approximately the same size and weight, each is equally likely to be violent. This assumption is unfounded. In same-sex domestic violence there is almost always one primary aggressor. Domestic violence is not a "fair fight" between equals, it is a systematic pattern of abuse and terror used by one individual in an intimate relationship to gain control over his/her partner. The myth of mutual combat also assumes that the gay domestic violence is *only* physical, whereas battering almost always includes other forms of violence such as psychological abuse, economic control and the destruction of property.

Relevant Issues Concerning Gay Domestic Violence

Isolation. Given the shame and stigma of victimization, battered gay men like other victims of domestic abuse are most often extremely isolated. Their status as homosexuals in an oppressively homophobic society, however, creates additional barriers that may further deter them from seeking help. Gay men, for example, are not likely to turn to their biological families for support. The shame of being battered may be compounded by their family's negative attitudes about homosexuality. Calling the police, which is increasingly seen as an option for (white, middle-class) heterosexual women, remains unthinkable for most gay men given the widespread homophobia of many police departments. Indeed, according to recent studies of anti-gay violence, the median number of lesbians and gay men who were victimized *by the police* was 20%.

Furthermore, there are no shelters for gay men in the United States, and most traditional domestic violence services locally and nationally offer no services for battered gay men. Finally, and perhaps most significantly, since the onset of the AIDS epidemic, many gay men have lost large numbers of friends. Thus the circle of intimate people to whom a battered gay man can turn for help may be very small or simply nonexistent. It is possible that the only person a battered gay man talks to about the abuse by his partner is the medical professional who treats his injuries.

> *"Gay domestic violence is not 'mutual combat.'"*

HIV infection. As most medical personnel are aware, AIDS is an extremely difficult disease to manage. It is unpredictable, disabling, often disfiguring and terminal. Nonetheless, HIV infection and/or stresses of caregiving for an intimate partner with AIDS do not cause gay domestic violence. Battering is a choice and other non-abusive behavioral choices are always available.

For many gay men, HIV complicates decisions about leaving an abusive partner. A battered gay man with HIV or AIDS may be reluctant to leave a partner who is periodically violent, because that partner may also be his primary caregiver. Conversely, a gay man being battered by a partner with AIDS may have great difficulty terminating the relationship due to feelings of responsibility for the abusive partner's well-being. It is essential for service providers to focus first on the safety of the battered partner and not to underestimate the potential for a person with AIDS to be violent and abusive. Believe what your patients tell you about the seriousness of the abuse they experience. If anything, they are likely to downplay the severity of their situation rather than exaggerate it.

Substance abuse. Research indicates that one in three gay men are substance abusers; a rate much higher than that of heterosexual men. Medical professionals working with battered gay men are likely therefore to encounter the problem of alcoholism or other drug abuse. It is important to understand and to convey to patients that substance abuse does not cause domestic violence though it is often used as an excuse or an explanation for battering. Batterers who abuse substances and eventually get clean and sober are just that: clean and sober batterers. Violence and addiction are two separate problems. Battered gay men with substance abuse problems should be referred to both drug treatment programs and to domestic violence support services.

Intervention

Identifying the abuse. The role of the medical profession in intervening in the escalating cycle of domestic violence is absolutely crucial. According to the American Medical Association, "The most important contribution physicians can make to ending abuse and protecting its victims is to identify and acknowledge the abuse."

There are certain indicators of abuse developed in reference to battered heterosexual women that are equally applicable to battered gay men. Among these indicators are a central pattern of injuries (to the face, head, chest and abdomen), defensive posture injuries, injuries that seem inconsistent with the explanation provided, a delay between the occurrence of the injury and treatment seeking, and frequent visits to medical facilities and/or vague complaints. . . .

It is not the responsibility of medical personnel to turn each patient's life around, but they are responsible for addressing the etiology of their patient's injuries and/or illnesses: in this case domestic violence. Like other victims of domestic violence, battered gay men are often extremely strong people who are actively seeking help to resolve the violence they live with. They have managed to survive in chronically dangerous conditions and, given the proper resources, have the capacity to escape their violent partners and live a full life without abuse. Your identifying the violence in their lives and asserting that it is unacceptable is the first step.

The Law and Battered Gay Men

A new California law [Assembly Bill 1652, Chapter No. 992] requires health practitioners to report to local law enforcement cases of domestic violence where some injury has occurred. This is a potentially dangerous law for battered gay men as it entails identifying oneself as gay to a legal system that has a long and ugly history of discriminating against lesbians and gay men. Even though California law now prohibits discrimination against lesbians and gays in housing and employment, such discrimination is rampant. Interacting with the criminal justice system may result in unwanted publicity around a man's homosexuality and/or HIV status that may mean the loss of his job, terminated health insurance, custody battles over his children, dishonorable discharge from the military, an increased risk for anti-gay violence and so forth.

> *"Like other victims of domestic violence, battered gay men are often extremely strong people . . . actively seeking help to resolve the violence."*

I fear this new law will deter many gay men from seeking medical attention and from disclosing information about domestic violence, particularly those gay men who are already considered "marginal" by mainstream society: low-income gay men, non-English-speaking or immigrant gay men and gay men of color. It is, however, the law, and medical personnel who do not comply with the law can be charged with misdemeanor violations.

Chapter 4

How Can Family Violence Be Reduced?

CURRENT CONTROVERSIES

Chapter Preface

"I come before you today as a 16-year veteran in the field of law enforcement. . . . I've been very fortunate to have experienced a wide variety of police duties, but by the grace of God and a strong mother, I'm speaking to you today in a police uniform and not the uniform of a convict. I was taught to be a criminal by a criminal. Let me explain."

As he stood before members of the House of Representatives Subcommittee on Health and the Environment, on April 19, 1993, Sergeant Mark A. Wynn recounted the story of his childhood spent with an alcoholic stepfather who had beaten his mother and terrorized him, his brother, and his sisters. He described the violence he had experienced as a child as being no different from that which he had encountered as a law officer contending with terrorists and hate groups such as the Ku Klux Klan. "The crime of family violence gives birth to the crime of the future," he told the panel emphatically. "The cycle of violence must be broken."

As social scientists and researchers pursue solutions to society's problems, they frequently find themselves face to face with the issue of violence. And in tracing violence to its roots they invariably turn their gaze to their own backyard or, to be precise, the home. "Being abused as a child is significantly related to higher rates of violent crimes as an adult," write authors Sally A. Lloyd and Beth C. Emery. "Children reared amid violence risk more problems in school and an increased likelihood of drug and alcohol abuse," journalists Michele Ingrassia and Melinda Beck report in a *Newsweek* feature story, adding that "of course" these children also risk repeating the abuse they suffered with their own offspring when they become parents.

Peeling back the layers of childhood to delve more deeply into the causes behind abuse, theorists examine nearly every factor conceivable. Biochemists searching for a biological or genetic link to violence suggest the answer lies in understanding the chemistry of the brain. Religious scholars, often joined by secular students of ethics, believe a rupture in the moral fabric of society is what ushers in abuse, with some pointing, further, to consumerism as the seed of the spiritual vacuum that fosters violence in the home.

Although much debate is waged over how it begins and how to stop it, family violence is, most people agree, a self-perpetuating legacy, handed down from one generation to the next. As one observer puts it, "The fist that breaks and smashes travels on through time, destroying more lives and bodies as it goes."

Police officer Wynn is an example of someone who successfully avoided a life of violence and crime against odds that were stacked against him. Another veteran of a childhood marked by family violence fared less well. Yet even as he sat in a prison cell awaiting sentencing for armed robbery, David A. Clark wrote of triumph—of being able to spare his now grown children from the "dark terror" of abuse that so devastatingly marred his own life. He explains why this "victory," he believes, will outlive all his failures: "The cycle of violence is broken." The following chapter examines possible solutions for preventing and ending family violence and the arguments exploring their viability.

The Catholic Church Should Combat Family Violence

by the National Conference of Catholic Bishops' Committee on Women in Society and in the Church and Committee on Marriage and Family Life

About the authors: *At the October 1992 National Conference of Catholic Bishops, the Committee on Women in Society and in the Church and the Committee on Marriage and Family Life jointly issued this statement*

As pastors of the Catholic Church in the United States, we join bishops in other countries, notably Canada and New Zealand, in stating as clearly and strongly as we can that violence against women, in the home or outside the home, is *never* justified. Violence in any form—physical, sexual, psychological or verbal—is sinful; many times it is a crime as well.

Abuse is a topic that no one likes to think about. But because it exists in our parishes, dioceses and neighborhoods, we present this statement as an initial step in what we hope will become a continuing effort in the church in the United States to combat domestic violence against women. This statement is our response to the repeated requests of many women and men around the United States to address the issue.

We write out of our desire to offer the church's resources to both the women who are battered and the men who abuse. Both groups need Jesus' strength and healing. We also write out of an awareness that times of economic distress such as the present, when wage earners lose their jobs or are threatened with their loss, often are marked by an increase in domestic violence.

Though we focus here on violence against women, we are not implying that violence against men or against youth or violence against the elderly or the unborn is any less vicious. In fact, violence against any person is contrary to Jesus' Gospel message to "love one another as I have loved you." When violence toward women is tolerated, it helps to set the stage for violent acts against other groups as well.

Excerpted from a joint statement of the U.S. National Conference of Catholic Bishops' Committee on Women in Society and in the Church and the Committee on Marriage and Family Life, as it appeared in *Origins*, vol. 22, no. 21 (November 5, 1992), under the title "When I Call for Help: Domestic Violence Against Women." Reprinted with permission.

Violence against women in the home has particularly serious repercussions. When the woman is a mother and the violence takes place in front of her children, the stage is set for a cycle of violence that may be continued from generation to generation.

A Violation of Christian Values

Domestic violence counselors teach that violence is learned behavior. In many cases men who become abusive and the women who are abused grew up in a home where violence occurred. In such a situation a child can grow up believing that violence is acceptable behavior; boys learn that this is a way to be powerful. Abuse counselors say that a child raised in a home with physical abuse is 1,000 times more likely to use violence in his own family. At the same time, 25 percent of men who grow up in an abusive home choose not to use violence.

We agree with the bishops of Quebec, Canada, in calling on the Christian community to "join forces with and complement the work of those associations and groups which are already involved in preventing and fighting this form of violence."

We also agree with the Canadian church leaders who stated that when men abuse women, they

> reflect a lack of understanding in our society about how men and women ought to relate to each other. They violate the basic Christian values of justice, equality, respect, dignity and peace; they go against the call to practical kindness, gentleness, faithfulness, mutual support and to love one another as ourselves.

. . . In the words of Barbara Ann Stolz, "Abuse, assault or murder are not less serious because they occur within the family. . . . Violence, whether committed against family members or strangers, is antithetical to the Judeo-Christian messages of love and respect for the human person."

As the U.S. bishops' ad hoc Committee for a Pastoral Response to Women's Concerns wrote, "a woman's dignity is destroyed in a particularly vicious and heinous way when she is treated violently.". . .

The Church Condemns Family Violence

A theme throughout Scripture, beginning with Genesis, is that women and men are created in God's image. As Pope John Paul II has said, "Both man and woman are human beings to an equal degree." In the New Testament, Jesus consistently reached out to those on the fringes of society, those without power or authority, those with no one to speak on their behalf. He taught that all women and men are individuals worthy of respect and dignity.

> *"Both the women who are battered and the men who abuse . . . need Jesus' strength and healing."*

Jesus unfailingly respected the human dignity of women. Pope John Paul II reminds us that "Christ's way of acting, the Gospel of his words and deeds, is a consistent protest against whatever offends the dignity of women." Jesus went out of his way to help the most vulnerable women. Think of the woman with the hemorrhage (Mark 5:25–34) or the woman caught in adultery (John 8:1–11). By his actions toward women in need, Jesus set an example for us today. Like him, we are called to find ways to help those most vulnerable women in our midst. We also need to find ways to help the men who want to break out of the pattern of abuse.

As a church, one of the most worrying aspects of the abuse practiced against women is the use of biblical texts, taken out of context, to support abusive behavior. Counselors report that both abused women and their batterers use Scripture passages to justify their behavior.

Abused women say, "I can't leave this relationship. The Bible says it would be wrong." Abusive men say, "The Bible says my wife should be submissive to me." They take the biblical text and distort it to support their right to batter.

> *"Even where the Bible uses traditional language to support the social order common in the day, [it] never ... condones the use of abuse."*

As bishops, we condemn the use of the Bible to condone abusive behavior. A correct reading of the Scriptures leads people to a relationship based on mutuality and love. Again, Pope John Paul II describes it accurately: "In the 'unity of the two,' man and woman are called from the beginning not only to exist 'side by side' or 'together,' but they are also called to exist mutually one for the other."

Even where the Bible uses traditional language to support the social order common in the day, the image presented is never one that condones the use of abuse to control another person. In Ephesians 5:21–33, for instance, which discusses relationships within the family, the general principle laid down is one of mutual submission between husband and wife. The passage holds out the image to husbands that they are to love their wives as they love their own body, as Christ loves the church. Can you imagine Jesus battering his church?

How to Help

Presented here are some practical suggestions to implement in your parish and diocese. . . .

For pastors and pastoral staff:

- Make your parish a safe place where abused women and men who batter can come for help.
- Learn as much as you can about domestic violence. Be alert for the signs of abuse among parish women.
- Join in the national observance of October as Domestic Violence Awareness Month. Dedicate at least one weekend during October to educate parish-

ioners about abuse and its likely presence in your parish.

- Make sure that parish homilies address domestic violence. If abused women do not hear anything about abuse, they think no one cares. Describe what abuse is so that women begin to recognize and name what is happening to them.
- If you suspect abuse, ask direct questions: Ask the woman if she is being hit or hurt at home. Evaluate her response carefully. Some women do not realize they are being abused or they lie to protect their spouse.
- In talking to an abused person, be careful of your language. Don't say anything that will bolster her belief that it is her fault and she must change her behavior. The victim is not to blame. The abuser must be accountable for his behavior.
- In marriage preparation education sessions, check couples' patterns of handling disagreements and their families' problem-solving patterns. Suggest postponing marriage if you identify signs of abuse or potential abuse.
- In baptismal preparation programs be alert that the arrival of a child and its attendant stress may trigger violent behavior.
- Keep an updated list of resources for abused women in your area.
- Have an action plan in place to follow if an abused woman calls on you for help. Build a relationship with police and domestic-violence agencies. Find a safe place for abused women.

Ultimately, abused women must make their own decisions about staying or leaving. It is important to be honest with women about the risks involved. Remember: Women are at a most dangerous point when they attempt to leave their abusers. Research provided by the National Coalition Against Domestic Violence indicates that "women who leave their batterers are at a 75 percent greater risk of being killed by the batterer than those who stay."

For educators and catechists:

- Make sure all teachers and catechists receive training in how to recognize abuse.
- Insist that teaching and texts be free of sexual stereotyping. Battering thrives on sexism.
- Try to include shelters for abused women and children on lists of service for confirmation classes and other service groups.
- Include information about domestic violence in human sexuality and family life classes.
- Sponsor parish workshops on domestic violence.

For liturgy committees:

- In parish reconciliation services, identify violence against women as a sin.
- Include intercessions for victims of abuse, for the men who abuse women and for those who help both victims and abusers.
- Strive to use inclusive language in liturgical celebrations as authorized.

For commissions on women and other women's groups:

- Include a list of names and phone numbers of parish contacts in parish bulletins and directories for abused women to call.
- Work to see that women as well as men are represented in parish leadership positions, e.g., on parish finance and pastoral councils.
- Offer free meeting space to support groups for abused women and for men who abuse.
- Spearhead education in your parish/diocese on crimes of violence against women.
- Look for resource people in your parish who can offer their expertise.

A Closing Prayer

This viewpoint has addressed the problem of violence against women in their homes. Such violence has repercussions on all residing there, even to the extent of setting up a situation for repeating violence in successive generations. Accordingly, we encourage all parents and all educators and catechists to teach children from the earliest ages that abuse is not appropriate behavior. As pastors of the church, we are dedicated to encouraging all that nurtures and strengthens family life.

One of the sources of healing we have in our lives as Christians is prayer. The psalms in particular capture the depth and range of human anguish and hope and reassure us of God's help. Psalm 31 may be an especially apt prayer for women who are dealing with abusive situations. With all of you we pray:

Have pity on me, O Lord,
For I am in distress;
With sorrow my eye is consumed;
My soul also and my body—
I am like a dish that is broken...
But my trust is in you, O Lord;
I say, You are my God.

Harsher Penalties Can Reduce Family Violence

by Casey G. Gwinn

About the author: *Casey G. Gwinn supervises the San Diego Office of City Attorney's Child Abuse and Domestic Violence Unit and has served as special deputy district attorney for felony domestic violence cases.*

For more than twenty years in this country, many have grappled with the complex issue of family violence. In the 1970s, the shelter movement developed to provide safe shelter for battered women and their children. Then, in the early 1980s, the shelter movement exercised its influence in the courts and state legislatures across the country. Class action lawsuits on behalf of battered women and legislation mandating arrest and aggressive law enforcement responses became commonplace. By the mid-1980s prosecutors and judges began to address their role in the appropriate response of the criminal justice system to family violence. Most recently, medical professionals, therapists, pastors, and the military community have joined coordinated strategies in many jurisdictions.

Clear consensus has developed in many jurisdictions that not only points the way toward effective intervention but brings with it reliable statistics to back the claim of effectiveness. The consensus in the criminal justice system context focuses around this clarion call: Aggressive arrest and prosecution policies, coupled with strong advocacy programs, in the context of a coordinated community response, can lead to effective intervention. Effective intervention is being defined as stopping the violence, making victims safer, and holding abusers accountable. Jurisdictions such as San Diego, California; Duluth, Minnesota; Quincy, Massachusetts; Knoxville, Tennessee; Newport News, Virginia; Seattle, Washington; and others have seen dramatic drops in recidivism and in domestic violence homicide rates through implementation of these strategies.

Many, however, believe that a gaping hole still exists in the intervention effort across the country. It is the role of the incarceration and jail system in stopping the violence, making victims safer, and holding abusers accountable. If domestic

Excerpted from "Can We Stop Domestic Violence?" by Casey G. Gwinn, *American Jails*, March/April 1995. Reprinted with permission.

violence is to be treated as a serious crime, then jail staff must play a role.

The stark reality of the need for the jail officer to do more faces off squarely with the traditional reluctance of jail staff to be in the business of habilitation/rehabilitation. But jail officers clearly must play a role in the effort to stop domestic violence in this country. It is time to propose the expansion of the role of the jail officer in domestic violence cases. It is time to call for proactive steps from the detention community to assist the domestic violence movement in our effort to stop domestic violence. . . .

More Serious than a Misdemeanor

The jail system plays a crucial role in society's decision to treat domestic violence as a serious crime. Historically, however, this message does not emanate from the jails of this country. If a domestic violence offender is booked and released simply because of the misdemeanor nature of the offense, the crime is minimized. We can say it is a "serious crime" until we are blue in the face but if it is not treated as a serious crime, the batterer will not receive that message. We must not allow the phrase "just a misdemeanor" or "only a misdemeanor" to creep into our vocabulary when we talk about domestic violence.

Nearly 90 percent of all domestic violence offenses nationally are handled as misdemeanors, yet the potential lethality and often the raw nature of the violence far surpass many felony offenses. Indeed, in ten years as a prosecutor handling both felonies and misdemeanors, I have never handled a felony domestic violence case that was as "serious" as many of the misdemeanor cases that I handle on a regular basis.

Policies which automatically allow domestic violence offenders to receive book-and-release simply because of the nature of the offense must end. Policies which make domestic violence offenders eligible for a "Sheriff's Own Recognizance Release" or some such similar policy should be reviewed. Across the country in recent years, many jurisdictions that I have trained in have identified policies in the jail system that return domestic violence offenders to the home with rarely even a judicial review. The result is the minimization of the offense and the increased likelihood of yet another violent episode.

> *"If [domestic violence] is not treated as a serious crime, the batterer will not receive that message."*

A study by researcher Larry Sherman proves this point. Sherman's study in Milwaukee also highlights the fallacies swirling around these issues. Sherman studied the effectiveness of arrest in domestic violence cases in Milwaukee between 1988 and 1992. He concluded that arrest was counterproductive because of the high level of recidivism following release from custody. His research, however, must be more carefully examined. It actually proves a quite different point.

In Sherman's study, the "long arrest" lasted only 12 hours, the "short arrest" lasted approximately 6 hours, and the control group was simply warned by officers at the scene not to commit another offense. Only 1 percent of the subjects in the study were prosecuted and convicted in court. It should come as no surprise that an individual held for only 12 hours, not provided with treatment, and not prosecuted would feel empowered to continue the violence upon release from "custody." His study actually proves the point made here. If the detention system minimizes the offense and is derelict, along with the rest of the system, in treating domestic violence as a serious crime, then offenders will continue *and* escalate their behavior upon release from jail.

The challenge for the detention facilities therefore becomes identifying ways in which domestic violence offenses are minimized or virtually "decriminalized." Certainly, informal or nonjudicial own recognizance release programs carry this message. Systems with extremely low bail amounts for domestic violence offenses often cause a similar result. But what of work furlough programs? Most jurisdictions do not allow work furlough for "violent" offenders. Yet domestic violence offenders routinely qualify for work furlough programs across the country. What message does this send to offenders? Every policy in a detention facility or jail that relates to domestic violence cases must be assessed in light of the question: "Is domestic violence treated as a serious crime by this facility?"

> *"If the detention system minimizes the offense . . . offenders will continue **and** escalate their behavior upon release from jail."*

Making Victims Safer

Jail officers must also acknowledge their role in providing for the victim's safety in a domestic violence case. Nearly 4,000 women are killed in this country every year in domestic violence homicides. Nearly 75 percent of these women are killed after separation in the relationship. By definition, incarceration creates separation in the relationship. It challenges the power of the batterer over the victim. Not surprisingly then, release from custody may well be the most dangerous time for victims of domestic violence. Unfortunately, many victims assume that when their attacker is arrested he will stay in jail. Sadly, we know this is not so. . . .

The jail system, therefore, must ask basic questions. What policies are in place for notifying a victim prior to the release of her assailant? What policies are in place which trigger notification if she requests it? What relationship exists between shelters and jails to allow safety planning and crisis intervention to occur during the critical period of incarceration? The answer to these questions, unfortunately, is usually "None."

These issues can often be addressed irrespective of fiscal constraints. Shelters, advocates, and volunteers exist in every jurisdiction who can assist in the creation and implementation of appropriate policies. Even putting aside the moral imperative for such policies, the potential liability for failure to notify and failure to protect in these circumstances looms on the horizon. Aggressive work is now being done across the country to assist victims in planning for their own safety upon the release from custody of their assailants. Jail systems need to join in this effort.

What Works?

There is a pressing need nationally for the jail and detention system in this country to begin working with researchers and domestic violence movement professionals to determine what works with domestic violence offenders. Does early release combined with monitoring reduce recidivism while saving money? Is work furlough as effective a deterrent as full-time incarceration? Does the length of a sentence correlate to long-term reductions in recidivism?

These questions have answers. First, however, we must ask the questions and then we must work to answer them. Pilot projects and limited duration studies even with rudimentary approaches can be extremely helpful in this process. In jurisdictions in which I consult across the country, I am challenging system professionals to start answering their own questions about effectiveness. For example, if a jurisdiction were simply to take a large sample of domestic violence offenders from work furlough and early release categories and study re-arrest rates over time it would have a basis for discussion. While researchers abhor such simplicity without control groups and the like, any data will elevate the discussion.

The potential for partnerships between local domestic violence community professionals and the jail system is significant. A jurisdiction that studied the significance of the length of a sentence in a domestic violence case, for example, would also find that incarceration may also increase the chances of the victim's seeking the assistance of an advocate and engaging in safety planning. It is common sense that an incarcerated batterer may have some level of diminished control over the contacts and conversations of a domestic violence victim, yet few jurisdictions study this interrelationship.

In San Diego, we have found that the victim is far more likely to talk to an advocate and begin the process of safety planning if the abuser is still in jail. We know from experience that our best contact with the victim is during the period of incarceration of the batterer. Yet, nationally, most jail systems are not studying how their policies might affect this dynamic. By bringing together those within a system that can study this issue, the process toward coordinated community response is greatly enhanced.

Treating Violence as a Choice

Perhaps the most significant arena for jail staff to have an impact lies in the area of treatment programs for batterers. Across the country, a consensus is emerging that focuses on a psychoeducational model of "treatment" for batterers. It was developed in Duluth, Minnesota, by Ellen Pence and Michael Paymar and is gaining acceptance across the country. The "Duluth Model" approach moves away from individual psychotherapy and rejects anger/stress management or substance abuse treatment as the core of the intervention. It focuses on violence as a choice, most often made by men in our society, and works at re-educating men to make different choices. It seeks to address issues of sex-role socialization and the related topics of male entitlement and male privilege.

The key component of the Duluth model program, however, triggers the consequences for making the wrong choices. Clearly, in domestic violence cases, the most significant negative consequence must be incarceration. If domestic violence is to be treated as a serious crime, and if offenders are going to be forced to make different choices, then the criminal justice system must impose serious consequences for continuing criminal behavior.

Improved Government Intervention Can Curb Family Violence

by **Donna E. Shalala**

About the author: *Donna E. Shalala is secretary of health and human services for the Clinton administration. The following viewpoint is excerpted from a speech delivered to the American Medical Association National Conference on Family Violence in Washington, D.C., in March 1994.*

The day after Christmas of 1993, Marsha Brewer-Stewart was found with a knife in her chest. Police say she was murdered by her husband, Gregory. Just seven months earlier, Marsha had stood by her husband's side in a suburban Chicago courtroom to try to clear him of attempting to kill her.

She had dismissed the episode as a drunken fit of rage. Police and prosecutors begged her not to post his bond, nor to move back with him, but like many women before her, she forgave him.

Then on December 26, 1993, Marsha called the police, desperate for help. The police called back, and the man who answered said nothing was wrong.

By the time a squad car arrived to check on her, Marsha was dead.

Hours later, her husband was charged with murder.

It's a common story. Studies show us just how common.

An Unacknowledged Epidemic

In this country, domestic violence is just about as common as giving birth—about four million instances of each.

Think about that—hopelessness and hope, equally weighted in our society—and all too often, intermingled in the same woman's life.

We know that *17 percent* of women interviewed in public prenatal clinics reported being assaulted during pregnancy.

We don't have precise numbers for all pregnant women.

We've asked the Centers for Disease Control and Prevention [CDC] to find

Excerpted from "Domestic Terrorism: An Unacknowledged Epidemic," a speech by Donna Shalala, delivered at the American Medical Association's National Conference on Family Violence in Washington, D.C., March 11, 1994.

out what the numbers are.

But we do know—all of us in this room know—that domestic violence is an unacknowledged epidemic in our country.

And yet we're still shocked when the "life of the party," an expert in his field, a pillar of the community, turns out to be a wife-beater.

We still find it remarkable that someone who wouldn't think of stomping up to the front office and beating his boss—for fear that he could be fired or worse, go to jail—will come home and punch his wife and children.

We find it remarkable that around four million women each year—*women* like Marsha Brewer-Stewart—are terrorized by the men they know.

Often the men they share their homes with—men who profess to love them.

> *"We're still shocked when the 'life of the party,' an expert in his field, a pillar of the community, turns out to be a wife-beater."*

We also find it remarkable that 19 children can be found helpless, hungry, and huddled together in a filthy Chicago apartment—a place where neighbors had endlessly tried to contact the authorities.

But in the end, a place where police entered only because they believed they would find drugs, not desperate children.

And we find it remarkable that an old man suffering from Alzheimer's Disease is abandoned at a racetrack by his own daughter.

These victims—these survivors—are all victims of a plague—the *same* plague.

They are united by their desperate need to know that we can help them. And they are united in their awareness that we have not yet devised a nationwide plan to take their abusers off the streets to prevent more beatings. . . .

Building Bridges

Time and again, these victims have slipped through our fingers in a system that all too often sends the vulnerable back into their hellish homes—until one day we greet them again in the emergency room if we're lucky, in the morgue if we're too late.

So we have come here today to accept the tough job of examining the causes and the consequences of family violence.

And we're here today to build bridges.

Because when bridges are built—the victims of family violence, and their advocates, cross them in droves. . . .

We all know the complexities of family violence. Much has been done about child abuse since the 1960s, when Dr. Henry Kempe discovered that although fear can provoke silence, a child's X-rays will speak volumes of a history of physical abuse.

Dr. Kempe helped open up our eyes.

Yet after all these years, we're only now coming together to seek real solutions.

We can all ask why. Why has it taken so long?

But better yet, we must ask:

How can we keep up this commitment to establish emotional and physical safety for those who are vulnerable?

And how can we effectively punish and change abusers of women, children, and the elderly?

Domestic Terrorism

Family violence has become as American as guns on our streets and murders in our movies.

It affects all Americans, regardless of background.

It plagues families where poverty, tension, unemployment, and discrimination are common.

But it is also found in wealthy suburbs and middle-income homes where advanced degrees are hanging on the walls.

It occurs among people who are isolated, and among those who have friends.

Violence is a sickness plaguing our entire society. . . .

Domestic violence is terrorism.

Terrorism in the home.

And that is what we should call it.

Domestic terrorism is a leading cause of injury to women in our country.

In fact, one in four women will be assaulted by a domestic partner in her lifetime.

And 60 percent of female homicide victims are killed by someone they know.

> *"[The] system . . . all too often sends the vulnerable back into their hellish homes."*

Often, these women are tracked down and killed—after separating from or divorcing their abusers.

Why do women stay?

Why do they take the relentless punching, and bruising, rather than move out into the world alone?

Because as the battered woman stays on in a battered relationship, her self-confidence drowns in the sea of violence.

And she begins to believe she is unworthy of help.

Unfortunately, because the danger increases for many women when they attempt to leave their abuser, they stay on, and on, and on.

A Cost Society Cannot Afford

It's an ugly, tragic story for millions of women today. And what's more, we're not even sure how many women and men, and often their children, opt for silent suffering and shame.

What we do know is that 20 to 30 percent of the injuries that send women to the emergency room stem from physical abuse by their partners.

Think about that:

Think about the staggering health care costs.

Think about the cost to society.

We see women in emergency rooms holding—almost clutching—the hand of their abusers.

They're holding onto their worlds.

They're holding onto their sole means of support. Their homes. Their possessions. And their neighborhoods.

And one of the great ironies may be that battered women hold on to the tragic illusion that by remaining in abusive homes, they can protect their children.

> *"We see women in emergency rooms holding—almost clutching—the hand of their abusers . . . their sole means of support."*

Tragically, studies show the exact opposite: in at least half the homes where women are being abused, there is also child abuse.

Sgt. Mark Wynn of the Nashville Police Department does not call violence in the home "abuse."

Like me, he calls it *terrorism.*

He should know.

Sgt. Wynn's stepfather was an alcoholic who regularly beat his wife.

At the age of 7, Sgt. Wynn and his brother unsuccessfully tried to poison their stepfather by pouring roach killer into his wine bottle.

This police officer credits the remarkable strength of his mother, and her love, for the fact that he emerged from this cycle of violence.

He says that his experience shows how children who frequently witness abuse against their mothers learn to avenge such behavior with violence.

But an eye for an eye only makes the whole world blind.

Working Together

We *must* provide alternatives.

We *can* take steps to protect all Americans against violence in the home.

All of you have been working tirelessly for this—but others maintain an eerie conspiracy of silence.

There will be no silence in the Clinton Administration.

As Secretary of Health and Human Services, I will speak out, call for legislation, and help find resources to solve the crisis of family violence.

All of America has to wake up to the very real consequences of this violence. . . .

We're going to work together—with nurses and doctors, with educators and mental health professionals, with advocates for battered women and advocates for battered children, with shelter providers and social service providers, with the courts and the Congress, with the police and the Justice Department.

We're all going to work together. It's time for action.

This requires public health and criminal justice professionals to work hand-in-hand—to educate, to intervene, and to deal with the problems before they become explosive.

We have to work with educators to develop conflict resolution curricula, so that early in life, our children learn that might doesn't make right, and that compassion is a sign of strength.

We have to raise our sons to grow into men who respect women and who understand that it is never, never "okay" to abuse girls or women.

The Government's Response

Until now, domestic violence was something the federal government didn't bring up.

We didn't think about it enough.

We didn't talk about it enough.

We didn't care about it enough.

The times have already changed.

In 1994, for the first time ever, the Clinton Administration and Congress allocated funds to the CDC with the aim of investigating—and reducing—violence against women.

Under Dr. David Satcher's leadership, the CDC has taken bold first steps.

We are collecting data on the scope of domestic violence. We are launching public awareness initiatives. And we are seeking creative solutions to the scourge of violence against women. . . .

But that's not all we're doing.

In 1993, we fought for and won the passage of the one-billion dollar Family Preservation and Support Initiative.

This effort is designed to strengthen families—and it also devotes resources to making sure that children are protected from danger.

> *"We have to work with educators to develop conflict resolution curricula, so that . . . our children learn that might doesn't make right."*

Family Preservation allows us to address the multiple factors that place families at risk, including joblessness, poor housing, and the need for day care.

It teaches parenting skills that can prevent blow-ups and fighting.

But I want to emphasize, this initiative aims to prevent problems, *not* to keep families together no matter what. Our commitment to Family Preservation and Support is historic. We have moved from an era of closing our eyes and denying our problems to doing the tough, hard work of saving families to save futures.

But that's still not all.

The Senate-passed version of the crime bill contains the Violence Against Women Act. [The Omnibus Crime Act of 1994 was signed into law on September 13, 1994.]

This act would authorize 1.8 billion dollars over five years to aid police, prosecutors, women's shelters, and community-prevention programs.

The bill gives me the authority to set up a national hotline for victims of domestic abuse.

And let me tell you, that's one grant I can't wait to make.

This hotline will save lives.

The Violence Against Women Act is a tremendous advance. And we must make sure it becomes law.

Police and Courts Must Lead the Way

So the federal government is finally showing strong leadership. But we also need you to lead us.

For one thing, we need medical professionals to help us train police departments. *Unless the police respond properly in a domestic violence case*—a woman who limps out of the hospital is probably returning to the same dangerous trap.

Well-trained police save lives. Domestic violence victims who call the police reduce their risk of being re-assaulted within the next six months.

When police respond properly at a domestic disturbance, the incidence of injury and fatality dramatically goes down.

While we're creating a hotline, while we're providing more shelter,

> *"We have moved from an era of closing our eyes and denying our problems to doing the tough, hard work of saving families to save futures."*

while we're educating the public, and while we're creating tougher penalties for abusers, police departments *must immediately adopt policies to take the control out of the hands of the abusers.*

We need tough laws that don't treat the victim like a criminal.

We need police departments in every community to be responsible for filing complaints on behalf of the victim—so the abuser cannot threaten retaliation to force her to drop the charge.

In Newport News, Virginia, mandatory arrest of offenders is a tough policy. But it has saved lives.

In 1984, 13 of 20 murders in Newport News were related to family violence.

One year after a mandatory-arrest policy was instituted, family violence homicides dropped almost 70 percent. In 1992, *no murders were related to domestic violence.*

We're also seeing big success in Quincy, Massachusetts.

Up in Quincy, former Chief Judge Al Kramer said arresting the perpetrator wasn't going far enough.

He assigned advocates to brief all battered women. And he sent convicted abusers into tightly supervised probation and batterers' treatment, as well as jail.

That's a huge contrast to a judge in another state. Only a few years back, he routinely opened his courtroom by saying to women: "Form a line to the left if you wish to drop a complaint against your husband."

It might be that the police and the courts are coming around—but not fast enough, and not systematically.

Health Care Plays a Pivotal Role

The same could be said about the health profession—there's progress, but not enough, and not systematically.

An advocate for battered women tells the story of one doctor, who typically identified two to three women a year who suffered from spousal abuse. Then he started asking questions.

He took the time to go beyond his routine, and show some compassion. And he found startling evidence of an epidemic:

Now, in the same practice, this doctor treats two to three women a week for spousal abuse.

> *"We need tough laws that don't treat the victim like a criminal."*

The American Medical Association's [AMA] medical guidelines for identifying and handling family abuse have proved to be invaluable to more than 6,000 doctors who took the time to call for this information.

But there are more than *400,000* practicing doctors in America. We cannot wait for each of them to call *us*. Each day, many silent victims continue to suffer.

A 1993 survey by the Commonwealth Fund found that 92 percent of women who were physically abused by their partners did *not* tell their doctors.

And the Family Violence Prevention Fund of San Francisco found that since the AMA guidelines were published—only *23* percent of California hospitals have trained emergency room staff to identify and help victims of spousal abuse.

We need more health professionals asking the right questions. . . .

Everyone Can Help

I challenge all of us to find more creative ways to pass on life-saving information to our colleagues. We must reach out to communities. We must share our knowledge with educators, with school counselors, with town officials, with law enforcement officers, with judges.

In the long run, that's what we have to do.

We have to elevate this issue to the national stage—and that means all of us have to take responsibility for doing even more in our own arenas.

Let me conclude by telling you about a child psychologist named Sandra Graham-Berman who took responsibility for even doing more.

Several years ago, she became aware of a support group for battered women.

But she heard that there was no professional support for their children.

On her own time and with her own money, she began a support group for the children of these battered women.

She began to see the girls and boys act out, talk out, and draw out their fears and their frustrations.

She helped them learn they are not alone in their pain. And she taught them that when mommy is in trouble—when she is being hurt by daddy—it's possible to get help by dialing 911.

A few years later, a shy 8-year-old girl walked in on a fight.

Her father—if you can believe it, a child psychiatrist—was beating her mother on the head with a hammer.

Try to imagine that.

Try to imagine what you would do.

Well, that little girl knew what to do.

She remembered the lesson taught her by a caring adult.

And so she went to that phone, picked it up, pressed 911 and saved her mother's life.

The father is in prison now.

And the family's trying their best to build a new life.

If that little girl can have the courage to pick up the telephone, surely we can have the courage to prevent such stories from happening.

Christian Beliefs Foster Family Violence

by Philip Greven

About the author: *Philip Greven is a professor of history at Rutgers State University of New Jersey and the author of several books, including* Spare the Child: The Religious Roots of Punishment and the Psychological Impact of Physical Abuse, *from which this viewpoint is excerpted.*

For many centuries, the Book of Proverbs has provided parents, preachers, and teachers with the basic aphorisms that have justified their commitment to corporal punishment of children. The verses are so familiar that they have become part of both Christian and secular culture, generation after generation, century after century. Ironically, the one aphorism that epitomizes the commitment to corporal punishment— "Spare the rod and spoil the child"—is not from the Bible at all [but rather from Samuel Butler's poem "Hudibras"], though it has that familiar proverbial ring. But the other aphorisms attributed to Solomon are equally well known and commonly cited, most often in the language of the early-seventeenth-century King James translation:

> Train up a child in the way he should go: and when he is old, he will not depart from it (Proverbs 22:6).

> Correct thy son, and he shall give thee rest; yea, he shall give delight unto thy soul (29:17).

> My son, despise not the chastening of the Lord; neither be weary of his correction: for whom the Lord loveth he correcteth; even as a father the son in whom he delighteth (3:11–12).

> In the lips of him that hath understanding wisdom is found: but a rod is for the back of him that is void of understanding (10:13).

> Chasten thy son while there is hope, and let not thy soul spare for his crying (19:18).

> Judgments are prepared for scorners, and stripes for the back of fools (19:29).

A whip for the horse, a bridle for the ass, and a rod for the fool's back (26:3).

He that spareth his rod hateth his son: but he that loveth him chasteneth him betimes (13:24).

Foolishness is bound in the heart of a child; but the rod of correction shall drive it far from him (22:15).

The rod and reproof give wisdom: but a child left to himself bringeth his mother to shame (29:15).

The blueness of a wound cleanseth away evil: so do stripes the inward parts of the belly (20:30).

Withhold not correction from the child: for if thou beatest him with the rod, he shall not die. Thou shalt beat him with the rod, and shalt deliver his soul from hell (23:13–14).

More than two thousand years of physical violence and painful assaults against the bodies, spirits, and wills of children have been justified by these proverbs, scattered through the Old Testament collection of sayings attributed to Solomon.

A Biblical Injunction

Other Old Testament texts lend additional support to the punishment and violence against children advocated in the name of King Solomon. In the book of Deuteronomy, for instance, Moses told the Israelites that

If a man have a stubborn and rebellious son, which will not obey the voice of his father, or the voice of his mother, and that, when they have chastened him, will not hearken unto them: Then shall his father and his mother lay hold on him, and bring him out unto the elders of the city, and unto the gate of his place; And they shall say unto the elders of his city, This our son is stubborn and rebellious, he will not obey our voice; he is a glutton, and a drunkard. And all the men of his city shall stone him with stones, that he die: so shalt thou put evil away from among you; and all Israel shall hear, and fear (Deuteronomy 21:18–21).

Thus, the price of filial disobedience is death. Moses' injunctions clearly mirrored the will of Jehovah, who often killed those he judged to be disobedient and rebellious. Chastisements, in the form of physical punishments with the rod, were often only the first stage in the progression of discipline from pain to death. . . .

The "Christian" Method of Discipline

Anglo-American Protestants have always been among the most vocal public defenders of physical punishments for infants, children, and adolescents. They have provided many generations of listeners and readers with a series of theological and moral justifications for painful blows inflicted by adults upon the bodies, spirits, and wills of children. These defenses remain crucial to any understanding of the earliest sources of suffering and violence in our lives and culture. It is no accident that the shelves of evangelical and fundamentalist Protestant bookstores throughout the land are filled with books advocating physical punishments as the "Christian" method of discipline, essential to the creation of morality, spirituality, and character, and vital, ultimately, to the salvation of souls.

Doing God's Will

The basic premise shaping contemporary fundamentalist-Protestant rationales for corporal punishment is simply that God has willed it and requires it. As Roy Lessin, author of *Spanking: Why, When, How?*, notes:

> Spanking is God's idea. He is the one who has commanded parents to spank their children as an expression of love. Spanking is not optional. It is an issue love cannot compromise. The question we face as parents is this: do we love God enough to obey Him, and do we love our children enough to bring into their lives the correction of spanking when it is needed?

Larry Christenson, whose book *The Christian Family* has sold more than a million copies throughout the world, observes in his chapter "God's Order for Parents":

> *God holds you accountable for the discipline of your children.* If you discipline and bring up your children according to His Word, you will have His approval and blessing. If you fail to do so, you will incur His wrath.

Christenson also insists that "The Scriptural method of discipline is simple and unequivocal: *the rod*." Similarly, J. Richard Fugate, a former administrator of a Christian school in Texas, the head of the Foundation for Biblical Research, and the author of *What the Bible Says about . . . Child Training*, answers the question "Why must we use a rod to chastise our children?" as follows: "The first and only reason that should be necessary is because God's Word says to use a rod. God has specifically established the rod as the symbol of human authority."

> *"More than two thousand years of physical violence . . . against the bodies, spirits, and wills of children have been justified by these [biblical] proverbs."*

The Rod as Salvation

Many advocates of corporal punishment are convinced that such punishment and pain are necessary to prevent the ultimate destruction and damnation of their children's souls. Susanna Wesley was certain in 1732 that

> religion is nothing else than doing the will of God and not our own: that the one grand impediment to our temporal and eternal happiness being this self-will, no indulgence of it can be trivial, no denial unprofitable. Heaven or hell

depends on this alone; so that the parent who studies to subdue it in his child works together with God in the renewing and saving a soul. The parent who indulges it does the Devil's work; makes religion impracticable, salvation unattainable, and does all that in him lies to damn his child body and soul forever.

Similarly, two and a half centuries later, the Reverend Jack Hyles wrote in his book *How to Rear Children*:

> *The parent who spanks the child keeps him from going to hell.* Proverbs 23:14, *"Thou shalt beat him with the rod, and shalt deliver his soul from hell."* A child who is spanked will be taught that there is a holy God Who punishes sin and wrong. Hence, he will learn to heed authority and obey the laws and rules. When he hears the Word of God he will obey what he hears and will accept the Gospel as it is preached. The parent has kept his child from hell by teaching him truths that can be learned only by discipline and the use of the rod.

The possibility of future punishments thus justifies the infliction of present pain. As Larry Christenson observes, "God has ordained issues of the greatest importance to hinge upon the discipline of the rod—even involving the child's eternal salvation.". . .

Physical Terror and Pain

In *The Christian Family*, Christenson asserts that "If the punishment is of the right kind it not only takes effect physically, but through *physical terror and pain*, it awakens and sharpens the consciousness that there is a moral power over us, a righteous judge, and a law which cannot be broken" [emphasis added]. Such words and phrases may slip by quickly and without comment in *The Christian Family*, but they can resonate ominously in a reader's mind long afterward. If "physical terror and pain" are a normal part of Christian discipline, evidence of "moral power," "righteous" judgments, and unbreakable laws, it should come as no surprise to be informed by him that

> *"Chastisements, in the form of physical punishments with the rod, were often only the first stage in the progression of discipline from pain to death."*

> As Christians, we live under the discipline of Christ. He disciplines us severely as often as we need it. His object is not to spare us pain, but to surely slay the will of the flesh. Yet He disciplines us with moderation. He does not afflict us willingly. And as soon as He sees that we bow down and acknowledge our faults, He comes to us with consolation: He lets us feel how great is His kindness! So He deals with us, and so we ought to deal with our children.

Thus Christenson, like so many others, rationalizes pain and suffering inflicted by adults upon their children. If God does it, so should we, and "physical terror and pain" will continue to be inflicted in the name of Jesus and Christianity. If the immense popularity of *The Christian Family* is any guide, the endless loop of punishments will continue, generation after generation, until such violent assaults and suffering are no longer rationalized and defended.

> *"Unconscious memories of pain, fear, and anger remain encoded in the cells of the brain and body for the remainder of life."*

The rationales for physical punishments always mirror the theologies of those who advocate such practices. But knowing what to do and why is not the same as actually doing it. This is why the rationales for physical punishment so often include advice to parents on the methodology of discipline. The theories about punishment are enforced by real blows, real pain, real fear, real suffering. Most advocates are also practitioners.

Punishment Begins in Infancy

According to many Christian advocates of physical punishments, pain should begin to be felt early in life, often in infancy and the first years of childhood, and should continue to be inflicted, in many cases even through adolescence, until children learn obedience and submission to parental authority or until their wills have been broken. The lessons of discipline frequently start long before children have the ability to speak, remember, or resist. Nevertheless, unconscious memories of pain, fear, and anger remain encoded in the cells of the brain and body for the remainder of life.

Protestant advocates of physical punishment often advise parents to begin inflicting pain while their children are still infants. Larry Christenson recommends that "Discipline should begin when the child is in the cradle." Roy Lessin agrees that children should be punished within the first two years, and that spankings can continue until children reach their teens, without ruling out the possibility of further spankings even in adolescence. J. Richard Fugate believes six-month-old children should be switched for disobedience, observing that "The parents' controlled use of pain is not cruel and will not cause the child to fear his parents personally. . . . If he chooses willfully to ignore the commands, he chooses to receive pain."

Spanking for Disobedience

Similar advice is to be found in *Christian Child-Rearing and Personality Development*, by an evangelical psychiatrist, Paul Meier, who has taught at the fundamentalist Dallas Theological Seminary and conducted seminars across the country on "Christian child-rearing and Christian counseling." Meier considers corporal punishment indispensable for discipline: "Verbal reproofs are sometimes adequate," he observes, "but if the child is openly rebelling, spanking is the most effective form of discipline." Meier's own experience as a parent confirms this principle: "My wife and I are both very loving and nurturing parents,

and yet we remember spanking our older son or slapping his hand for open re-
bellion many times during those crucial twenty-one months (15th to 36th
months)." He believes that they fostered their son's "independence and explo-
ration" at the same time, while "spanking him for willful disobedience." Meier
comments, "I've heard a lot about the terrible threes, but I think we drove a lot
of the terrible threes out of him when he was still two, because his third birth-
day brought on a new era of relative peace, although he still needed an occasional spanking.". . .

Beverly La Haye, who has given Family Life seminars with her husband, the
Reverend Timothy La Haye (who once was a leader of Moral Majority), offers
[additional] advice in her book *How to Develop Your Child's Temperament*. She
urges parents who have spanked their child once to repeat their spankings as often as necessary to teach the child who continues to cry after the initial punishment not to voice feelings of "anger" and "rage." Her advice seems to be
designed to train children to suppress their feelings of resentment and resistance, an emotional control brought about by parental blows, violence, coercion, and the purposeful hurting of the child. Given her general commitment to
breaking children's wills and the use of rods in punishing children's bodies,
such advice is not surprising.

Leaving Marks

Given the intensity and duration of many punishments, the issues of both pain
and physical marks indicative of the suffering of the child being assaulted by
spankings, whippings, and beatings confront every advocate of corporal punishment. In his book *Dare to Discipline*, James Dobson [a psychologist and the
director of the multimillion-dollar organization Focus on the Family] assures
his readers that "It is not necessary to beat the child into submission; a little bit
of pain goes a long way for a young child." Lessin acknowledges that "there
may be times when spanking with a rod can leave marks on a child's bottom,
especially if several spankings are needed within a brief period of time. However," he adds, "these marks are temporary and should not become a source of
discouragement to parents. It is better for children to carry a few temporary
marks on the outside than to carry
within them areas of disobedience
and wrong attitudes that can leave
permanent marks on their character."
Similarly, Larry Tomczak [a charis-
matic from a Polish Catholic background and author of the book *God,
the Rod, and Your Child's Bod: The
Art of Loving Correction for Christian Parents*] cautions parents: "Keep in
mind that 'posterior protoplasmic stimulation' can cause some redness on the
skin. This is nothing to get upset about! These marks are only temporary," and

> *"Protestant advocates of
> physical punishment often
> advise parents to begin
> inflicting pain while their
> children are still infants."*

they are preferable to keeping "improper attitudes inside that can leave permanent scars later in life." Christenson
acknowledges the pain of punishments—"the object being to cause
the child enough pain to rouse whole-
some fear"—but he is silent concerning the possibility of physical marks
or wounds as a result of the applica-
tion of rods to children's bodies.

> *"Most advocates hesitate to acknowledge in print the full extent of the bodily harm that physical punishments can cause."*

Fugate, however, directly acknowledges the virtual inevitability of some
physical marks on children's bodies as a result of corporal punishments. He observes:

> Children vary as to the number and intensity of strokes they require before
> they will submit. Some children are ready to give in when they first see the
> switch. . . . However, the child who has not yet learned to trust his parent's
> commitment to his obedience, or who is exceptionally willful[,] will require
> more frequent and more intense whippings. Such a child is likely to require
> enough strokes to receive stripes or even welts. Some children have very sen-
> sitive skin that will welt or even bruise quite easily. Parents should not be
> overly concerned if *such minor injuries do result from their chastisement as it
> is perfectly normal* (2 Samuel 7:14; Psalms 89:32; Proverbs 20:30). However,
> parents should be careful that their use of the rod is not excessive and that the
> actual size of the rod is reasonable. Making stripes on a child is not the objec-
> tive of chastisement, but parents *must realistically expect them to be a neces-
> sary by-product* of the child's rebellion on some occasions [emphasis added].

Children's bodies often bear silent witness to the marks left by the rod or other
implements: reddened skin; stripes; welts; bruises; broken skin, cartilage, and
sometimes bone; and bleeding. Fugate, at least, is candid about the "minor injuries" that he finds "perfectly normal." Most advocates hesitate to acknowledge
in print the full extent of the bodily harm that physical punishments can cause.
Whether "minor" or major, such injuries are common when adults inflict pain
purposefully and intensely on the bodies of infants, children, or adolescents.

Inflicting Pain vs. Abuse

Given the infliction of pain often repeated for subsequent offenses against the
authority and will of parents, and given the virtual inevitability of some physical evidence of the force of the blows required to inflict this pain, the question
of potential abuse at times arises in the minds of corporal-punishment advocates. Dobson, for example, is very sensitive to the possibility of abuse arising
from corporal punishments, as he notes in his book *The Strong-Willed Child*.
However, he remains an advocate of painful punishments, whether with belts or
other things.

Roy Lessin, too, declares that "child abuse should be despised by every parent." Nevertheless, he adds that

> in rejecting even the thought of child abuse, parents must be careful not to reject God's way of providing loving correction through spanking. This is not to be confused with child abuse. Parents must guard against the fear that loving discipline is a form of child abuse. And they also must be careful not to become critical and wrongly judge parents who do provide this discipline.

Lessin also contends that "The *failure* to provide loving discipline through spanking is also a form of child abuse" because "it affects eternal issues as well as temporal issues." The fear of hell remains a central, if often implicit, justification for corporal punishments and pain in this present life, and makes the infliction of pain through spankings both necessary and nonabusive, in the opinion of those who share Lessin's convictions.

The limits of corporal punishment falling short of child abuse in the opinion of many advocates sometimes can extend very far, however. Paul Meier, writing as a Christian psychiatrist, replies to parents who say "that spanking simply doesn't work for their child" by insisting that "the spanking has to hurt; and it may need to be repeated a number of times for the same offense." He adds, "I am not advocating bruising the child; in fact I consider slapping his face or hitting him with a fist to be child abuse and provoking him to wrath. . . . But remember the words of Solomon," Meier cautions, invoking one of the direst of the proverbs: ["Withhold not correction from the child: for if thou beatest him with the rod, he shall not die"]. "God is almost mocking us here," he notes, "for being afraid to spank."

> *"Where . . . are parents to draw the line between discipline and child abuse?"*

Where then, are parents to draw the line between discipline and child abuse? If spanking often needs to be repeated while slapping and hitting with fists are unacceptable even though being beaten with rods is biblically approved, it is not surprising that Meier, like so many advocates of physical punishments, has difficulty setting forth a clear distinction between acceptable methods of punishment and unacceptable forms of abusive discipline. Since coercion and assault are inherent in physical discipline, is it any wonder that advocates of physical punishments have difficulty distinguishing abusive from nonabusive levels of pain and violence?

A More Moderate Approach

Many Christians, especially "once-born" mainstream Protestants, have been and continue to be disturbed by the readiness of so many "twice-born" Christians to inflict suffering and pain in the name of discipline, and dismayed by the severity of many assaults associated with physical punishments, which often seem excessive, undesirable, and even deplorable. More moderate Protestants have always advocated gentleness, reasoning, and respect for the selfhood of children.

Wishing to bend rather than to break children's wills, such moderates usually perceive themselves as being in the middle between the extremes of severity and indulgence. Nevertheless, the vast majority of parents have shared a deeply rooted conviction that physical punishments are necessary at some point if the goals of the parents or other adults are to be fulfilled and accomplished. . . .

The long-standing tradition of ambivalence among Christian moderates . . . who both oppose and advocate physical punishments and painful discipline, is evident today throughout D. Ross Campbell's *How to Really Love Your Child*, written from the perspective of a mainstream, nonfundamentalist Christian psychiatrist. Campbell's viewpoint reflects a self-conscious alternative to the ardent advocacy of the rod found in so many books by fundamentalists and evangelicals. . . .

A Nonpunitive Interpretation of the Bible

Campbell takes note of the "punishment trap" so many parents encounter, which arises in part because of the writing, speaking, preaching, and teaching of advocates of physical punishments. He observes:

> Few plead for a child and his real needs. Too many today are dogmatically calling for children to be punished, calling it discipline, and recommending the harshest, most extreme form of human treatment. Most perplexing of all, many of these advocates call this a biblical approach. They quote three verses from the book of Proverbs (Prov. 23:13; 29:15; 13:24) to totally justify beating a child. They neglect to mention the hundreds of Scripture verses dealing with love, compassion, sensitivity, understanding, forgiveness, nurturing, guidance, kindness, affection, and giving, as though the child has little or no right to these expressions of love.

Campbell's reading of the Bible, which implicitly opposes the use of the rod, provides a scriptural context for his declaration that "Corporal punishment degrades, dehumanizes, and humiliates a child." He also notes that "using corporal punishment as a principal means of behavioral control is dangerous" because "it drastically alleviates guilt." It also affects the formation of conscience. "If you want to prevent your child from developing a normal responsible conscience which will enable him to *control himself*, build your relationship with him on a punitive basis. Control his behavior primarily by spanking and scolding, especially spanking."

Campbell is disturbed by the "frightening advent of violence in all modes of mass communication, especially television"; he asks, "is it any wonder child abuse and all other forms of violence have become a national disgrace?". . .

A Last Resort

Despite the detrimental effects that he has outlined so cogently and persuasively, Campbell, like most moderates, is a reluctant advocate of physical punishments. Perceiving himself as part of the middle ground, he takes note of parental confusion when caught between "disciplinarians (actually punishment-oriented) on one side and advocates of vague, difficult-to-follow programs on the other," polarities that enable him to argue for a more moderate form of discipline, which yet relies at some point on force, coercion, and pain. "Yes, punishment and techniques are at times necessary, quite helpful, and often good, but let's face it, they are not the best; appropriate love and guidance are."

Campbell recommends that "Punishment is occasionally necessary but because of its negative effects from overuse, punishment should be used *only as a last resort*." Thus he joins the long tradition of people who are willing, under pressure, to resort to "physical force" despite their preference for controlling "a child's behavior in the most gentle, most considerate, and most loving way possible."

Disobedience Remains the Issue

For Campbell, as for most moderates, the crucial issue that ultimately justifies the infliction of pain and the use of physical punishments involves obedience and willfulness. "Defiance," he believes,

> is one of the few indications for punishment. Defiance is openly resisting and challenging authority—parental authority. It is stubbornly refusing to obey. Of course defiance, as well as any misbehavior, cannot be permitted. At these times, punishment is often indicated, and such times occasionally occur no matter what we do.

Centering as it does upon resistance to authority and the refusal of a child to obey, this statement is virtually indistinguishable from countless others by fundamentalist and evangelical advocates of harsh punishments. . . .

The tradition of severity combined with gentleness thus continues, a child's defiance and a parent's desperation being sufficient reasons to resort to force, violence, and pain. All the earlier arguments are put aside, especially those acknowledging the degradation, dehumanization, and humiliation experienced by children who are corporally punished. Physical punishment thus remains at the core of Christian discipline even for a psychiatrist who is not an advocate of the rod.

The use of physical punishment is still the "last resort" today for most moderates and mainstream Protestants, just as it always has been. Religious rationales for physical punishments have been, and remain, among the most powerful and influential theoretical justifications for violence known in the Western world. For generations, they have woven the threads of pain and suffering into the complex fabric of our characters and our cultures.

Harsher Penalties Will Not Reduce Family Violence

by George J. Bryjak

About the author: *George J. Bryjak is a professor of sociology at the University of San Diego.*

A host of politicians [are] calling for significantly greater punishments for . . . domestic violence. These individuals, some of whom are advocates of the "three strikes and you're out" philosophy, . . . struggle to outdo each other in their attempts to ratchet up existing penalties for spousal abuse.

Many legislators are reluctant to pass up what appears to be an all too politically rare win-win situation. Increasing the punishment associated with the violation of any criminal law is fiscally painless—at least in the short run. Unlike putting more police on the streets or building new prisons (crime reduction strategies that typically come with hefty price tags, accompanied by talk of raising taxes), it takes nothing more than a sufficient number of signatures to increase the punishment associated with any crime.

In addition, this most recent get-tough-on-crime attack plays well with one's constituents. With the exception of wife batterers, who could possibly object to increasing the punishment for this offense?

Raising Penalties Will Decrease Punishment

Unfortunately, raising the penalty for spousal abuse will have little long-term effect on reducing this very undesirable behavior. And if the punishment for this offense is raised too high, incidents of wife battering could very well increase.

Twenty years of research indicate that increasing the severity of a penalty without also increasing the certainty of being apprehended and punished has minimal deterrent effect on deviant behavior. Even the most severe punishment is unlikely to dissuade those would-be criminals who believe there is little chance they will be arrested and successfully prosecuted.

Then there is the phenomenon that has been referred to as "the neutralization of severe sanctions." If, for example, the punishment for felonious wife beating

George J. Bryjak, "Harsher Penalties Are No Cure for Abuse," *San Diego Union-Tribune*, July 10, 1994. Reprinted by permission of the author.

were increased to six months or one year in prison (first offense, no parole), we could expect some police officers (perhaps a sizable number) to view this new penalty as too severe. As a result, they might arrest offenders in only the most serious and dangerous cases, leaving the majority of spousal abusers free to inflict still more pain upon their wives.

> *"Society would be much better served if law enforcement agencies gave spousal abuse a higher priority rather than . . . resorting to overly tough sanctions."*

This problem would not necessarily be solved by a mandatory arrest policy—a policy stating that an officer must make an arrest if he or she has reasonable cause to believe that a felony has been committed. Excessive sanctions could be neutralized by juries. Jurors may well conclude that even though the defendant apparently beat his wife, the state-mandated punishment does not fit the crime; that is, the punishment is a greater injustice than the injuries suffered by the victim. We could well end up with a significant number of men who, in fact, did abuse their wives but nonetheless are deemed legally innocent by sympathetic courts.

Thus, exaggerated penalties for wife battering will permit some men guilty of that crime to escape punishment. Worse yet, overly stiff penalties ironically could contribute to *higher* rates of abuse.

According to the logic of deterrence theory, as the certainty of punishment resulting from fewer arrests and convictions (because of overly severe sanctions) goes down, the incidence of wife beating will go up.

Another problem with strengthening sanctions is that the victims themselves may be reluctant to call the police. While these women would most certainly welcome intervention by the authorities, they may not want abusive boyfriends and husbands to be imprisoned for a prolonged period, especially if these individuals are the sole or principal providers for their families. They also may fear retribution from in-laws who will be none too happy about seeing a brother or son incarcerated.

Unfortunately, a woman's failure to call authorities in the early stages of an abusive relationship may contribute to an ongoing pattern of more serious abuse.

How Society Can Be Better Served

There are at least two ways to prevent people from engaging in undesirable behavior.

The first, as noted, is by the threat of punishment, with the certainty of punishment being the overriding factor. Society would be much better served if law enforcement agencies gave spousal abuse a higher priority rather than attempting to remedy the situation by resorting to overly tough sanctions. Currently, 25 states require that an individual who violently attacks someone during a domestic dispute be arrested. All states should have this provision.

However, relying on punishment is not the most effective mechanism for substantially reducing abuse of women in the home. Brutalization of females in this country is but symptomatic of a much larger problem—gender inequality. The best way to diminish the physical abuse of women is to significantly reduce the deviant motivation that feeds this behavior.

In a review of the literature on 90 peasant societies around the world, David Levinson found that wife beating is the most common form of family violence occurring in 76 of these groups. He discovered that one of the strongest predictors of this form of violence against women was "sexual economic inequality."

No doubt this inequality in the form of females having lower wages and less opportunity for occupational advancement, coupled with working women still performing most if not all household chores when both husbands and wives work, are factors contributing to wife beating in modern industrial states as well.

If we want to end the physical and mental degradation of women, moving toward gender parity in the workplace would go a long way toward mitigating the feelings of superiority that so many men have regarding women, attitudes that contribute to a sense of having the right to control females—by force if necessary.

Unfortunately, it is much easier for politicians (as well as others) to rely solely on the "punishment response" regarding the problem of battered women than to work toward bringing about true economic and social gender equality.

This solution involves making fundamental changes in how we believe women should be treated, as well as implementing significant structural changes across society's major institutions.

Government Intervention Undermines the Family

by Allan Carlson

About the author: *Allan Carlson is the president of the Rockford Institute, a conservative research organization concerned with religious ethics and social change, and the publisher of the institute's monthly magazine* Chronicles.

The 1992 election season opened with hopes high for an intelligent debate of family issues. The 1991 *Final Report* of the National Commission on children (on which I served) seemed to have broken the moral and political logjams that had long prevented this dialogue. The commissioners had decided, after extensive argument, to avoid the mistake of earlier children's commissions, which had treated children as an independent constituency group needing its own government services. Instead, we agreed to focus on children in families and to find ways to strengthen the latter. On the great question of "whose children are they?" the official answer, at least, would be: they belong to their parents, not to the government.

Pro-Family Consensus Is Short-Lived

Affirmed by a unanimous, bipartisan vote, the report emphasized that children's well-being depends primarily on the status of their fathers and mothers and that a stable marital union of self-sufficient adults is the superior setting in which to raise children. The report gave notice to the negative effects of government intervention on families and focused on the dramatic shift of the income and payroll tax burdens onto the backs of families. Its primary recommendation was a tax-cut for families raising children, to be achieved through a new $1,000 per child tax credit. Given these dominant themes, the more traditionalist members of the panel took a certain pride in winning over the support of liberal members like Jay Rockefeller, Bill Clinton, and Marian Wright Edelman.

But the achievement was short-lived. Already on the day of the final vote, the Richard Darman–George Bush White House was frantically working to sabotage the report, worried that the endorsement of a tax-cut by Republican ap-

Allan Carlson, "Uncle Sam's Child," *Chronicles*, January 1993. Reprinted by permission of *Chronicles*, a publication of the Rockford Institute, Rockford, Illinois.

pointees to the commission would somehow upset the hallowed "budget agree-ment" with Congress. Soon after, the presidential electoral debate veered back to distorted themes of the past. Mr. Quayle opened with the stale Republican canard that the "media elite" of Hollywood is the cause of family miseries, a variation of neoconservative "new class" theory. Ignoring the facts, Mr. Bush then traced the family's breakdown to the Great Society programs of the 1960's (another staple neoconservative theme). He also transformed "family values" into a metaphor for gay-bashing, the 1992 version of "San Francisco Democrats," used to good effect four years earlier. Mr. Clinton responded with a sterile defense of single-motherhood as a lifestyle choice and an open em-brace of "gay rights." His wife, meanwhile, defended her advocacy of chil-dren's rights and of enhanced state intervention in families.

History of Anti-Family Sentiment

It may be, though, that this deterioration of the 1992 "family values" debate derived from a deeper weakness in liberal democratic theory. Since Thomas Hobbes first laid out the ideological premises for a society based on the status and rights of the individual, the family has had a tenuous foundation in Western political theory. For Hobbes, family relations were simply an exercise in power, where selfish parents claimed "dominion over the infant" by their superior size and strength. Recoiling from this brutal frankness, John Locke tried to put a hu-man face on the Hobbesian scheme. He carved out "a sort of rule or jurisdic-tion" for parents over children, and he found in childrearing a practical justifi-cation for marriage. Yet the emancipation of the young should occur early on, he continued, and the marriage, its function gone, should "dissolve itself." John Stuart Mill was less positive. In his famed essay on women's rights, he called the family system of his day oppressive, the seedbed of despotism, and the source of human misery, "which swells to something appalling."

Relative to family life, the genius of the American Constitution of 1787 lay in its avoidance of ideology and its devotion to authentic federal principle. Family issues of marriage, divorce, children, inheritance, education, mutual sup-port, and welfare were not questions for the new federal government. These were questions reserved to the

"[Children] belong to their parents, not to the government."

states, where Christian conceptions of patriarchy, charity, and shared obligation and Common Law understandings of family and community governance could, and did, hold sway.

Like so much else in our constitutional system, this view of the family began to falter during the Jacksonian period. The first juvenile reformatory in the United States, the New York House of Refuge, opened its doors in 1825. With delegated police powers allowing it to institutionalize children virtually at will, the House of Refuge blurred distinctions between poor, neglected, and delinquent children. The needed legal underpinning for a full-blooded reform school "movement" came from Pennsylvania. In 1839, that state's Supreme Court ruled that the Philadelphia House of Refuge could incarcerate a girl over her parents' objections and without formal legal proceedings. The Court based its decision on a new legal principle: *parens patriae*, or "the parenthood of the state." Under England's chancery laws, *parens patriae* had allowed the Crown to assume a parental role to protect the estates of wealthy orphans. But the Pennsylvania Court expropriated the term to justify the termination of parental rights, reasoning: "May not the natural parents, when unequal to the task of education or unworthy of it, be supplanted by the *parens patriae*, or common guardianship of the community?"

> *"Family issues [in the eighteenth century] . . . were questions reserved to the states, where Christian conceptions of patriarchy, charity, and shared obligation . . . [held] sway."*

Emergence of the Child Savers

Buoyed by this denial of both the Common Law and the natural rights of parents, the Child Saving movement gained momentum. The Child Savers soon linked up with the budding social work profession and the progressive spirit, and together they all spawned the juvenile justice system. "Parents could no longer shield themselves behind *natural* rights," one early enthusiast said. Without a formal hearing or other consideration of due process, hundreds of thousands of American children would be seized by the Child Savers and incarcerated in reform or "industrial" schools, all for "the welfare of the child," a lone actor in an individualistic world.

The state courts soon elevated *parens patriae* into a doctrine superior to any constitution, conferring sweeping powers. As the Illinois Supreme Court reasoned in 1882:

> It is the unquestioned right and imperative duty of every enlightened government, in its character of *parens patriae*, to protect and provide for the comfort and well-being of such of its citizens as, by reason of *infancy, defective understanding, or other misfortune or infirmity*, are unable to take care of themselves. The performance of this duty is justly regarded as one of the most important of governmental functions, *and all constitutional limitations must be so understood and construed so as not to interfere with its proper and legitimate exercise* [emphasis added].

So energized, the concept quickly spread beyond the "child protection" arena. The late 19th-century proponents of mandatory state schooling, for example, ridiculed attention to "the sacred rights and personal privileges" of parents. Court decisions on mandatory attendance laws ruled that the principle of *parens patriae* took precedence over the rights of parents.

But *parens patriae* demanded still more. Franklin D. Roosevelt's Committee on Economic Security, in its 1935 report, recommended creation of a comprehensive Social Security Act, to replace the support once offered by "children, friends, and relatives." Congress concurred. In its 1937 decision declaring the Social Security Act constitutional, the U.S. Supreme Court turned to the parental state ideal for justification: "The *parens patriae* has many reasons—fiscal and economic as well as social and moral—for planning to mitigate disasters that bring these burdens in their train." Government had an obligation to plan and care for its children.

Indeed, the progressive spirit viewed the natural or biological family as the residue of another age. As a leading social historian from the period put it, "American history consummates the disappearance of the wider familism and the substitution of the parentalism of society." Prominent sociologists, such as William Ogburn and Ernest Groves, documented the "deinstitutionalization" and "disorganization" of the family, as it passed virtually all of its function over to state and charitable authorities, experts better able to manage children and give meaning to adults. At Herbert Hoover's 1930 White House Conference on Children, one leading participant called for recognition of an emerging new being: "Uncle Sam's Child," an entity "who belongs to the community almost as much as to the family," a "new racial experiment," and a citizen of "a world predestinedly moving toward unity." These human experiments in utopian democracy had been liberated from the disabling ties of the prescientific, predemocratic age and had become malleable agents for the better world order to come.

The Family Resurges

The full impact of the Parenting State was delayed, though, by Depression and war, followed by the strangest of developments—"The 50's." For a remarkable 15 years, 1946–1961, the utopian dreams of social engineers for a "familial state" were put on hold. Families appeared to grow stronger and more independent, as GIs and their brides poured into the mushrooming Levittowns of what Henry Luce called "a new America." The divorce rate went down and the birthrate soared, while the Child Savers beat a retreat. Sociologist Talcott Parsons saw the baby boom and the sprawling new suburbs as signs of the "upgrading" of the American family. The "household engineer" bonded to "the organization man" in a "companionate marriage" focused on "personality adjustment" became the new model, one celebrated and reinforced by Luce, Walt Disney, Ozzie Nelson, and other imagemakers from the era. Indeed, neoconservative theory later elevated this time-dependent family system into the "traditional family" of modern lore, over which political battles in the 1990's are still being fought.

> *"Without a formal hearing or . . . due process, hundreds of thousands of American children would be seized by the Child Savers."*

In truth, the family system of the 50's was fragile, transitory, and incapable of being reproduced. The peculiar psychology and economics of postwar America, combined with distinctive anti-communist and antistatist fervors, had checked for a time the ambitions of *parens patriae*. But its agents and sustaining laws were still in place. The Child Savers simply refocused, for a decade or so, on "the scourge of juvenile delinquency," with James Dean unwittingly providing them

> *"'Reporting laws,' requiring doctors, teachers, and social workers to report suspected cases of child abuse . . . denied the existence of natural parental rights."*

with the perfect cover. Rapid public school growth to accommodate the baby boomers preoccupied education officials, while Social Security became a tame, and seemingly cheap, presence in American life.

This halcyon age collapsed in the 1960's, though, as it had to at some point, and the old trends and their parasitical "professions" came roaring back. Marriage rates tumbled while divorce rates soared. Illegitimacy spread rapidly among white Americans (it was already common among blacks), while marital fertility collapsed. The "sexual revolution" came out from under the covers, where it had been heating up since the American libido was drafted in 1942, to do battle with the arthritic and thinning legions of Christian decency. The family itself fell into disrepute, pummeled by neo-Malthusians, neofeminists, neo-Marxists, and neopagans alike.

Government Intrusion Through Child Abuse Investigations

Sensing their opportunity, the Child Savers returned. In 1962, several clever advocates coined the phrase "battered child syndrome." Soon *Life, The Saturday Evening Post, Good Housekeeping*, and other bored organs of the 50's synthesis began thumping the drums with articles like "Parents Who Beat Children" and "Cry Rises From Beaten Babies." The emerging late 20th-century American mind, awash in sensation and cheap sentiment, lurched to the proffered solution. Between 1963 and 1967, all 50 states adopted "reporting laws," requiring doctors, teachers, and social workers to report suspected cases of child abuse. Like Child Saving tools of the past, these laws essentially denied the existence of natural parental rights and the Common Law. Accused parents faced a presumption of guilt (often involving seizure of their children) until they could prove their innocence. Other ancient legal protections—including the husband-wife privilege—were scrapped, in service to a great new crusade.

In fact, in the very year when this new "crisis" took form, fewer than 5,000 cases of physically abused children could be counted nationwide. By 1968, the number was still only 6,617. Yet a kind of inflation, in social statistics as well as money, soon occurred. By 1981, the official number reached 85,000; by 1986, 250,000; and today, over one million.

To believe the Child Savers, Americans are now battering their children at a level unprecedented in human history. On the one hand, the actual incidence of serious physical and sexual abuse probably is rising. However, this appears to be a consequence of the already shattered domestic order. A rapidly growing number of children are living in homes where the natural father is absent, due to illegitimacy, abandonment, or divorce. Many of these households also contain "live-in" boyfriends, who tend to behave in brutal fashion toward children of the earlier male.

On the other hand, the Child Saving crusade has relentlessly aimed its machinery at intact families. Spurred on by twisted feminist theories of patriarchal oppression, state agents have whipped up public hysteria, generating over one million *false* accusations of abuse each year. Healthy American families are subjected to the real abuse of state investigations into their structure and character, a special kind of terror unique to the sentimental totalitarianism of late 20th-century America.

> *"Government schools serve as the prime instrument for . . . subvert[ing] the bonds and sense of continuity of each family."*

State schools serve as the primary instruments of scrutiny and indoctrination. From the earliest grades, children are taught by public officials to be suspicious of their parents' touches and told how to register complaints over parents' actions with public officials. Federally funded School-Based Multi-Disciplinary Teams enter schools to ferret out "abusing families." These cadres of social workers and psychologists have the power to examine a family's source of income, history, living conditions, attitudes, self-image, spousal relations, impulse control, and degree of community involvement. Those falling short of federal standards face therapy, loss of children, and formal criminal charges.

Indeed, it is primarily through the state's schools that *parens patriae* continues its drive to displace the autonomous family. As Princeton sociologist Norman Ryder has conclusively shown, government schools serve as the prime instrument for communicating a "state morality" and a "state mythology" designed to subvert the bonds and sense of continuity of each family. "Families" are allowed to exist only as they become agents of the state, dutifully providing room and board to the state's children.

G. K. Chesterton explained, decades ago, what was at stake here. "The ideal for which the family stands . . . is liberty," he wrote. "It is the only . . . institution that is at once necessary and voluntary. It is the only check on the state that is bound to renew itself as eternally as the state, and more naturally than the state."

Reclaiming the Functions of Family

For the 1990's, the most important front in the ongoing contest between the liberal state and the family may be "homeschooling." Embracing but a handful of children thirty years ago, homeschools now educate at least a half-million children; the actual number is probably over a million, and growing. These families have pulled their children out of state schools, seeking to defend the integrity of their distinctive history and moral message from the leveling impulses of the state. At the same time, these families act on the instinctive knowledge that their existence as autonomous entities requires a reclaiming of powers and functions from *parens patriae*. This "refunctionalization," in turn, changes the family's nature, often restoring the sense of "household" and economic community lost decades ago.

Not surprisingly, *parens patriae* has turned its full fury on these latter-day rebels. Authorities in many states have mobilized neglect and abuse laws alongside truancy laws to harass or imprison parents and to force their children back into the government's schools. Yet the number of dissenters continues to grow, forming a new kind of underground movement against the overweening ambitions of the parental state.

The reconstruction of family life in America cannot be based on the "companionate" model of the 1950's, as the neoconservative dream would have it. This "traditional family" represented no more than a brief pause, inherently unstable, in the transfer of power and authority from the autonomous family of the 19th century to the triumphant *parens patriae* of the 20th. More certainly, the current liberal dream of public daycare and expanded "family services" represents a plan for the final destruction of the state's only real rival. Instead, the survival of the American family depends on those families able and ready to reclaim the functions and the powers, such as education, that are naturally theirs. The critical battles will be fought in hamlets and cities throughout the land, as individuals wake up and shake off their shackles, rediscovering that their liberty, like the liberty of their neighbors, rests on their covenants of marriage and parenthood.

Bibliography

Books

Louise Armstrong — *Rocking the Cradle of Sexual Politics: What Happened When Women Said Incest.* Reading, MA: Addison-Wesley, 1994.

Ellen Bass and Laura Davis — *The Courage to Heal: A Guide for Women Survivors of Child Sexual Abuse.* New York: Perennial Library, 1988.

Douglas J. Besharov, ed. — *Family Violence Research and Public Policy.* Washington, DC: AEI Press, 1991.

Children's Express; Susan Goodwillie, ed. — *Voices from the Future: Our Children Tell Us About Violence in America.* New York: Crown, 1993.

Dorothy Ayers Counts, Judith K. Brown, and Jacquelyn C. Campbell, eds. — *Sanctions and Sanctuary: Cultural Perspectives on the Beating of Wives.* Boulder, CO: Westview Press, 1992.

James C. Dobson — *The New Dare to Discipline.* Wheaton, IL: Tyndale House, 1992.

Joanne Ross Feldmeth and Midge Wallance Finley — *We Weep for Ourselves and Our Children: A Christian Guide for Survivors of Childhood Sexual Abuse.* San Francisco: HarperSanFrancisco, 1990.

Vincent J. Fontana and Valerie Moolman — *Save the Family, Save the Child: What We Can Do to Help Children at Risk.* New York: Dutton, 1991.

John C. Gonsiorek, Walter H. Bera, and Donald LeTourneau — *Male Sexual Abuse: A Trilogy of Intervention Strategies.* Thousand Oaks, CA: Sage Publications, 1994.

David Island and Patrick Letellier — *Men Who Beat the Men Who Love Them: Battered Gay Men and Domestic Violence.* Binghamton, NY: Haworth Press, 1991.

Peter G. Jaffe, David A. Wolfe, and Susan Kaye Wilson — *Children of Battered Women.* Thousand Oaks, CA: Sage Publications, 1993.

Nancy Kilgore — *Every Eighteen Seconds: A Journey Through Domestic Violence.* Volcano, CA: Volcano Press, 1993.

Jordan I. Kosberg and Juanita L. Garcia, eds. — *Elder Abuse in World-Wide Perspective.* Binghamton, NY: Haworth Press, 1995.

Bibliography

Elaine Leeder	*Treating Abuse in Families*. New York: Springer Publishing Co., 1994.
David Levinson	*Family Violence in Cross-Cultural Perspective*. Newbury Park, CA: Sage Publications, 1989.
Cloé Madanes with James P. Keim and Dinah Smelser	*The Violence of Men*. San Francisco: Jossey-Bass, 1995.
Alice Miller	*For Your Own Good: Hidden Cruelty in Child-Rearing and the Roots of Violence*. London: Virago, 1987.
Mark Pendergrast	*Victims of Memory: Incest Accusations and Shattered Lives*. Hinesburg, VT: Upper Access, 1995.
Vimala Pillari	*Scapegoating in Families: Intergenerational Patterns of Physical and Emotional Abuse*. New York: Brunner/Mazel, 1991.
Claire Renzetti	*Violent Betrayal: Partner Abuse in Lesbian Relationships*. Newbury Park, CA: Sage Publications, 1992.
William Stacey, Lonnie R. Hazlewood, and Anson Shupe	*The Violent Couple*. Westport, CT: Praeger, 1994.
Larry Tifft	*Battering of Women: The Failure of Intervention and the Case for Prevention*. Boulder, CO: Westview Press, 1993.
Lenore E. Walker	*Terrifying Love: Why Battered Women Kill and How Society Responds*. New York: Harper & Row, 1989.
Richard Wexler	*Wounded Innocents: The Real Victims of the War Against Child Abuse*. Buffalo: Prometheus Books, 1990.

Periodicals

Charles J. Aron	"In Defense of Battered Women: Is Justice Blind?" *Human Rights*, Fall 1993. Available from 750 N. Lake Shore Dr., Chicago, IL 60611.
Sandra Barwick	"Not Men Only," *Spectator*, June 1, 1991. Available from PO Box 1310, Long Island City, NY 11101.
John Bradshaw	"To the Rescue of Recovery," (letter to the editor) *Harper's*, January 1992.
Katy Butler	"Clashing Memories, Mixed Messages," *Los Angeles Times Magazine*, June 26, 1994. Available from Times Mirror Square, Los Angeles, CA 90053.
Jessica Collins	"Kids Hurting Kids for Sex," *Insight*, August 10, 1993. Available from 3600 New York Ave. NE, Washington, DC 20002.
Ellis Cose	"Truths About Spouse Abuse," *Newsweek*, August 8, 1994.
Jerome Cramer	"Why Children Lie in Court," *Time*, March 4, 1991.

James Cronin   "False Memory," *Z*, April 1994. Available from 116 St. Botolph St., Boston, MA 02115.

Joyce Dougherty   "Women's Violence Against Their Children: A Feminist Perspective," *Women & Criminal Justice*, 1993. Available from the Haworth Press, 10 Alice St., Binghamton, NY 13904-1580.

Susan Douglas   "Blame It on Battered Women," *Progressive*, August 1994.

Katherine Dunn   "Truth Abuse," *New Republic*, August 1, 1994.

Jean Bethke Elshtain   "Women and the Ideology of Victimization," *World & I*, April 1993. Available from 3600 New York Ave. NE, Washington, DC 20002.

Ted Gest with Betsy Streisand   "Still Failing Women?" *U.S. News & World Report*, June 19, 1995.

Erica Goode et al.   "Till Death Do Them Part?" *U.S. News & World Report*, July 4, 1994.

Kathleen M. Heide   "Why Kids Kill Parents," *Psychology Today*, September/October 1992.

Randi Henderson   "The Tangled Net of Memory," *Common Boundary*, November/December 1993. Available from PO Box 445, Mt. Morris, IL 61054.

Ellen L. Hopkins   "Abusing the Rights of Parents," *Newsweek*, October 18, 1993.

Michele Ingrassia and John McCormick   "Why Leave Children with Bad Parents?" *Newsweek*, April 25, 1994.

Nicholas Lemann   "The Vogue of Childhood Misery," *Atlantic,* March 1992.

John Leo   "Is It a War Against Women?" *U.S. News & World Report*, July 11, 1994.

Marc Mannes   "Seeking the Balance Between Child Protection and Family Preservation in Indian Child Welfare," *Child Welfare*, March/April 1993. Available from 440 First St. NW, Washington, DC 20001-2085.

Jill Neimark   "Why Doctors Won't Help Battered Women," *Glamour*, November 1992.

Sandy Pittman   "America's Children in Trouble," *Bulletin of the Park Ridge Center*, January 1991. Available from 676 N. St. Clair, Suite 450, Chicago, IL 60611.

Donald F. Schwarz et al.   "A Longitudinal Study of Injury Morbidity in an African-American Population," *JAMA*, March 9, 1994. Available from the AMA, 515 N. State St., Chicago, IL 60610.

Lisa Sigler   "The Incest-Survivor Controversy," *Z*, September 1993.

Roxanne Snider   "Lolita's Not to Blame," *New Internationalist*, February 1993. Available from PO Box 1143, Lewiston, NY 14092.

Thomas Sowell   "Long on Claims, Short on Evidence," *Forbes*, November 23, 1992.

Bibliography

David Ramsay Steele   "Partial Recall," *Liberty*, March 1994. Available from PO Box 1181, Port Townsend, WA 98368.

Karen D. Stout   "Intimate Femicide: A Study of Men Who Have Killed Their Mates," *Journal of Offender Rehabilitation*, vol. 19, no. 3/4 1993. Available from the Haworth Press, 10 Alice St., Binghamton, NY 13904-1580.

Becky Sweat   "The Painful Secret of Elder Abuse," *Plain Truth*, March 1991. Available from 300 W. Green St., Pasadena, CA 91123.

Neil Websdale   "Female Suffrage, Male Violence, and Law Enforcement in Lane County, Oregon, 1853 to 1960: An Ascending Analysis of Power," *Social Justice*, Fall 1992. Available from PO Box 40601, San Francisco, CA 94140.

Mark A. Wynn   "The Crime of Family Violence," *Christian Social Action*, September 1993. Available from 100 Maryland Ave. NE, Washington, DC 20002.

Cathy Young   "Abused Statistics," *National Review*, August 1, 1994.

Organizations to Contact

The editors have compiled the following list of organizations concerned with the issues debated in this book. The descriptions are derived from materials provided by the organizations. All have publications or information available for interested readers. The list was compiled on the date of publication of the present volume; names, addresses, and phone numbers may change. Be aware that many organizations take several weeks or longer to respond to inquiries, so allow as much time as possible.

Center for the Prevention of Sexual and Domestic Violence (CPSDV)
936 N. 34th St., Suite 200
Seattle, WA 98013
(206) 634-1903
fax: (206) 634-0115

CPSDV is an educational resource center that works with both religious and secular communities throughout the United States and Canada to address issues of sexual abuse and domestic violence. The center offers workshops concerning clergy misconduct, spouse abuse, child sexual abuse, rape, and pornography. Materials available from CPSDV include the quarterly journal *Working Together*, the book *Violence in the Family—a Workshop Curriculum for Clergy and Other Helpers*, the booklet *Keeping the Faith: Questions and Answers for the Abused Woman*, and the monograph *The Speaking Profits Us: Violence in the Lives of Women of Color*.

Childhelp U.S.A.
6463 Independence Ave.
Woodland Hills, CA 91370
(818) 347-7280
fax: (818) 593-3257

Childhelp works toward the prevention and treatment of child abuse. The organization provides residential care and counseling services for abused and neglected children through its group and foster homes. It promotes public awareness of child abuse issues and offers a child abuse hotline that services North America. Its publications include the book *Child Abuse and You* and the periodic *Child Help Newsletter*.

Emerge: Counseling and Education to Stop Male Violence
2380 Massachusetts Ave., Suite 101
Cambridge, MA 02140
(617) 422-1550

Emerge works to prevent domestic violence by providing counseling services and training workshops for batterers. It also conducts research and disseminates information and referrals. Publications available from Emerge include an annual newsletter and the papers "Counseling Men Who Batter: A Pro-Feminist Analysis of Treatment Models" and "The Addicted or Alcoholic Batterer."

End Violence Against the Next Generation, Inc. (EVANGI)
977 Keeler Ave.
Berkeley, CA 94708
(510) 527-0454

EVANGI views corporal punishment as the primary cause of violence. The organization asserts that youths are taught violence by the actions of their parents and teachers. It further contends that the consequences of spanking and other forms of physical punishment range from mild to rampant aggression. EVANGI publishes articles, booklets, and the books *Corporal Punishment Handbook* and *The Influence of Corporal Punishment on Crime*.

False Memory Syndrome Foundation (FMSF)
3401 Market St., Suite 130
Philadelphia, PA 19104
(215) 387-1865
fax: (215) 387-1917

FMSF believes that many "delayed memories" of sexual abuse are the result of false memory syndrome (FMS). In FMS, patients in therapy "recall" childhood abuse that never occurred. The foundation seeks to discover reasons for the spread of FMS, works for the prevention of new cases, and aids FMS victims, including those it believes have been falsely accused of abuse. FMSF publishes the *FMS Foundation Newsletter*, the booklet *The False Memory Syndrome Phenomenon*, and the books *Confabulations* and *True Stories of False Memories*.

Family Research Laboratory (FRL)
University of New Hampshire
126 Horton Social Science Center
Durham, NH 03824-3586
(603) 862-1888
fax: (603) 862-1122

Since 1975, FRL has devoted itself primarily to understanding the causes and consequences of family violence and to working to dispel myths about family violence through public education. It publishes numerous books and articles on women's violence against men, the physical abuse of spouses or cohabitants, marital rape, and verbal aggression. Books available from FRL include *When Battered Women Kill* and *Physical Violence in American Families: Risk Factors and Adaptations to Violence in 8,145 Families*.

Family Violence and Sexual Assault Institute (FVSAI)
1310 Clinic Dr.
Tyler, TX 75701
(903) 595-6600
fax: (903) 595-6799

FVSAI is a nonprofit corporation committed to networking, education, and the dissemination of information to reduce and prevent family violence and sexual assault. It publishes the quarterly *Family Violence and Sexual Assault Bulletin*, the *Spouse/Partner Abuse Bibliography (Original)*, and *Sexual Abuse/Incest Survivors: A Categorized Bibliography and Reference List*.

Family Violence Prevention Fund (FVPF)
383 Rhode Island St., Suite 304
San Francisco, CA 94103
(415) 252-8900
fax: (415) 252-8991

FVPF is a national nonprofit organization concerned with domestic violence education, prevention, and public policy reform. It works to improve health care for battered women and to strengthen the judicial system's capacity to respond appropriately to domestic violence cases. The fund publishes brochures, action kits, and general information packets on domestic violence as well as the books *Domestic Violence: The Law and Criminal Prosecution, Domestic Violence: The Crucial Role of the Judge in Criminal Court Cases—a National Model for Judicial Education*, and *Domestic Violence in Immigrant and Refugee Communities: Asserting the Rights of Battered Women*.

Focus on the Family
8605 Explorer Dr.
Colorado Springs, CO 80920
(719) 531-3400

Focus on the Family believes that reestablishing the traditional two-parent family will end many social problems. The organization publishes the monthly magazine *Focus on the Family Citizen* and the resource list *Information on Abuse*, which lists books, audio tapes, and information sheets related to family violence.

Illusion Theatre
528 Hennepin Ave., Suite 704
Minneapolis, MN 55403
(612) 339-4944
fax: (612) 337-8042

Illusion Theatre is an educational and theatrical organization that works to prevent child sexual abuse. The theatre creates, performs, and distributes theatrical productions that address social issues such as sexual abuse, interpersonal violence, and AIDS. Illusion Theatre publishes sexual abuse prevention materials, a semiannual newsletter, and the video *No Easy Answers*.

Metro Action Committee on Public Violence
Against Women and Children (METRAC)
158 Spadina Rd.
Toronto, ON M5R 2T8
CANADA
(416) 392-3135
fax: (416) 392-3136

METRAC works to prevent all forms of violence against women and children. It educates governments and the public about the harmful effects violence has on women, children, and the whole community. In addition, METRAC promotes research on violence, services for survivors, and legal system reform. Its publications include information packets and the books *Sexual Assault: A Guide to the Criminal System, Violence-Free Schools: Sexual Assault Prevention Manual*, and *Discussion Paper: Developing a Safe Urban Environment for Women*.

Movement for the Establishment of Real Gender Equality (MERGE)
10011 116th St., #501
Edmonton, AB T5K 1V4
CANADA
(403) 488-4593

MERGE works to end gender discrimination and stereotyping. It contends that publicity about family violence is biased toward women and ignores the male victims of spousal abuse. MERGE disseminates educational information on gender issues, including the pamphlet *Balancing the Approach to Spouse Abuse*.

National Center on Women and Family Law (NCWFL)
799 Broadway, Suite 402
New York, NY 10003
(212) 674-8200

The center monitors and analyzes legal developments pertaining to domestic violence and family law issues. NCWFL operates the National Battered Women's Law Project and conducts research on domestic violence. It produces numerous publications, including research findings and a national newsletter for advocates of victims of domestic violence.

National Council of Juvenile and Family Court Judges (NCJFCJ)
PO Box 8970
Reno, NV 89507
(800) 527-3223
fax: (702) 784-6160

NCJFCJ offers juvenile-justice professionals information and technical assistance on topics including child abuse and neglect, the foster care system, and custody disputes. The council operates the Resource Center on Domestic Violence: Child Protection and Custody, a national resource center funded by the U.S. Department of Health and Human Services. NCJFCJ publishes the quarterly *Juvenile and Family Court Journal*, the monthly *Juvenile and Family Court Digest*, and the quarterly magazine *Juvenile and Family Justice Today*.

National Resource Center on Child Sexual Abuse (NRCCSA)
106 Lincoln St.
Huntsville, AL 35801
(800) 543-7006

NRCCSA is funded by the National Center on Child Abuse and Neglect of the U.S. Department of Health and Human Services and is operated by the National Children's Advocacy Center. In addition to its toll-free information line, the center publishes a newsletter, information papers, monographs, and bibliographies on child abuse and neglect issues.

National Victims Resource Center (NVRC)
Box 6000
Rockville, MD 20850
(800) 627-6872

Established in 1983 by the U.S. Department of Justice's Office for Victims of Crime, NVRC is the primary source of information for crime victims. It answers questions by using national and regional statistics, a comprehensive collection of research findings, and a well-established network of victim advocates and organizations. NVRC distributes all Office of Justice Programs publications on victim-related issues, including a resource packet dedicated to domestic violence issues.

Index